"Bernard and Ron's passion for food and culinary travel jumps off the pages. This book is wonderfully organized and well written with recipes that are unique and delicious. The photographs are truly luscious enough to eat. This is a book that I will not only read from cover to cover again, but will also have fun cooking with!"

—SONDRA BERNSTEIN
Proprietor, the girl & the fig, Sonoma
Author, *the girl & the fig cookbook*

"Traveling Chefs Bernard Guillas and Ron Oliver take us on an amazing adventure around the globe. They are two of the most authentic and passionate chefs I know, and have generously shared their personal stories, favorite recipes and a magnificent taste of our world today."

—INGRID CROCE
Restaurateur, Croce's Restaurant & Jazz Bar, San Diego
Publisher/author, *Thyme in a Bottle*,
and *The San Diego Restaurant Cookbook*

"What a treat, my two favorite things, food and travel, beautifully executed in *Flying Pans*. Bernard and Ron with the help of Greg Bertolini (an extremely talented photographer) bring to life the sights, smells and tastes of their exotic travels. This book inspired me with beautiful recipes and heartfelt stories."

—ISABEL CRUZ
Chef/owner, Isabel's Cantina, San Diego
Author, *Isabel's Cantina*

"Chef Bernard and Chef Ron have a passion for life and travel. With this book they translate that passion into a language we all understand—food. The recipes here are creative and witty, much like the chefs. Follow them through their journey of life and enjoy every bite."

—GAVIN KAYSEN
Executive Chef, Café Boulud, New York

"Anyone who loves to travel will enjoy the pleasures of *Flying Pans*—a remarkable culinary journey. This cookbook reflects the special passion and devotion Chef Bernard Guillas and Chef Ron Oliver have for fine cuisine and exploring the globe."

—GRACE YOUNG
Author, *The Wisdom of the Chinese Kitchen*,
and *The Breath of a Wok*

"I knew Bernard and Ron were troubadours at heart, but never realized the extent of their travels. Joining them on this culinary voyage through forty countries is quite a ride, and I don't even need my passport! I thoroughly enjoyed the culturally inspired recipes, anecdotes, and the magnificent photography of *Flying Pans*."

—PIERRE CHAMBRIN
Executive Chef, The White House, 1990–94
Presently Executive Chef, St. Louis Club

"I love how each recipe in this vibrant book pays homage to the country that inspired its creation. Bernard and Ron show that they are ready for an episode of Iron Chef with their creative colorful dishes that take us to all corners of the world. *Allez cuisiner!*"

—CHRISTINE CUSHING
Chef, food stylist, and host,
"Christine Cushing Live" on Food Network Canada
Author, *Dish it Out*, *Fearless in the Kitchen*, and *Pure Food*

"*Flying Pans* by Bernard Guillas and Ron Oliver is more than just a cookbook. The two talented chefs take you on an amazing culinary journey all over the world. Every recipe is magnificently photographed by Gregory Bertolini and styled by the chefs themselves. . . . I expected to like this book, in fact I love it!"

—JEANNE JONES
Syndicated columnist, author,
Jeanne Jones' Homestyle Cooking Made Healthy

"*Flying Pans* is an exciting, rich culinary tour of indigenous cuisine from around the globe. Through the immensely talented, creative style of Chef Bernard and Chef Ron, you are able to explore widely varied fresh flavors woven with their cultural roots. I especially enjoyed their unique stories and perspectives of the people they meet and the history they uncover. *Flying Pans* is a great addition to your culinary and travel library."

—JIMMY SCHMIDT
Chef/owner, Rattlesnake Restaurants
Author, *Jimmy Schmidt's Cooking Class*,
and *Cooking for All Seasons*

FLYING PANS

TWO CHEFS, ONE WORLD

BERNARD GUILLAS

RON OLIVER

PHOTOGRAPHY BY
GREGORY BERTOLINI

CABIN FEVER PRESS

Cabin Fever Press
208 W 23rd Street, Suite 1016
New York, NY 10011

ISBN 978-0-9824283-1-3

R & B Food and Culture Production
525 Summerview Circle
Encinitas, California, 92024

PASSION IS THE SECRET THAT BRINGS
ADVENTURES AND MAGIC TO COOKING!
SHARE THE LODE!
life is Delicious! *Bernard*

SPICE UP YOUR LIFE
IN THE KITCHEN AND
AROUND THE WORLD!
HAPPY COOKING... *Chef RON*

CONTENTS

THANKS/MERCI

One of the most important ingredients in writing this cookbook was the selfless participation and support from our family, friends, and peers in the industry. Our sincerest thanks and gratitude goes to your generous contributions. The success of this project is stamped with your special spirit.

LA JOLLA BEACH & TENNIS CLUB

As the chefs of the La Jolla Beach & Tennis Club, Inc. and the Marine Room Restaurant, we have been privileged to work with some outstanding people over the years. All of the owners and Board of Directors have been supportive of our creative and culinary search for innovative approaches to cooking and presenting the items that we serve to our guests. Special thanks to our general manager, John Campbell, for his vision, experience and guidance. By encouraging us to travel and learn, this book became possible.

MACY'S SCHOOL OF COOKING
SAN DIEGO'S MACY'S WEST

Thank you for generously welcoming us into your kitchen to shoot the photos for the book. Our deepest thanks go to Jonna Talbott and Jennie Van Meter from Special Events for making this possible. With access to every imaginable piece of cookware, linen, china, and glassware, we were like kids in a candy store. We particularly want to thank the staff of the Housewares Department for helping us to find the perfect plateware to bring each dish to life during our six months of shooting.

SPECIALTY PRODUCE
THE HARRINGTON BROTHERS

Thank you for providing us with all the fruits, vegetables, herbs, and exotics. To our favorite produce girls, Julie Hosler and Amiko Gubbins, "merci mille fois" for gathering and delivering the best ingredients from our local farms.

HAMILTON MEAT COMPANY
MICK HAMILTON
JONATHON SACHS

Thank you for delivering the precious "hooves" and "wings" straight to our door, always with a firm handshake and a smile.

SANTA MONICA SEAFOOD
ANTHONY CIGLIANO
SUE LUCCHINO

Thank you for providing us with the freshest fruit of our oceans for the Sea Fare chapters. We appreciate your commitment to the sustainability of natural resources from the world's waters.

CABIN FEVER PRESS

To our publishers, Gregory Bertolini and Jane Van Gelder, we owe a debt of gratitude. Their creativity, artistic vision, and guidance transformed our dream into a reality. They steered and shaped this project every step of the way from concept to photography to finished book. Without them, *Flying Pans* would not have been possible.

PHOTOGRAPHER AND PRINCIPAL
Gregory Bertolini

PUBLISHING DIRECTOR
Jane Van Gelder

FOOD STYLIST
Cindy Epstien

DIGITAL TECHNICIAN
Ken Sadlock

SPECIAL THANKS TO

KITCHEN PHOTO SHOOT TEAM
For sweating it out with us in the kitchen and helping wash the dishes!

Tony Sunga, Kevin Michaels, Cristina Smith, Kristine Fredericks, Lisa Oliver

CONTRIBUTING EDITORS
For helping us to say things when the words wouldn't come out right!

TEXT
Mark Wischkaemper, Maria Montana, Brandon Hernandez, Donna Long Knierim

RECIPES
Clarissa Flamenco, Pam Wischkaemper

RECIPE TESTERS
With their fine palates and insightful comments

BARONA VALLEY CASINO COOKING SCHOOL
Chef Dean Thomas, Chef Jim Phillips, and their culinary team

SAN DIEGO CULINARY INSTITUTE
Chef Larry Lewis and his culinary students

FRIENDS AND FAMILY
Donna Long Knierim, Jonna Talbott, Karen Lanning, David Trygstad, Kate and Doreen Palmiere, Brandon and Heather Hernandez, Isabel, Kaley, and Jazmin Oliver

TWO CHEFS, ONE WORLD

Most of our acquaintances, peers, staff, and even family and friends call each of us "Chef"—some out of respect, some out of obedience, and others (like our moms) out of endearment. But we know ourselves simply as Bernard and Ron—two cooks together in one world. We are energized by the beauty of life, the art of cooking, the discovery of travel, and the passion of the human race. We are on a journey that began long before we met and is not even close to being over.

The pursuit of our passion is an exciting, unpredictable, and rewarding voyage. We both feel very fortunate to be engaged in this lifelong pursuit. Although we are two very different people with opposite personalities, we share a fascination for exploring and an unquenchable thirst for the knowledge of discovery. We have a burning desire to share those revelations with as many people as will listen.

Shortly after meeting, we compared stories and found we were both avid travelers guided by food as a compass to foreign lands. Writing this book is our way to invite you on an exploration of different cultures, told through food and life stories. For you, it is a guide to creating interesting and conversation-starting cuisine for friends and family.

We hope our recipes will inspire you to spend more time in the kitchen, but we have also designed them to be approachable enough for today's hectic lifestyles. We love creating fancy presentations and want to show you some really neat ideas. Whether you follow the recipes exactly or make changes, your personal touch will be present in the final dish because you are cooking it. Be proud of your results.

When you cook without boundaries or the fear of failure, and are guided by your passion for food and sharing it with those you love, that passion is contagious. Your guests will feel the warmth and the care in the final product. No ingredient is as delectable and effective as your good intentions. This is one of the core values behind *Flying Pans*.

We created the recipes with a genuine, heartfelt adoration for a practice, a medium, and, most importantly, people. It is our sincere hope that these values translate beautifully in your own kitchen and create a foundation for exploration, enjoyment, emotion, and ecstasy at your table. Welcome aboard this voyage of the senses. We are pleased you came and hope you enjoy the journey.

Here is a bit of our story.

BERNARD

I was raised in a family of farmers. My two uncles were a baker and a butcher. I grew up on the coast of Brittany with my grandmother who was a fantastic cook. We had a garden and raised rabbits, chooks, and geese. I learned a lot from her. Every Friday we made crêpes and galettes for the family. I loved cooking, baking, and butchering (but not so much cleaning). At the age of 15, I decided that cooking was my calling because it came naturally to me. I thought it would be a great craft, as well as an excuse to travel the world. I made the decision to skip culinary school and do an apprenticeship at Le Bretagne with my mentor, Georges Paineau. The artistic aspect and hands-on opportunities were appealing to me.

As a youngster, my family traveled every summer. I remember running wild with my sisters in the souks of Morocco and picnicking on St. Brelade beach on Jersey Island. At age 19, I moved to French Guyana to work at a Breton restaurant in Kourou at the basin of the Amazon River. For three weeks, I lived in a local village in the heart of the jungle. Talk about going back to the grassroots! Fishing on the river bank brought the true meaning of "out of the water and into the pot." Or out of the jungle and onto the spit roast!

Pierre Chambrin, former chef of The White House, brought me to The United States, which was a dream come true. This is my home now and the starting point for all my travels. On Prince Edward Island, I gathered mussels that reminded me of my childhood. In India, I cooked goat on a sabre in a tandoori oven. In Australia, I fell in love with the Adelaide Central Market's artisanal cheeses and outback honey. I discovered the hawker centers in Singapore and noodle bars in Taipei. By sailing the oceans on the Regent Seven Seas Cruise Line, I have globetrotted our beautiful planet.

Farmers do marvels by growing bountiful organic fruit, vegetables, and herbs. The soul of any community, great or small, is its market. This is where people from all walks of life gather to procure their food for the day, to socialize, and to interact with the region's farmers, ranchers, fishermen, and artisans. The market provides a snapshot of a people, their environment, and the wonderful products that stem from both of those entities. I am a very inquisitive chef, always searching for the unknown—new ingredients, techniques, spices, and wines.

Chefs are like scientists, artists, and magicians. A white canvas is replaced by a sleek white plate. On our palette, we use the natural color of ingredients and textures to awaken all of the senses. It is a journey through the magic of cooking.

The role of a chef is to create a feast for the senses—telling the tale of a region and its people via taste, texture, scent, and sight. I am always striving to discover new styles of cuisine with original cultural roots.

RON

As a child, my family's obsession with tasty food and our habit of gathering in the kitchen inspired me to cook. Years before I was tall enough to see above the counter tops, I would spend hours absorbing the sounds, aromas, and orchestrated movements surrounding me. Those experiences sparked the curiosity and excitement I still feel every time I step into a kitchen. I often close my eyes and revisit those very first impressions of cooking—the rhythmic tapping of efficient knife work, the steel-on-steel swoosh of hand-whipped cream, or the clinking of dishes as the table is prepared in anticipation.

I encourage people to see cooking as a multi-sensory activity. Sautéed onions passing through the golden-brown stage to the threshold of caramelization can be judged purely by smell. With a little awareness, you can establish the stage of reduction in a saucepan behind you by using your ears. To have a successful relationship with the foods you are cooking, it helps to be a great listener.

I don't think this is a mysterious craft. We are all born with the intuition that makes a great cook. All it takes is some confidence. My mom was the best cook I ever met until she took culinary classes. Then she started questioning herself too much in the kitchen. I encouraged her to take a step back and rediscover how to follow her instincts. She's the best cook in the world again!

Curiosity and the excitement of new experiences, making new friends, and gaining new perspectives on life are what fuelled my appetite for travel. Thinking about all of my destinations, the high plain region of Bolivia remains my favorite place in the world. The natural features of the land exude mystery and the indigenous people have many stories to tell, if only given a chance.

When in foreign lands, I always want to see what is around the next corner. That has led to a lot of trouble at times but has also created rewarding experiences. When I travel I want to be with the local people, to experience life and food as they do. Food brings people together. It is a common bridge capable of connecting any two people, no matter who they are or where they are from. It is easy to interact with strangers when you know a little something about their cooking. Just through a simple expression of interest, many people have embraced me and acted as my official culinary tour guide in their land. The sense of pride and excitement I see in people when sharing their native foods is more precious than the taste could ever be, no matter how delectable.

My culinary excursions have not only led me to discover native ingredients and cooking methods. The perspective I've gained towards life from one destination crosses over to the next. The idea that food is a gift from the earth and a sustainer of life, that cooking is an act of love, and that eating is socially unifying, are all concepts I've learned through travel.

"We are energized by the beauty of life, the art of cooking, the discovery of travel, and the passion of the human race. We are on a journey that began long before we met and is not even close to being over. It is an exciting, unpredictable, and rewarding voyage."

THE CULINARY JOURNEY

GATHERING

The term *hors d'oeuvres*, which means "outside the work," was developed by French architects to describe a structure not included as part of a building's master design. In 1903, legendary gastronomist Georges Auguste Escoffier borrowed the term for his cookbook, *Le Guide Culinaire* to describe edibles offered outside the scope of a formal meal.

The tradition of preparing little noshes for a gathering of guests dates much farther back than the days of Escoffier and has roots spanning far beyond France. In Morocco, the opening act to a meal is called *meze*. Across the Atlantic, Mexicans enjoy an array of savory snacks called *botanas*. In Russia, pre-meal nibbles of cured meats, fish, and vegetables called *zakusi* are served buffet-style along with the much beloved regional spirit—vodka.

Every culture has developed its own fermentation and distillation methods, but each region's indigenous food resources lend their distinctive flavors. This is the essence that forms the base for drinks such as martinis and mojitos, which give a nation's citizens unique beverages to enjoy and share proudly with the rest of the world.

Precursory treats and spirited libations go hand-in-hand with any occasion where friends and family meet to relive old memories and create new ones.

SOUPS

Soups provide nourishment and fuel to face the day, warming both body and soul. Their delicious, earthy flavors are derived from a region's native ingredients, providing a telling snapshot of a people's diet and culinary traditions.

Contrary to popular belief, soups are not one of the oldest staples of mankind's diet. It wasn't until the advent of leak-proof cooking vessels that man was able to boil water, much less cook with it. Clay pots, which conduct and maintain heat, provide the model upon which today's stock pots, Dutch ovens, and slow-cookers are based.

Soups tend to be viewed as rustic in nature. While that is true in some cases, many of the world's most popular soups are extremely refined, the product of countless revisions to achieve the perfect balance of flavors and textures.

Soups are deeply engrained in the history and evolution of the world's cultures. Each civilization has its signature concoctions guided by products inherent to the land. Hearty stews and chowders are favored in cold weather, while chilled soups like gazpacho are popular in warmer climates. In some countries, particularly where physical labor is a part of daily life, soup isn't just a dinnertime delight. It's a breakfast mainstay, providing much-needed nutrients for the work to come.

Whether for sustenance or culinary expression, soup equals comfort. A tasty bowl of soup has a magical way of nourishing and energizing the people we cook for, warming the souls of both the giver and the receiver.

SALADS

Mélanges of tender greens with farm fresh produce dressed in herbed emulsions or vinaigrettes have secured a place in our hearts and on our tables as the dish we call salad. Adding tasty cultural influences and an unlimited variety of ingredients opens up a whole world of opportunity.

Around the globe, any dish built on a medley of ingredients, adorned with a flavor-enhancing condiment, can be considered a salad.

The word *salad* is derived from the Latin term *salata*, which dates back centuries and literally means "salted." From the beginning, the flavors of freshly-harvested produce were subtly heightened with sea salt and herbs. These seasonings were difficult to apply until the introduction of fluid conveyances such as cold-pressed oils, vinegars, and fruit juices, making it possible to adhere the seasonings to the main ingredients. This novel cooking technique was the birth and inspiration for our modern day dressings.

Nowadays, the word *salad* still remains, but its definition has evolved. In Europe, a formal salad course is built into the traditional meal structure and each country's take on that is uniquely centered on the local harvest. Whether tossed in a bowl or stacked high for an eye-catching, upscale presentation, the sky is the limit for salads. The key to flavor is to keep things simple, using the freshest, top-quality ingredients and allowing their natural goodness to shine.

SEA FARE

Beneath the surface of our azure waters lies an entire universe of marine life and edible treasures. Nothing tastes as pure and delicious as seafood plucked straight from its native waters. Whether it's sweet crab, raw tuna, buttery diver scallops, or freshly shucked oysters, seafood boasts an expansive array of potent and altogether scrumptious sensations. These unique qualities are reflected in the diets and food cultures of the world's coastal communities.

It is ideal to present fish and shellfish early in a meal's progression, when lighter, palette-teasing dishes are most welcome. Many cooking methods showcase the natural flavors of seafood. Curing adds saltiness while infusing the aromas of blended herbs and spices. Smoking adds an underlying warmth and richness. Pickling contributes a pronounced brightness and tart intensity. All of these processes were developed as preservation techniques in times when refrigeration was not an option. What was invented out of necessity is now practiced almost purely for pleasure!

Freshness, quality, and safety are paramount when purchasing seafood. To ensure you get all three, it's important to seek out reliable sources. Once you've located a quality fishmonger, get to know them. They have their fingers on the pulse of the local waters, knowing which fish and shellfish are in season. Ask them which varieties represent the best of each day's catch. You'll gain a friend in the business and the peace of mind that you have the absolute freshest, best-tasting seafood possible.

WINGS

Chickens, turkeys, ducks, and their feathered friends serve as the dietary backbone for civilizations in every part of the world. Adding to the worldwide popularity of poultry are the countless numbers of ways in which it can be prepared.

In India, birds are skewered on spits and roasted whole in huge ceramic ovens called tandoors. Chinese cooks use a reverse vacuum mechanism to separate a duck's skin from the meat to ensure extra crispiness for their traditional Peking duck. In the Republic of Georgia, quail are cooked by pressing them under hot stones with aromatic herbs until crispy. In Tennessee, folks have taken to the tradition of deep-frying whole turkeys.

These global preparations are all unique, but each has been devised to achieve the primary goal common to poultry cookery—the heavenly combination of flavorful skin matched with juicy, succulent meat. The fact these specific results can be reached via such diverse methods speaks to the versatility of poultry. Birds mesh well with just about any ingredient in the world, and are a valued staple for people of all nationalities.

On festive occasions like Thanksgiving, turkeys, geese, ducks, and game hens will delight your guests, leaving their taste buds pleasantly piqued and their appetites hungry for more.

HOOVES

While cows supply us with one of the world's most valuable liquid assets, milk, the steer performs the heavy labor necessary for farming. It's no wonder bovines are considered sacred creatures in India. But cows are not the only animals who serve as beasts of burden. Throughout Asia, water buffalo cultivate rice fields, while in Italy they give milk for the prized mozzarella. In Europe, goats and sheep contribute their own unique-tasting milk for tart French chèvre and Spain's zesty sheep's milk manchego.

Providing a butcher counter's worth of cuts, beef, pork, lamb, and game are hearty and nutritious enough to single-handedly sustain us throughout the year. Starting in winter we prepare braised roasts, stews, and other one-pot wonders. Each packs enough protein and warmth to fight off the season's bitter chill. Temperatures and tastes gradually shift during summer with grilled and barbecued specialties such as steaks, ribs, burgers, and sausages.

Talk to your butcher about origin and ranching methods when buying meats. Our favorites are organically or naturally raised products from local farms. A good butcher can help you be adventurous in the kitchen by recommending different cuts and teaching you about the quality grades of meats.

HOME SWEET HOME

Whether serving an elegant crème brûlée or a frosted wedge of homemade cake, it's no coincidence that a dinner party's mood hits its festive peak at dessert time. Sweets arouse and heighten the senses, making a perfect endnote to the symphonic delights of an exquisite meal.

The world's most famous desserts can be traced back to their birthplaces, but regional twists imparted over time are every bit as important to their heritage.

Classic French apple tarte tatin becomes quince tart in the region of Cotignac. A traditional lemon curd originates in England, but is prepared as a tart in the United States. A French vanilla pot de crème becomes Italian with cherries and Amarone.

Desserts such as cobblers, pies, and bars provide people a chance to beautifully showcase the products of their local harvest. The same goes for a region's crafted treats. Belgium, Switzerland, and Austria, all renowned for their top quality chocolate, have no shortage of recipes for cakes, tortes, truffles, and soufflés. All of these delicious recipes are well-suited to the home kitchen. After all, that's where the majority of them were invented.

Bold, lavish, dynamic flavors. Soft, inviting, ooey-gooey textures. Sumptuous inspiration. Desserts have it all!

GATHERING

AHI TUNA LOLLIPOP 25

LEMONGRASS SPEARED DIVER SCALLOPS 27

KURA RIVER SALMON 28

MARRAKECH CHICKEN SKEWERS 31

BAKED NORTH PACIFIC OYSTERS 32

JAVANESE BEEF SATAY 35

MAPLE SCENTED CRIMINI MUSHROOMS 37

PRESERVED FIG AND HAZELNUT BRUSCHETTA 38

BAJA SHRIMP BISQUE SHOOTER 40

BLEU D'AUVERGNE GRAPE TRUFFLE 43

HYPNOTIC BLUES 44

ORANGE BLOSSOM FIZZ 44

STRAWBERRY ROSE 44

BELLE ÉPOQUE 44

ORCHARD BEE 44

"BUDDHA'S HAND" SAKE 46

GRAIN OF PARADISE HIBISCUS 46

LAVENDER CITRONELLE 46

HOT CHILE CACAO 46

AQUAVIT POMEGRANATE 48

MAOTAI GINGER KUMQUAT 48

CUCUMBER GRAPPA 48

GUAYAMA PASSION 48

TURKEY

Oguz Kosebalaban, an expert in Ottoman cuisine, invited my wife Isabel and me to his posh apartment on the Asian side of Istanbul for a banquet of authentic Turkish dishes. The best part of the story is that this same evening was our first time meeting Oguz in person. I had struck his acquaintance over the internet while researching the history of sardine canneries on the Gallipoli peninsula. One month later, he welcomed us to his country and his home, treating us like family.

The evening was a culinary journey through the many nuances and inspirations of true Turkish cuisine, with Oguz citing historical influences along the way. My favorite preparation was a kebab called *alinekani*, ground lamb patties sandwiched between unpeeled slices of eggplant, roasted over charcoal. The high heat burns the eggplant's skin, providing a smokey accent to the seasoned meat.

Gallipoli is where my grandfather was born and raised in a mansion on the ocean's edge. His father owned a sardine cannery and a fishing boat fleet that brought enough riches to tutor his son in classical Turkish music and eight foreign languages. At the beginning of World War I, all the luxuries were confiscated and my grandfather found himself on the streets begging for a piece of flatbread. As required by law, he joined the army, but was held back to play his beautiful music to the sargeants while the rest of the men were sent to fight. None of the others, not a single one, returned alive.

Knowing how much I adore eggplant, Oguz prepared another special but simple kebab using a rare, banana-shaped eggplant called "goat's ear," known to grow only in a small village outside of the Gaziantep strip, his mother's region. He showed us how his mom used to drain yoghurt through silk scarves to make a thick, tangy cream for the succulent grilled eggplant. Next, he drizzled pomegranate vinegar over a bowl of crushed walnuts, onions, mint, tomato cubes, and red peppers to create a local specialty called Infidel Mountain Salad.

For Turks, hospitality is an art form, conversing is a favorite pastime, and life is celebrated often with food, drink, and music. This is something I learned at a young age by observing my grandfather. I especially remember the chanting songs he played on his ud, the fervor with which he pounded his ring-adorned hand on the dining room table while telling stories, and the eggplant, pomegranates, olives, and feta cheese that were never absent from the table when visitors were expected.

I was told by the elders of my family that my great-grandfather's cannery is still in operation in Gallipoli. I wasn't able to confirm it, but we asked Oguz to take us out to the peninsula. We saw working canneries at the ocean's edge and fishing boats passing by on Dardenelle Straight. It seemed natural to wonder if the spot where I was standing had ever felt the passing-by of my ancestors. Perhaps they were on their way to a gathering, to celebrate life and enjoy great food and bang their hands on the table with fervor while sharing great stories.

—RON

FIJI

On the Islands of Fiji, we were met with a smile and the word *"bula"* from the locals. The warmth we discovered was not only from the sun, but from the hospitality and infectious friendliness of the people. *Bula* is a word similar to *aloha* in Hawaii and is used often to say "hello," "welcome" and "cheers." This recipe is a great way to welcome you to our book. It is inspired by our fishing experience in Fiji—enjoying ruby red ahi tuna, sushi-style, right on the boat, before returning to shore to a great big *"bula!"*

—RON AND BERNARD

AHI TUNA LOLLIPOP
Ginger Macadamia Sauce

MAKES 12

GINGER MACADAMIA SAUCE

½ cup mint leaves
½ cup cilantro leaves
3 tablespoons seasoned rice vinegar
1½ tablespoons teriyaki sauce
1 teaspoon sambal chile sauce
1 tablespoon freshly grated ginger
1 lemon, juiced
¼ cup toasted macadamia nuts
¼ cup macadamia oil
to taste sea salt and freshly ground black pepper

Rough chop mint and cilantro leaves. Place in blender with rice vinegar, teriyaki sauce, sambal, ginger, lemon juice and macadamia nuts. With blender running, slowly drizzle in macadamia oil until well incorporated. Season with salt and pepper. Transfer to serving bowl.

AHI TUNA

1 pound ahi tuna, sushi-grade #1
¼ cup pomegranate juice
1 teaspoon sesame oil
⅛ teaspoon togarashi pepper
¼ teaspoon sea salt
12 skewers, 2 inches long

Cut tuna into 12 equally sized cubes. Whisk remaining ingredients in mixing bowl. Transfer to small shallow dish. Add tuna. Refrigerate 5 minutes. Turn tuna over. Refrigerate 5 minutes. Transfer tuna to paper towel-lined plate to absorb excess liquid. Place one skewer down center of each tuna cube.

PRESENTATION

¼ teaspoon togarashi pepper
6 shiso leaves

Sprinkle togarashi atop tuna. Arrange on large serving platter. Lay shiso leaves in center of platter. Place bowl of ginger macadamia sauce atop.

JAPAN

Coming down from Niseko Higashiyama mountain, I was reminded of the Alps by the Bavarian style cottages that dotted the countryside. I ended up in the seaside town of Saroma, where I tried squid ink ice cream for the first time. Good stuff! The next morning, in the crowded alleys of one-hundred-year-old Nijo market in Sapporo, hairy crabs, oysters, sea urchins, and live scallops made a tasty breakfast with hojicha green tea. Saroma scallops are considered to be among Japan's best. Always sear scallops over high heat, without crowding the skillet. This will maximize caramelization and flavor. —BERNARD

LEMONGRASS SPEARED DIVER SCALLOPS
Seaweed Wrap, Wasabi Cream

MAKES 12

SCALLOPS

¼ **cup** almond meal
1 teaspoon chopped thyme leaves
¼ **teaspoon** togarashi pepper
¼ **teaspoon** sea salt
1 nori sheet, cut crosswise into 12 ¼-inch strips
12 large scallops, size u-10, tendon removed
1 tablespoon grapeseed oil
1 stalk lemongrass, cut into 12 4-inch spears
to taste sea salt and freshly ground black pepper

Preheat oven to 400°F. In small mixing bowl, combine almond meal, thyme, togarashi, and sea salt. Set aside. Tightly wrap one nori strip around each scallop. Add grapeseed oil to skillet over high heat. Lightly season scallops with sea salt and pepper. Sear four scallops at a time for 30 seconds on each side. Transfer to baking sheet. Skewer each scallop horizontally with lemongrass spear. Top with almond mixture. Bake 2 minutes or until warm in the center and slightly underdone.

WASABI CREAM

2 tablespoons wasabi powder
2 tablespoons sake wine, cold
2 tablespoons mayonnaise
2 tablespoons sour cream

In small mixing bowl, combine wasabi powder and sake to form a paste. Whisk in remaining ingredients. Transfer to squeeze bottle.

PRESENTATION

Arrange scallops on warm serving platter. Dot wasabi cream beside each.

REPUBLIC OF GEORGIA

I was overcome with the joy, laughter, and celebration sparked by our arrival at my friend Koko's family house in Tblisi. Hospitality is a way of life and every celebration is a special gathering. Koko's mom, Lali, spent the entire week preparing the feast in honor of her son's return. His father, Teimuraz, gathered the wine for the *tamada*, a traditional toasting ceremony. Lali brought a basket of oyster mushrooms from the Tblisi market to make blinis for the sturgeon caviar. If you can't find osetra caviar, substitute with tobiko, salmon or paddlefish roe. —BERNARD

KURA RIVER SALMON
Osetra Caviar, Oyster Mushroom Griddle Cakes

MAKES 12

GRIDDLE CAKES

1 tablespoon olive oil
¼ cup minced shallots
2 cups diced stemmed oyster mushrooms
¼ teaspoon paprika
½ cup whole wheat flour
1 teaspoon baking powder
½ teaspoon sea salt
¼ teaspoon black pepper
1 large egg
¼ cup milk
2 tablespoons melted unsalted butter
to taste sea salt and freshly ground black pepper
2 tablespoons unsalted butter

Add olive oil to skillet over medium heat. Add shallots, oyster mushrooms and paprika. Cook, stirring often, until liquid from mushrooms evaporates. Set aside to cool. Combine dry ingredients in large mixing bowl. In separate bowl, beat egg and milk together. Whisk in dry ingredients. Fold in mushrooms and melted butter. Adjust seasoning. Place large non-stick skillet over medium heat. Add ½ teaspoon butter. Ladle ⅓ cup batter into pan. Cook until puffed and dry around edges. Flip. Cook to golden brown. Set aside. Repeat with remaining butter and batter. Cut each pancake into mini cakes, using 2-inch round cookie cutter. Set aside.

SALMON

1 pound fresh salmon fillet, boneless, skinless
⅛ teaspoon hot paprika
2 tablespoons tangerine juice
2 teaspoons olive oil
2 tablespoons finely chopped chives
½ teaspoon finely chopped mint leaves
to taste sea salt and freshly ground black pepper

Cut salmon into ¼-inch cubes. Transfer to mixing bowl. Toss with paprika, tangerine juice, olive oil, chives, and mint. Season with salt and pepper. Cover. Refrigerate.

PRESENTATION

2 ounces osetra caviar

Using small spoon, mound salmon on top of each griddle cake. Transfer to serving platter. Garnish with osetra caviar.

As a seven-year-old boy traveling through Morocco with my family, I was stunned by the beauty of the snow-capped Atlas Mountains, rose gardens, palm groves, and exotic red buildings. I was visiting Marrakech when I discovered the Moroccan brochettes called kabobs. In July, the wind and hot sun of the Sahara desert drenched the city. Every morning we went shopping in the Medina where the souks and the Kasbah are located. All of my senses were awakened by the colors, fragrances, piles of tajines, cool babouches, and food stalls. Vendors prepared hummus, fried falafel, and grilled mergez sausage. My favorites were the kabobs of lamb and chicken with preserved lemon. —BERNARD

MARRAKECH CHICKEN SKEWERS
Fennel Date Relish

MAKES 12

CHICKEN

12 6-inch bamboo skewers
4 6-ounce chicken breasts, boneless, skinless
1 tablespoon freshly grated ginger
2 tablespoons chopped cilantro
½ teaspoon paprika
¼ teaspoon cumin
1 tablespoon minced garlic
¼ cup olive oil

½ cup minced white onion
¼ cup lemon juice
1 teaspoon sambal chile paste
¼ teaspoon sea salt
1 pineapple
** canola oil spray
1 tablespoon toasted sesame seeds

FENNEL DATE RELISH

1 large bulb fennel, trimmed
½ cup pitted dates, ¼-inch diced
¼ cup peeled, finely diced pineapple
¼ cup chopped smoked almonds
2 tablespoons extra virgin olive oil
1 tablespoon cider vinegar
1 tablespoon minced mint leaves
to taste sea salt and freshly ground black pepper

Soak bamboo skewers in water for 1 hour prior to use. Cut each chicken breast into 3 equally sized strips. In a large mixing bowl, combine ginger, 1 tablespoon cilantro, paprika, cumin, garlic, olive oil, onion, lemon juice, chile paste, and salt. Add chicken. Combine well. Cover. Refrigerate 2 hours. Cut pineapple into one 2-inch thick wheel. Lay on cutting board. Slice ¼-inch from one side to create base. Stand on serving platter. Thread one chicken strip onto each bamboo skewer. Place grill pan over medium high heat. Spray with canola oil. Sear chicken 2 minutes on each side or until done. Sprinkle with sesame seeds and remaining cilantro. Insert skewers into pineapple. Serve with fennel date relish.

Thinly slice fennel crosswise using sharp knife or vegetable slicer. Add to mixing bowl. Combine with remaining ingredients. Season with salt and pepper. Transfer to serving bowl.

I stood outside a charming, wood-beamed, red house at the base of a hill in the Niagara peninsula. It was December, and the barren trees were only skeletons of their autumn glory. For miles on end, leafless grapevines held tightly to barely frozen clusters of small, pink icewine grapes. I popped one in my mouth, savoring the juice as it defrosted on my tongue. The long winter freeze dehydrated the grapes, concentrating the sugar and the flavor. Earthy and sweet icewine elevates classic hollandaise sauce to a new level. —RON

BAKED NORTH PACIFIC OYSTERS
Lump Crab Meat, Icewine Hollandaise

MAKES 12

OYSTERS

1 tablespoon unsalted butter
½ cup finely chopped leeks, white part only
¼ cup finely diced fennel
½ cup lump crab meat, shelled
3 tablespoons crème fraîche
to taste sea salt and freshly ground black pepper
12 fresh raw oysters, washed
¼ cup seasoned bread crumbs
2 teaspoons olive oil
2 tablespoons chopped parsley leaves

Preheat oven to 375°F. Melt butter in large skillet over medium heat. Add leeks and fennel. Cook 5 minutes without browning, stirring often. Transfer to mixing bowl. Refrigerate until chilled. Fold in crab meat and crème fraîche. Season with salt and pepper. Shuck oysters, discarding top shells. Remove all shell fragments from meat. Transfer oysters to baking sheet. Place generous mound of crab meat mixture on each oyster. Combine bread crumbs, olive oil, and parsley in small mixing bowl. Sprinkle generously on top of crabmeat. Bake 8 minutes or until hot in center.

HOLLANDAISE

½ cup icewine
3 tablespoons Meyer lemon juice
4 large egg yolks
pinch cayenne pepper
¾ cup melted unsalted butter, hot
to taste sea salt and freshly ground black pepper

Add icewine and lemon juice to saucepan over medium heat. Reduce to ¼ cup. Cool to room temperature. Transfer to blender. Add egg yolks and cayenne pepper. Blend at medium speed 1 minute or until frothy. With blender running, pour in hot butter in slow steady stream. Blend 20 seconds or until thick and smooth. Season with salt and pepper. Transfer to serving dish.

PRESENTATION

1 cup rock salt

Spread rock salt evenly on warm serving platter. Arrange oysters on platter. Serve with hollandaise.

INDONESIA

Bartering through the hawker-lined streets of Semawis, the air was clouded with sweet and smokey aromas. Beef skewers were grilled over bright red coals and slathered with fragrant peanut sauce and sizzling chiles. This satay experience was quite a contrast to the serenity of Borobudur Temple, where I had spent the morning, but was equally enlightening. Cashews, almonds, macadamias, and pecans are a great substitute for peanuts in the dipping sauce. —BERNARD

JAVANESE BEEF SATAY
Chile Peanut Dipping Sauce

MAKES 12

MARINADE

1 tablespoon grapeseed oil
1 teaspoon grated ginger
1 teaspoon crushed garlic
2 teaspoons brown sugar
1 Thai chile, seeds removed, sliced
½ teaspoon shrimp paste
1 lime, zested, juiced
½ cup coconut milk
1 pound trimmed center-cut filet mignon

Add grapeseed oil to skillet over medium heat. Add ginger, garlic, brown sugar, chile, shrimp paste, and lime juice. Cook 1 minute, stirring constantly. Whisk in coconut milk. Bring to simmer. Remove from heat. Refrigerate until chilled. Cut filet mignon into 12 equally sized cubes. Add to marinade. Toss to coat. Cover. Refrigerate 3 hours.

CHILE PEANUT SAUCE

¼ cup peanut butter
1 tablespoon rice vinegar
½ tablespoon honey
½ teaspoon freshly grated ginger
1 tablespoon lime juice
2 tablespoons soy sauce
½ teaspoon sambal chile sauce
1 tablespoon chopped cilantro
1 tablespoon finely chopped green onions
1 tablespoon sesame oil

In mixing bowl, whisk peanut butter, rice vinegar and honey until creamy. Add remaining ingredients. Whisk until smooth. Transfer to squeeze bottle.

PRESENTATION

1 tablespoon grapeseed oil
12 Asian spoons
12 leaves cilantro
1 tablespoon toasted sesame seeds

Transfer beef from marinade to paper towel-lined plate. Add grapeseed oil to large skillet over medium high heat. Quickly sear beef on all sides, cooking to desired doneness. Transfer to spoons. Garnish with peanut sauce, cilantro and sesame seeds.

Driving from San Diego to Maine, I took a detour to the mushroom capital of the world. Who would've thought it would be Kennett Square in Chester County, Pennsylvania? Eighty mushroom farms in a 25-mile radius—that's a lot of fungus! It is where underground caves and tunnels snake below the earth, sheltering countless varieties of growing mushrooms. The weekend following Labor Day, at the annual Mushroom Festival, the town's population swells like a cremini becoming a portobello. Creminis are fun for the whole family—just stuff, bake, and eat. —RON

MAPLE SCENTED CREMINI MUSHROOMS

Turkey Sausage, Maytag Blue, Pomegranate Sherry Reduction

MAKES 24

MUSHROOMS

24 cremini mushrooms, 2-inch cap
2 tablespoons olive oil
2 tablespoons sherry vinegar
2 tablespoons maple syrup
1 teaspoon chopped fresh thyme leaves
to taste sea salt and freshly ground
  black pepper

Preheat oven to 400°F. Remove stems from mushrooms. Wipe clean with dry cloth. Add remaining ingredients to large mixing bowl. Whisk to emulsify. Add mushrooms. Coat thoroughly. Cover. Marinate 20 minutes. Place mushrooms upside down on baking sheet. Cook 5 minutes or until tender. Set aside.

TURKEY SAUSAGE

1 pound turkey sausage (about 4 links)
1 tablespoon finely chopped parsley
  leaves
⅓ cup finely diced sun-dried plums
1 tablespoon finely chopped chives
1 teaspoon Cajun spices
to taste sea salt and freshly ground
  black pepper

Remove sausage meat from casings. Discard casings. Crumble meat into mixing bowl. Combine with parsley, plums, chives, and Cajun spices. Season with salt and pepper. Fill mushroom caps with mixture.

REDUCTION

½ cup pomegranate juice
¼ cup maple syrup
¼ cup sherry vinegar
½ vanilla bean, chopped

Combine all ingredients in saucepan over medium heat. Bring to simmer. Reduce to syrup consistency. Strain through fine sieve. Cool. Set aside.

PRESENTATION

6 chives
¼ cup crumbled Maytag blue cheese

Bake mushrooms 10 minutes or until cooked through. Transfer to warm serving dish. Immediately top with blue cheese. Drizzle with pomegranate sherry reduction. Cut chives on bias into 1-inch sticks. Place 1 chive atop each mushroom.

At a time when almost everyone I knew was off to Venice and Tuscany, I found myself in a tiny village called Frondarola in the region of Abruzzo, Italy. The town stands proudly atop a high slope overlooking the hillside panorama. The people in these parts are fond of bruschetta, and they enjoy it in traditional style (grilled bread rubbed with garlic and olive oil) or with toppings like spicy red peppers, beans, herbs, and cured meats. Bruschetta is fun when served in build-your-own style. It creates a buzz and lively conversation. This is my California version. —RON

PRESERVED FIG AND HAZELNUT BRUSCHETTA
Goat Cheese, Ciabatta

SERVES 8

FIG AND HAZELNUT TAPENADE

1 cup diced, stemmed sun-dried figs
¾ cup Marsala wine
¼ teaspoon star anise, ground
⅓ cup chopped, pitted Kalamata olives
2 tablespoons hazelnut oil
2 tablespoons balsamic vinegar
1 teaspoon chopped lemon thyme leaves
½ cup toasted chopped hazelnuts
to taste sea salt and freshly ground black pepper

Add figs, Marsala and star anise to saucepan over medium heat. Cook until liquid evaporates and figs are soft, about 5 minutes. Transfer to mixing bowl. Combine with remaining ingredients. Season with salt and pepper. Transfer to serving dish.

CIABATTA CRISP

1 loaf ciabatta bread
¼ cup extra virgin olive oil
½ teaspoon flaky sea salt

Preheat oven to 300°F. Slice ciabatta crosswise ¼-inch thick. Lay slices on baking sheet. Brush with olive oil. Sprinkle with sea salt. Bake 15 minutes or until crispy and lightly golden. Transfer to wire rack. Cool.

PRESENTATION

2 teaspoons lemon juice
1 tablespoon hazelnut oil
1 tablespoon minced shallots
to taste sea salt and freshly ground black pepper
2 cups arugula leaves, washed, patted dry
1 11-ounce log goat cheese

Add lemon juice, hazelnut oil, shallots, salt and pepper to mixing bowl. Whisk to emulsify. Toss in arugula. Arrange on platter with goat cheese, ciabatta, and fig tapenade.

MEXICO

One morning in San Felipe, the early sun bounced off the choppy sea like sparkling emeralds while small fishing boats, called *pangas*, came to shore with prized Mexican white shrimp. The seabirds, hoping for an easy snack, had competition when I was there. During the San Felipe Shrimp Festival, the malecón is jammed with food stalls selling their fare. Every preparation of shrimp imaginable was accompanied by Mariachi music and tequila. One señorita in national colors served a crema de camarón with a hint of chile. Just like tequila, one shot will do you. —RON

BAJA SHRIMP BISQUE SHOOTER
Citrus Foam, Fennel Pollen Spices

MAKES 18

THE BISQUE

2 pounds shrimp, heads on, medium size
¼ cup grapeseed oil
½ cup chopped celery
½ cup chopped white onion
1 tablespoon chopped garlic
1 bay leaf
4 thyme sprigs
½ cup flour
2 tablespoons tomato paste

1 teaspoon shrimp paste
½ cup Riesling wine
½ cup diced tomatoes
3 quarts shellfish stock
1 cup heavy cream
to taste sea salt
pinch cayenne pepper
2 tablespoons peach schnapps

Coarsely chop shrimp. Add grapeseed oil to large stock pot over high heat. Roast shrimp until shells are golden brown. Lower heat to medium. Add celery, onion, garlic, bay leaf, and thyme. Cook 5 minutes, stirring often. Stir in flour, tomato paste, and shrimp paste. Cook 5 minutes, stirring occasionally. Add wine, tomatoes, and shellfish stock. Bring to simmer. Cook 30 minutes. Strain through coarse sieve, pressing on solids to extract maximum flavor. Discard solids. Return liquid to pot. Bring to simmer. Add heavy cream. Cook 5 minutes or until bisque thickens, whisking often. Season with sea salt and cayenne pepper. Blend with immersion blender until smooth. Strain through fine sieve. Whisk in peach schnapps. Keep hot.

CITRUS FOAM

⅓ cup heavy cream
2 tablespoons lemon juice
pinch sea salt

Place all ingredients in mixing bowl. Whip until frothy and lightly thickened. Transfer to squeeze bottle.

PRESENTATION

1 tablespoon chef Bernard's M'Ocean fennel pollen blend

Pour shrimp bisque into eighteen 2-ounce shot glasses up to ½-inch from rim. Squeeze citrus foam on top. Sprinkle with fennel pollen.

The ancient vineyard of Saint Pourçain is in the Auvergne region, a vast open space surrounded by majestic volcanic mountains. Hearty vines of Gamay, Pinot, and Tressailler grapes foreshadowed the spicy fresh wines awaiting my arrival. I joined the harvest and picked grapes until dusk. Afterward, we all gathered at the winery where the enticing smell of freshly baked bread mingled with the aroma of the oak-fueled fire. Wheels of local pride— bleu d'Auvergne cheese, black walnuts, grapes, and bottles of wine adorned the table. *Laissez le bon temps rouler!* —RON

BLEU D'AUVERGNE GRAPE TRUFFLES
Rolled in Toasted Walnuts

MAKES 36

36 medium red or green seedless grapes
⅔ cup cream cheese
½ cup bleu d'Auvergne cheese or your favorite blue cheese
1 cup finely chopped toasted walnuts

Wash grapes well. Pat dry. Using wooden spoon, beat cream cheese and bleu d'Auvergne in mixing bowl until smooth. Spread walnuts in shallow dish. Generously coat each grape with cheese mixture. Roll in walnuts. Refrigerate 30 minutes. Transfer to serving bowl.

BUBBLES

ORANGE BLOSSOM FIZZ

SERVES 6

¼ **cup** Elysium Orange Blossom wine
¼ **cup** Mandarin Imperial® liqueur
¼ **cup** tangerine juice
6 sprigs lemon thyme
1 bottle blanc de blanc sparkling wine
6 blackberries, each skewered
6 6-ounce champagne flutes

Combine Orange Blossom, Mandarin Imperial, tangerine juice, and thyme sprigs in small bowl. Infuse 15 minutes. Divide mixture among flutes. Fill with sparkling wine. Garnish with blackberry skewer and thyme sprig.

HYPNOTIC BLUES

SERVES 6

¾ **cup** Hypnotic® liqueur
1 bottle brut champagne
6 raspberries, each skewered
6 sprigs spearmint
6 6-ounce champagne flutes

Divide Hypnotic® liqueur among champagne flutes (2 tablespoons per glass). Fill flutes with champagne. Garnish with raspberry skewer and mint sprig.

ORCHARD BEE

SERVES 6

1 green apple
½ **teaspoon** lemon juice
4 teaspoons honey
¼ **cup** brandy
¼ **cup** peach schnapps
¼ **cup** apple juice
1 bottle cremant sparkling wine
18 leaves oregano
6 6-ounce champagne flutes

Scoop 6 balls of apple with melon baller. Toss with lemon juice. Combine honey, brandy, peach schnapps and apple juice in small mixing bowl. Stir well. Divide among flutes. Fill with sparkling wine. Garnish with apple ball and oregano leaves.

STRAWBERRY ROSE

SERVES 6

1 cup thinly sliced strawberries, stemmed
1 tablespoon granulated sugar
¼ **cup** vodka
½ **teaspoon** rose water
1 bottle champagne rosé
6 whole strawberries
6 6-ounce champagne flutes

Add sliced strawberries, sugar, vodka, and rose water to small mixing bowl. Toss to coat. Cover. Refrigerate six hours. Stir to dissolve sugar. Strain through fine sieve. Reserve strawberries for another use. Add 1 tablespoon strawberry rose syrup to each flute. Fill with champagne. Garnish each with one whole strawberry.

BELLE EPOQUE

SERVES 6

1 pink grapefruit
1 tablespoon "Chef Bernard's Zen-sational" fennel pollen spices
¼ **cup** absinthe liquor
⅓ **cup** pink grapefruit juice
2 tablespoons Campari® liqueur
1 teaspoon granulated sugar
1 bottle prosecco sparkling wine
6 6-ounce champagne flutes

Zest grapefruit into six 3-inch long strips. Reserve for garnish. Peel grapefruit. Cut into segments. Thread 1 segment onto each skewer. Dip edge of segment in fennel pollen spice. Set aside. Whisk absinthe, grapefruit juice, Campari®, and sugar in small mixing bowl until sugar dissolves. Divide among flutes. Fill with prosecco. Garnish with grapefruit skewer and zest.

MARTINIS

GRAIN OF PARADISE HIBISCUS

SERVES 4

2 cups dried hibiscus flowers
1 teaspoon grain of paradise black peppercorns
1½ cups water
¾ cup granulated sugar
1 tablespoon oregano leaves
2 cups Hendrick's® gin
12 pickled onions
4 sprigs oregano

Combine hibiscus flowers, peppercorns, water, and sugar in small saucepan over medium heat. Simmer slowly 15 minutes. Remove from heat. Add oregano leaves. Cover. Steep 20 minutes. Strain through fine sieve. Refrigerate until well chilled. Combine 1 cup hibiscus syrup with gin in mixing bowl. Stir well. Transfer half of mixture to martini shaker. Add 12 ice cubes. Shake 15 seconds. Strain into 2 frosted martini glasses. Repeat process. Skewer 3 onions onto each oregano sprig for garnish.

HOT CHILE CACAO

SERVES 4

2 tablespoons cocoa powder
1 tablespoon chile powder
2 tablespoons turbinado sugar
1 tangerine
1¼ cups Van Gogh® Dutch chocolate vodka
¾ cup Absolut® mandarin vodka
½ cup cranberry juice
¼ cup Lillet®
4 sprigs mint

Combine cocoa powder, chile powder, and sugar in small mixing bowl. Spread evenly onto plate. Cut tangerine in half. Rub cut side around rims of glasses. Dip rims into cocoa mixture. Set aside. Combine chocolate vodka, mandarin vodka, cranberry juice, and Lillet® in large mixing bowl. Squeeze in remaining tangerine. Stir well. Transfer half of mixture to martini shaker. Add 12 ice cubes. Shake 15 seconds. Strain into 2 martini glasses. Repeat process with remaining vodka mixture. Garnish with mint sprigs.

LAVENDER CITRONELLE

SERVES 4

3 stalks lemongrass
½ cup water
⅔ cup granulated sugar
6 sprigs lavender
¼ cup honey crystals
¼ teaspoon ground star anise
1 teaspoon flaky sea salt
½ lemon
⅓ cup lemoncello liqueur
1½ cups vodka
12 anchovy-stuffed olives

Cut lemongrass into 3-inch long pieces, discarding the hard bottom root. Crush pieces with mallet. Add water, sugar, lemongrass and 2 sprigs lavender to sauce pot over medium heat. Simmer two minutes. Remove from heat. Steep 30 minutes. Strain through fine sieve. Refrigerate until well chilled. Combine honey crystals, star anise, and flaky sea salt in small mixing bowl. Spread evenly onto plate. Rub cut side of lemon around rims of glasses. Dip rims into honey crystal mixture. Set aside. Combine lemongrass syrup, lemoncello, and vodka in mixing bowl. Stir well. Transfer half of mixture to martini shaker. Add 12 ice cubes. Shake 15 seconds. Strain into 2 martini glasses. Repeat process. Skewer 3 olives onto each of the 4 remaining lavender sprigs for garnish.

"BUDDHA'S HAND" SAKE

SERVES 4

1 cup sake
1 cup Hangar One® citron "Buddha's Hand" vodka
¼ cup lime juice
½ cup tangerine juice
¼ cup ZEN® Green Tea liqueur
8 slices crystallized ginger

Add sake, vodka, lime juice, tangerine juice, and green tea liqueur to mixing bowl. Stir well. Transfer half of mixture to martini shaker. Add 12 ice cubes. Shake 15 seconds. Strain into 2 frosted martini glasses. Repeat process. Add 2 slices crystallized ginger to each glass.

MOJITOS

MAOTAI GINGER KUMQUAT

SERVES 4

4 large shiso leaves
¼ cup sugar
8 kumquats, chopped
½ cup goji berry juice
1½ cups Maotai® liquor or Jamaican Appleton® rum
to top ginger beer
4 kumquats, whole
2 tablespoons goji berries
4 sprigs amaranth flower

In large mortar, crush shiso, sugar, and chopped kumquats to coarse paste. Stir in goji berry juice. Transfer to large mixing bowl. Whisk in Maotai® liquor. Strain through fine sieve. Divide into highball glasses filled with ice. Top with ginger beer. Cut slit into one end of each whole kumquat. Slide kumquats onto rims of glasses. Garnish with goji berries and amaranth flower.

CUCUMBER GRAPPA

SERVES 4

1 stalk lemongrass
2 teaspoons fennel seeds
24 mint leaves
¼ cup granulated sugar
½ cup verjus
½ cup cucumber juice (juiced skin-on)
1 cup grappa
½ cup lemoncello liqueur
¼ cup finely diced cucumber
1 bottle sparkling water
4 sprigs mint
4 cucumber slices, ¼-inch thick

Cut bottom 2 inches of lemongrass stalk into thin slices. Cut top part into quarters lengthwise to make swizzle sticks. Reserve. In mortar, crush lemongrass slices, fennel seeds, mint leaves, and sugar to a paste. Stir in verjus. Transfer to large mixing bowl. Combine with cucumber juice, grappa, and lemoncello. Strain through fine sieve. Divide into highball glasses filled with ice. Sprinkle with diced cucumber. Top with sparkling water. Garnish with mint sprigs, cucumber slices, and lemongrass swizzle sticks.

AQUAVIT POMEGRANATE

SERVES 4

16 leaves opal basil
¼ cup turbinado sugar
12 whole white peppercorns
½ cup lime juice
1 cup aquavit
½ cup Pama® pomegranate liqueur
½ cup pomegranate juice
to top soda water
4 sprigs opal basil
4 lime wedges

In large mortar, crush basil, sugar, and peppercorns until sugar dissolves. Stir in lime juice. Transfer to large mixing bowl. Stir in aquavit, pomegranate liqueur, and pomegranate juice. Strain through fine sieve. Divide mixture into highball glasses filled with ice. Top with soda water. Garnish with opal basil sprig and lime wedge.

GUAYAMA PASSION

SERVES 4

24 mint leaves
8 pods green cardamom
¼ cup turbinado sugar
¼ cup lime juice
1 cup Caribbean vanilla rum
½ cup passion fruit juice
½ cup spiced rum
⅓ cup coconut milk
to top tonic water
4 sprigs mint
4 sugar cane swizzle sticks
pinch ground allspice

In mortar, crush mint leaves, cardamom, and sugar until sugar dissolves. Stir in lime juice. Transfer to large mixing bowl. Combine with vanilla rum, spiced rum, and passion fruit juice. Whisk in coconut milk. Strain through fine sieve. Divide into highball glasses filled with ice. Top with tonic water. Garnish with mint sprigs, sugar cane swizzle sticks, and allspice.

SOUPS

LIMERICK CHICKEN SOUP   55

GREEN LIP MUSSEL CHOWDER   57

CHILLED CARROT TANGERINE VELOUTÉ   59

CADIZ SUMMER GAZPACHO   60

PORTOBELLO MUSHROOM BISQUE   63

OREGON GOAT CHEESE WALNUT SOUP   64

LEMON VERBENA SCENTED MATZOH BALL SOUP   66

BUTTERCUP SQUASH NECTAR   69

FRANCE

I stepped off the train all alone, and he was the only person waiting at station. I walked towards him skeptically, wondering if I disembarked at the right stop. "Patrik?" I asked in my best French accent. "Oui, oui, bienvenue en France," he replied. *Okay,* I thought. *Cool!*

On our way to Patrik's home in the Brittanic village of Pleucadeuc, staring out the car window was like looking into the pages of a European romance novel. Square combed fields of yellow flowers, small winding roads, and storybook towns with cathedral-roofed houses floated by.

The dining room table was the nucleus of Patrik's home. His wife Celine served multi-course dinners nightly and he matched the dishes with a progression of wines and spirits. I clearly recall the vibrance of Celine's smoked salmon pâté and macedoine vegetable salad, paired by Patrik with an Alsatian Riesling. The table is where we bonded and became close friends. It is where, while writing down Celine's recipe for vanilla crème caramel, I turned from an unknown visitor to an adopted family member. When Patrik set a brandy snifter of his homemade orange and coffee bean liqueur, called *44,* in front of me, I concluded that in all of France, I had come to the right house.

Pleucadeuc is a small town with a big heart. Next to the church is restaurant Chez Titi where I found Chef Didier in the kitchen sautéeing veal kidneys with speedy choreography and a yell of "hooplah" at the climactic flaming of the brandy. I joined Didier and his staff one afternoon for their daily employee meal at a picnic table right in the middle of the kitchen. We watched Didier pull the contents of a classic Pot-au-Feu out of a huge steaming cauldron. "Hooplah!" he yelled when a huge cut of tender beef nearly bent his two-pronged fork, as if fishing a giant marlin. Our mouths watered in anticipation as Didier sliced off the appropriate number of portions before returning the meat to its simmering sea. Each plate was completed with a mélange of vegetables and topped with a ladle of aromatic broth. I imitated my fellow diners by garnishing the dish with a pinch of pure sea salt and a slather of grainy mustard. It was at Didier's kitchen picnic table that I realized how saintly simplicity can be.

The meal was interrupted repeatedly by Didier, who jumped up from the table every time an order came in from the dining room, darting here and there, cooking, spicing, tasting, and presenting dishes, like a cross between a whirlwind and a ballerina.

Upon returning to Patrik and Celine's house, they expressed their delight at Didier's hospitality. When it came time for me to depart, they drove me back to the train station, gave me a kiss and a bottle of 44 and acted as if they were sending their only son off to college. What beautiful people, I thought. I knew at that moment that I might never see them again, but hoped that someday our paths would cross, and that there would be food involved.

—RON

Soda bread is well-associated with Irish heritage, but I didn't know if I would really find a lot of it traveling through Ireland. To my pleasant surprise, it is quite popular, at least in restaurants, where I found it served in many ways. Chefs showcase the bread in its original, rustic form with a bowl of hot soup, or refine it as part of an upscale bread basket. Either way, for me soda bread is a must-eat in Ireland. Its heartiness is a natural accompaniment to soulful soups. Being neutral in flavor, the bread willingly accepts any herb, spice, or ingredient you feel like introducing. How about cumin seeds and raisins? The best part of soda bread is the leftovers, toasted with butter and jam on a cold morning. In other words, make extra and give me a call the next day.—RON

LIMERICK CHICKEN SOUP
Sun Dried Currant Soda Bread

SERVES 6 FAMILY STYLE

CHICKEN SOUP

1 five-pound organic chicken, quartered
4 quarts vegetable stock
1½ teaspoons sea salt
1 teaspoon black peppercorns
4 sprigs thyme
2 bay leaves
1 cup diced celery
2 cups sliced leeks, white part only, washed
2 cups trimmed, peeled, diced carrots
1 pound red bliss potatoes, quartered
1 cup peeled, diced turnips
3 large egg yolks
¾ cup plain yogurt
2 cups washed, coarsely chopped spinach leaves
to taste sea salt and freshly ground black pepper

Rinse chicken thoroughly inside and out under cold running water. Transfer to 10-quart stock pot. Add vegetable stock, salt, peppercorns, thyme, and bay leaves. Bring to simmer. Cook 1 hour or until fully cooked. Carefully transfer chicken to cutting board to cool. Strain broth through fine sieve. Return 2 quarts broth to pot. Add celery, leeks, carrots, potatoes, and turnips. Simmer 20 minutes. Meanwhile, remove meat from bones. Discard skin and bones. Pull meat apart into shreds. Add meat to vegetables. Cook 5 minutes, skimming fat from surface with ladle . Remove soup from heat. Whisk egg yolks and yogurt in mixing bowl. Stir into soup. Add spinach. Season with salt and pepper. Transfer to large soup tureen.

SODA BREAD

** canola oil spray
4 cups all-purpose flour, sifted
¾ cup dried currants
1 tablespoon caraway seeds
1½ teaspoons granulated sugar
1 teaspoon baking soda
¾ teaspoon sea salt
½ teaspoon baking powder
⅓ cup unsalted butter, softened
1½ cups buttermilk
2 large eggs, beaten

Preheat oven to 375°F. Spray 8-inch square baking pan with canola oil. In large bowl, combine flour, currants, caraway seeds, sugar, baking soda, salt and baking powder. Cut butter into flour mixture. Stir in buttermilk and eggs. It is very important not to over mix. Turn out dough onto lightly floured surface. Knead briefly. Place in prepared baking pan. Bake 40 to 45 minutes or until golden brown and skewer inserted into center comes out clean. Remove from oven. Cool 5 minutes. Unmold. Transfer to serving platter.

NEW ZEALAND

Driving through the mountainous area of New Zealand's North Island after visiting the Kumeu River Winery, we arrived at our vacation home in the rural seaside town of Keri keri. The oldest wooden and stone buildings, weathered by the ocean, have survived since the 1820s, bringing character to the entire region. At the local supermarket, large, transparent glass bins housed the giant emerald green mussels, found only on the coast of New Zealand. We bought a couple of kilograms with veggies and herbs and made a soup on that chilly night. This experience reminded me of my childhood in Brittany when the family would gather at the seashore to collect black mussels and shuck oysters right on the beach at low tide. Depending on the season, I substitute cockles, clams, or oysters for the mussels.—BERNARD

GREEN LIPPED MUSSEL CHOWDER
Paprika Herb Croutons

SERVES 6

MUSSEL SOUP

3 pounds green lipped mussels, scrubbed, de-bearded
1 cup white wine
3 kaffir lime leaves
3 sprigs thyme
1 pod star anise
¼ cup olive oil
1 bulb fennel, chopped
1 cup chopped white onion
1 cup chopped leek, white part only, washed
3 cloves garlic, minced
2 cups peeled, diced sweet potatoes
¼ teaspoon ground turmeric
1 quart half and half
1 tablespoon cornstarch
½ cup dry sack sherry
2 tablespoons chopped flat leaf parsley
to taste sea salt and freshly ground black pepper

Soak mussels in cold water for 30 minutes to purge the sand. Add wine, lime leaves, thyme, and star anise to large sauce pot over high heat. Bring to a boil. Add mussels. Cover. Cook 3 minutes without opening the lid. Rotate mussels from bottom to top using slotted spoon to cook evenly. Cook additional 3 minutes or until mussels open. Transfer mussels to large bowl, discarding any that do not open. Remove meat from shell. Reserve 12 mussels and shells for garnish. Cut remaining mussels into quarters. Set aside. Strain liquid through fine sieve. Set aside. Add olive oil to large saucepan over medium heat. Add fennel, onion, leeks, and garlic. Cook 3 minutes without browning, stirring often. Add potatoes, reserved mussel liquid, turmeric, and half and half. Bring to simmer. Cook 10 minutes. Whisk cornstarch and sherry in small mixing bowl. Stir into chowder. Simmer 5 minutes. Fold in chopped mussels. Season with salt and pepper.

HERB CROUTONS

6 slices multigrain bread, crust removed, ½-inch cubed
2 tablespoons olive oil
1 teaspoon chopped thyme leaves
1 teaspoon chopped parsley leaves
¼ teaspoon salt
½ teaspoon sweet paprika

Preheat oven to 300°F. Toss all ingredients together in large mixing bowl. Transfer to baking sheet. Bake 15 minutes or until golden and crisp.

PRESENTATION

12 reserved mussels and shells
6 sprigs fresh dill

Ladle soup into warm bowls. Garnish with mussels, shells, croutons, and dill.

TAHITI

Flying over the island of Tahiti in a helicopter is an experience. The beauty of the deep blue sea, waterfalls, forests, and lush valleys surrounded by mountainous peaks made me forget the rotor blades above my head. Hopping from island to island, we landed at the Hanoa Plantation on the island of Raiatea where crops of taro, sugarcane, papaya, pineapple, and bananas are farmed. Five varieties of vanilla are the jeweled crown of the island. Nine months after pollination, the vanilla bean is harvested, laid in the sun and cured for six months. I brought back half a pound, a small fortune, to create this summer favorite recipe at the Marine Room. After scraping the seeds, seal the pods in a container of sugar to flavor your morning coffee or tea.—BERNARD

CHILLED CARROT TANGERINE VELOUTÉ
Rock Lobster Salad, Vanilla Oil

SERVES 6

THE SOUP

2 tablespoons grapeseed oil
½ cup chopped celery
1 bulb fennel, chopped
1½ pounds chopped peeled carrots
1 cup diced peeled sweet potato
¼ cup sweet vermouth
1 cup tangerine juice
1 cup vegetable stock
⅛ teaspoon hot chile powder
½ teaspoon sea salt
pinch saffron threads
½ cup heavy cream
1 cup carrot juice
to taste sea salt and ground white pepper

Add oil to stock pot over medium heat. Add celery, fennel, carrots, and sweet potato. Cook 5 minutes, without browning, stirring often. Add vermouth, ½ cup tangerine juice, vegetable stock, chile powder, sea salt and saffron. Cover. Simmer 20 minutes or until vegetables are soft. Remove from heat. Stir in cream. Working in batches, purée in blender until smooth. Strain through fine sieve. Refrigerate until well-chilled. Whisk in carrot juice and remaining tangerine juice. Season with salt and pepper.

ROCK LOBSTER SALAD

1 gallon water
1 teaspoon sea salt
2 6-ounce rock lobster tails
2 tablespoons hazelnut oil
½ teaspoon vanilla oil
1 tablespoon sweet vermouth
1 teaspoon minced chives
1 tablespoon julienned mint leaves
to taste sea salt and freshly ground black pepper

Bring water and salt to boil in large pot over high heat. Drop in lobster tails. Return to simmer. Cook 5 minutes. Transfer to ice bath. Remove shell. Devein. Cut into small cubes. Transfer to mixing bowl. Combine with remaining ingredients. Season with salt and pepper.

VANILLA OIL

2 vanilla beans
1 teaspoon vanilla extract
3 tablespoons hazelnut oil

Cut vanilla bean in half lengthwise. Scrape seeds into small mixing bowl. Whisk in vanilla extract and hazelnut oil. Reserve ½ teaspoon vanilla oil for lobster salad. Set aside remainder for presentation. Reserve vanilla pod for another use.

PRESENTATION

¼ cup alfalfa sprouts

Ladle soup into chilled soup bowls. Place lobster salad in center. Top with sprouts. Drizzle vanilla oil over soup.

SPAIN

I don't make a habit of visiting the same place twice. There is too much to see in this world. But Cadiz is a place I would go to over and over if given the choice. Surrounded by water on three sides, it is the oldest continuously inhabited city in the western world. The ambience and architecture, with golden domes and narrow streets, reminded me of a Middle Eastern setting. The city's lengthy evolution parallels the long, eventful history of one of the regions most popular dishes—gazpacho. What started as bread, garlic, and oil pounded to a paste is now what you see here—a beautiful tomato soup with a Cadiz-inspired seafood garnish. Gazpacho is made hundreds of ways throughout Spain. Join the fun and be a part of the ever-evolving creativity — R O N

CADIZ SUMMER GAZPACHO
Pico Del Mar

SERVES 6

GAZPACHO

3 cups diced ripened heirloom tomatoes
¼ cup chopped red onion
2 tablespoons extra virgin olive oil
1 cup vegetable stock, chilled
2 cloves garlic, sliced
1 tablespoon sherry vinegar
1 hot chile pepper, seeded, chopped
1 cup peeled, seeded, finely diced cucumber
¼ cup minced scallions
2 tablespoons chopped basil leaves
¼ cup gin
to taste sea salt and freshly ground black pepper

Place tomatoes, onions, olive oil, vegetable stock, garlic, vinegar, and chile pepper in blender. Pulse 15 seconds or until coarsely blended. Transfer to mixing bowl. Stir in remaining ingredients. Season with salt and pepper. Cover. Refrigerate 2 hours.

PICO DEL MAR

2 quarts water
1 teaspoon salt
12 large shrimp, size u-15
½ cup lump crabmeat, shelled
1 lemon, zested, juiced
1 tablespoon walnut oil
2 tablespoons toasted sunflower seeds
to taste sea salt and freshly ground black pepper

Bring water and salt to boil in large pot over high heat. Add shrimp. Return to simmer. Cook 2 minutes or until slightly underdone. Transfer to ice bath. Peel and devein shrimp, leaving tail on. Transfer to mixing bowl. Toss with remaining ingredients. Season with salt and pepper. Cover. Refrigerate until chilled.

PRESENTATION

6 sprigs basil
9 yellow teardrop tomatoes, halved
2 tablespoons extra virgin olive oil

Ladle gazpacho into chilled soup plate. Arrange shellfish in center. Garnish with basil and teardrop tomato halves. Drizzle with olive oil.

ITALY

In Umbria, the village of Montone celebrates the Festa del Bosco, a slow food festival that brings together cooks, food artisans, farmers, and academics to promote world food sustainability. This area is known for its truffles and porcini mushrooms that grow under giant oak trees. Taking our willow basket and walking stick to the woods, we gathered a potpourri of mushrooms. Back at the village, our forager guide, Maria, inspected the harvest carefully for mis-picked specimens. We were safe! We had a funghi fiesta of risotto, salads, and soup paired with a bottle of the finest Amarone. Brush or peel your mushrooms until clean, but avoid washing them as they will absorb water and lose flavor. Pulverizing dried porcinis, morels, or chanterelles in your spice grinder will fortify the taste of your bisque.—BERNARD

PORTOBELLO MUSHROOM BISQUE
Truffle Oil, Pine Nuts, Lemon Mascarpone

SERVES 6

MUSHROOM BISQUE

8 large portobello mushrooms
¼ cup olive oil
½ cup diced pancetta
½ cup chopped peeled shallots
5 cloves garlic, chopped
¼ cup all purpose flour
1 cup diced peeled celery root
1 tablespoon chopped marjoram
6 cups vegetable stock
½ cup heavy cream
¼ cup dried porcini mushrooms
¼ cup Marsala wine
pinch nutmeg
to taste sea salt and freshly ground black pepper

Remove stems from mushrooms. Scrape and discard gills using small spoon. Cut caps into 1-inch pieces. Set aside. Add oil, pancetta, shallots, and garlic to large stock pot over medium heat. Cook 3 minutes, stirring often. Add flour. Cook 1 minute. Add portobello, celery, and marjoram. Cook 5 minutes, stirring occasionally. Add stock and cream. Bring to simmer. Cook 20 minutes. Add dried porcinis to spice grinder. Process to a powder. Transfer to small mixing bowl. Whisk in Marsala and nutmeg. Add to soup. Cook 1 minute. Working in batches, transfer mixture to blender. Puree until smooth. Transfer back to stock pot. Return to low simmer. Season with salt and pepper.

LEMON MASCARPONE

3 tablespoons mascarpone cheese
½ teaspoon lemon zest
2 teaspoons chopped tarragon leaves
to taste sea salt and freshly ground black pepper

Add all ingredients to mixing bowl. Beat with wooden spoon until smooth. Season with salt and pepper.

PRESENTATION

2 tablespoons toasted pine nuts
6 sprigs marjoram
1 tablespoon truffle oil

Ladle bisque into warm soup bowls. Spoon mascarpone in center. Garnish with pine nuts and marjoram. Drizzle with truffle oil.

Seeing a plywood plank painted with the words "Pick Ur Own" by the side of the road has always meant an obligatory stop for my family when traveling scenic routes through the United States. Even before we had kids, and much more now that we do, we always stop. There is no better way to spend long driving days than snacking on just-picked berries or cracking walnuts one at a time by pounding them with an empty wine bottle against the dashboard. Oregon is one of our favorite road trips. Summer berries are followed by tree fruits in late August and nuts in the fall. Artisan cheeses are plentiful. This recipe melds the beauty of Oregon's produce in one simple dish. —RON

OREGON GOAT CHEESE WALNUT SOUP
Granny Smith Apple

SERVES 6

SOUP

1 tablespoon unsalted butter
½ cup chopped shallots
1 cup sliced leeks, white part only, washed
4 granny smith apples, cored, diced
1 quart vegetable stock
1 quart half and half
1 pound Yukon gold potatoes, peeled, chopped
2 leaves sage
1 teaspoon lemon thyme leaves
1 teaspoon sea salt
1½ cups crumbled organic goat cheese
½ cup toasted walnut halves
to taste sea salt and freshly ground white pepper

Melt butter in stock pot over medium heat. Add shallots, leeks, and apples. Cook 5 minutes without browning, stirring often. Add stock, half and half, potatoes, sage, thyme, and salt. Simmer 20 minutes or until potatoes are tender. Remove from heat. Transfer one third of soup to blender with one third of goat cheese and walnuts. Purée until smooth. Season with salt and white pepper. Transfer to stock pot over low heat. Repeat process.

APPLE

2 granny smith apples, cut into matchsticks
2 tablespoons cider vinegar
2 teaspoons honey
⅓ cup chopped toasted black walnuts
2 teaspoons minced chives
pinch freshly grated nutmeg
to taste salt and freshly ground black pepper

Gently toss all ingredients in mixing bowl. Season with salt and pepper.

PRESENTATION

6 sprigs lemon thyme

Ladle soup into warm soup bowls. Arrange green apple mixture in center. Garnish with lemon thyme.

ISRAEL

The Sephardic Jews of the Middle East, my grandfather's people, brought the influence of aromatic spices and herbs to the foods of Israel. The Ashkenazic Jews of Eastern Europe, my grandmother's side, brought sweeter ingredients like root vegetables and dinner pastries. My mom must have inherited the Sephardic side. When she makes Matzoh ball soup—she doctors it up big time, plucking verbena leaves from the garden, throwing in some hot chiles, and mixing sesame seeds into the matzoh ball mix. I throw some parsnips into the broth just to keep grandma's side happy. With a little creativity this can be a year-round soup that everyone can enjoy. It's nourishing, filling, and versatile. Matzoh ball soup—not just for Passover anymore.—RON

LEMON VERBENA SCENTED MATZOH BALL SOUP
Pickled Radish

SERVES 6 FAMILY STYLE

BROTH

1 tablespoon canola oil
6 scallions, white part only
6 cloves garlic, crushed
3 whole cloves
1 teaspoon black peppercorns
1 small red chile pepper, sliced
1 cup diced peeled parsnips
1 cup chopped celery
2 quarts chicken stock
½ teaspoon kosher salt
1 cup curly parsley leaves
to taste kosher salt and freshly ground black pepper

Add oil to large stock pot over medium heat. Add scallions, garlic, cloves, peppercorns, chile pepper, parsnips, and celery. Cook 10 minutes or until lightly browned, stirring often. Add chicken stock, kosher salt, and parsley. Simmer 30 minutes, skimming foam often. Strain through fine sieve. Return broth to clean pot over low heat. Season with salt and pepper.

MATZOH BALLS

4 large eggs
1 teaspoon kosher salt
½ teaspoon freshly ground black pepper
¼ cup chopped parsley leaves
1 tablespoon chopped lemon verbena leaves
2 tablespoons toasted sesame seeds
¼ cup canola oil
¼ cup soda water
1 cup matzoh meal

Beat eggs thoroughly in large mixing bowl. Add kosher salt, pepper, parsley, lemon verbena, and sesame seeds. Stir in oil, soda water, and matzoh meal. Cover. Refrigerate one hour. Bring 4 quarts lightly salted water to boil in large pot. Using palms of hands, gently roll 18 matzoh balls. Place on cookie sheet lined with oiled plastic wrap. Drop balls into boiling water. Return water to simmer. Cover. Cook 20 minutes. Transfer matzoh balls to soup tureen. Ladle hot broth over.

PICKLED RADISH

6 red radishes, thinly sliced
1 tablespoon white wine vinegar
1 teaspoon honey
to taste kosher salt and freshly ground black pepper

Toss all ingredients in small mixing bowl. Season with salt and pepper. Set aside.

PRESENTATION

2 scallions, green part, sliced on bias
18 smoked almonds whole

Transfer matzoh balls to soup tureen. Ladle hot broth over. Garnish with pickled radish, almonds and scallions.

BRAZIL

Floating on the Amazon River in an old wooden sailboat, I arrived at the hot, humid, and rainy city of Manaus. You can't even jump in the water to cool off without becoming lunch for the piranhas. Feeling under the weather, my local guide took me to the medicine man who gave me a bowl of deep purple-colored açai berry juice. For centuries, indigenous tribes in the Amazon River basin have used the açai berry, a rainforest fruit known for its healing powers. Traditionally, fresh açai berry clusters are crushed to make wine. For sipping, I prefer to infuse a bottle of white rum with 1 cup dried açai berries, ½ cup cacao nibs, 1 tablespoon black peppercorns, and 1 split vanilla bean. Refrigerated for 3 months, this makes the sexiest potion. —BERNARD

BUTTERCUP SQUASH NECTAR

Spiced Rum, Açai Berries, Fromage Blanc

SERVES 6

SQUASH NECTAR

- **2 3-pound** kabocha squash, halved, seeded
- **2 tablespoons** brown sugar
- **2 tablespoons** unsalted butter
- **½ cup** minced shallots
- **⅛ teaspoon** each ground cinnamon, clove, nutmeg, cayenne pepper
- **1 cup** dry vermouth
- **2 quarts** vegetable stock
- **1 stalk** lemongrass, split
- **2 tablespoons** maple syrup
- **1 teaspoon** grated fresh ginger
- **¼ cup** heavy cream
- **to taste** sea salt and freshly ground white pepper

Preheat oven to 350°F. Place squash on baking sheet, cut side up. Sprinkle flesh with brown sugar. Bake 35 minutes or until tender. Remove from oven. Cool. Scoop flesh from shell. Set aside. Melt butter in large pot over medium heat. Add shallots. Cook 2 minutes without browning, stirring often. Add cinnamon, clove, nutmeg, and cayenne pepper. Cook 1 minute, stirring often. Pour in vermouth. Bring to simmer. Add squash, stock, and lemongrass. Simmer 25 minutes. Discard lemongrass. Purée soup in blender until smooth. Strain through sieve into pot. Whisk in maple syrup, ginger, and cream. Bring back to simmer. Season with salt and pepper.

PRESENTATION

- **¼ cup** açai berries
- **¼ cup** apple juice
- **3 tablespoons** vanilla spiced rum
- **6 teaspoons** fromage blanc
- **6 sprigs** chervil

In small bowl, soak açai berries in apple juice for 10 minutes. Ladle nectar into warm soup cup. Drizzle with rum. Spoon fromage blanc in center. Garnish with açai berries and chervil.

SALADS

MUMBAI

I gazed over the scenic waters of the Arabian Sea as I left the fashionable, up-market area of Juhu in "Bollywood." The air was dusty and humid as I crossed the busy street with my friend, Tarun Varma, from the JW Marriott, to grab a frosted glass of freshly squeezed sugar cane juice at Kapil Tea House. Today I would experience *Aamchi Mumbai* which means the "real essence" of the city's authentic cuisine and lifestyle.

Hailing a rickshaw, we traveled through enormous traffic jams created by thousands of people going in and out of the city. We visited the Taj Mahal Palace & Tower, an architectural marvel that brings together Moorish, Oriental and Florentine styles with panoramic views of the Gateway of India. We visited Ghandi's home and the Babu Amichand Panalal Adishwarji Jain Temple, the most beautiful temple in Mumbai, flanked by two stone elephants and housing a dome with painted zodiac.

After a short taxi ride, we arrived at the mystical landmark of Haji Ali Dargah tomb on a tidal islet off the coast of Worli. At the constantly crowded Haji Ali Circle, the iconic Juice Centre is a popular roadside vendor. We tasted thirst-quenching fresh fruit concoctions made from vibrant and colorful papaya, watermelon, pineapple, mango, coconut, and exotic spices.

Throughout Mumbai, the streets are dotted with make-shift stalls and rickety carts with people preparing food. We went on a street-food-hopping excursion, tasting mutton biryani at Bhendi Bazaar, khaboosh roti at Colaba Causeway, chanawallahs at Gateway, vada-paav baakdas at Fountain, and swati snacks on Tardero Road.

We ended up at the famous shopping arcade of Bandra on Hill Road to experience the famous khaman dhoklas made with chana dal served with grated coconut, mustard seeds, and curry pattas. Tikhi mithi chutneys made with spices and tamarind are the perfect sidekick to the mind-blowing pani puri, famous for its tang, that explodes in the mouth with all its glory. I tasted it all!

With the rising mercury levels, we decided to keep cool by enjoying sliced cucumbers seasoned with sea salt, red chile powder, homemade masala spices, and a glass of iced lime water.

Later that evening we went to Chowpatty Beach, famous in Mumbai for its carnival atmosphere where the old and young alike gather to enjoy the action. You might catch a film shoot or street play, see an amazing gymnast in yogic postures making a quick buck, an old lady in a bright sari reading the fortune of a newlywed couple, or a monkey show crowded with kids screaming and laughing. This is where I first enjoyed Mumbai's most popular sweet snacks made of crisp, puffed rice and semolina doused in pungent chutneys, all scooped up on a flat, fried puri. Add this to your list of what an ideal life should be—eating at the beach with the warm sea breeze ruffling your hair.

—BERNARD

Here is one of the first signature dishes Bernard and I crafted together for The Marine Room. Over the years we have served it at some of the top cooking venues in the United States—Aspen Food and Wine Festival, James Beard House in New York, and the Ahwahnee Hotel's Chef Celebration in Yosemite. The main attraction of this recipe is Redwood Hill's chèvre-style goat cheese from Sebastopol, California. If necessary, you can substitute another high quality chèvre. To optimize the flavor and texture of the finished custard, remove from refrigerator 30 minutes before serving. —RON

REDWOOD HILL GOAT CHEESE BRÛLÉE
Tupelo Honey Verjus Dressing

SERVES 4

CUSTARD

4 dates, pitted, quartered
¼ cup crumbled goat cheese
2 tablespoons cream cheese, soft
2 large egg yolks
1 cup heavy cream
2 tablespoons chopped parsley leaves
1 tablespoon finely chopped shallots
2 tablespoons white port wine
to taste sea salt and freshly ground black pepper

Preheat oven to 250°F. Line bottom of four 4-ounce ceramic ramekins with dates. Combine remaining ingredients in blender. Process at medium speed until smooth. Strain through fine sieve. Season with salt and pepper. Divide evenly among ramekins. Transfer to large roasting pan lined with paper towels. Pour hot water into the pan halfway up sides of ramekins. Bake 45 minutes or until set but still jiggly in the center. Remove custard cups from pan. Cool to room temperature. Refrigerate.

FIG COULIS

1 cup diced sun-dried mission figs
⅓ cup maple syrup
¼ teaspoon star anise powder
1 tablespoon balsamic vinegar
½ cup port wine
¼ teaspoon freshly ground black pepper

Combine all ingredients in saucepan over medium-low heat. Cover. Simmer 10 minutes. Transfer to food processor. Purée until smooth. Strain through coarse sieve. Transfer to squeeze bottle.

TUILE

¼ cup grated Asiago cheese
¼ cup chopped walnuts
½ teaspoon freshly ground black pepper

Preheat oven to 350°F. Combine cheese, walnuts and black pepper in mixing bowl. Line large baking sheet with parchment paper or silicone baking pad. Spread 2 tablespoons mixture evenly into 4-inch round cookie cutter. Repeat process to make 4 tuiles. Bake 5 minutes or until golden crisp. Transfer to cooling rack.

PRESENTATION

2 roma tomatoes
2 cups mixed spring greens
20 sprigs chives
4 sprigs chervil
4 sprigs dill
2 tablespoons olive oil
2 tablespoons verjus
1 teaspoon tupelo honey
1 teaspoon minced shallots
to taste sea salt and freshly ground black pepper
2 tablespoons turbinado sugar

Cut tomatoes crosswise into ½-inch slices. Scoop pulp from center to form rings. Equally divide greens and herbs into 4 bouquets, securing each with 1 tomato ring. Combine olive oil, verjus, honey, shallots, salt and pepper in mixing bowl. Whisk to emulsify. Drizzle over greens. Sprinkle thin layer of sugar over brûlée. Caramelize to golden brown with sugar torch. Stand greens behind brûlée. Place tuile in between. Squeeze fig coulis onto plate.

PERU

The main reason I went to Huancayo was to see the very town that inspired this dish. After leaving Lima by train, rising to 15,000 feet, and passing through 69 tunnels and 58 bridges (yes, I counted them), we settled in Huancayo, the culinary mecca of the Peruvian Andes. I was amazed at the different colors and shapes of potatoes in the outdoor markets—orange, purple, red, swirled, yellow, white, finger-shaped, caterpillar-shaped, kidney-shaped, and more. "Potatoes in the style of Huancayo" is a regional dish of boiled potatoes smothered with cheese sauce. It is typically served with sliced onions, boiled eggs, and corn on the side. I like to serve all the components on one platter with the sauce on the bottom to showcase the beautiful color of Peruvian purple potatoes. —RON

HUANCAYO PURPLE POTATO SALAD
Pickled Red Onions, Queso Fresco Sauce

SERVES 6 FAMILY STYLE

SAUCE

1 tablespoon canola oil
1 cup chopped, seeded yellow bell pepper
1 teaspoon granulated sugar
¼ teaspoon ground turmeric
½ teaspoon chile powder
½ cup half and half
2 large egg yolks
¼ cup lemon juice
½ pound queso fresco cheese, crumbled
1 teaspoon coarse sea salt
⅛ teaspoon freshly ground black pepper

Add oil to skillet over medium-low heat. Add bell pepper, sugar, turmeric, and chile powder. Cook 3 minutes, stirring often. Pour in half and half. Bring to simmer. Whisk yolks and lemon juice in large mixing bowl. Whisk bell pepper mixture into yolks. Transfer mixture to blender. Add cheese, salt and pepper. Purée at medium speed until smooth. Transfer to shallow bowl. Refrigerate until chilled.

CORN AND POTATOES

2 ears sweet corn, shucked
2 pounds purple potatoes, washed
1 tablespoon lemon juice
3 tablespoons olive oil
to taste sea salt and freshly ground black pepper

Bring 2 quarts lightly salted water to boil. Add corn. Cook 5 minutes. Remove from water. Cool. Return water to simmer. Add potatoes. Cook 15 minutes or until tender. Drain in colander. Rinse under cold water. Refrigerate until chilled. Cut potatoes crosswise into ¼-inch thick slices, discarding end pieces. Slice corn crosswise into 1-inch thick wheels. Transfer potatoes and corn to cookie sheet. Whisk lemon juice, oil, salt and pepper in mixing bowl. Brush onto both sides of corn and potatoes.

PICKLED RED ONIONS

1 medium red onion
1 tablespoon red wine vinegar
¼ teaspoon coarse sea salt

Slice onion into ⅛-inch thick wheels. Separate into rings. Toss with red wine vinegar and sea salt. Set aside for 5 minutes.

PRESENTATION

6 hard-boiled eggs, peeled, quartered
18 whole black olives
18 sprigs parsley
to taste sea salt and freshly ground black pepper

Spoon sauce over entire surface of large ceramic serving platter. Arrange potatoes and corn atop. Garnish with eggs, olives, onion rings, and parsley sprigs. Sprinkle with salt and pepper.

BELGIUM

The concept of creating fine food using beer as an ingredient became clear to me when traveling through Belgium. At the annual beer festival in Brussels I had a five course mushroom tasting paired with a progression of ten different styles of beer. The earthy, nutty, and caramel flavors of Belgian beer are such a nice complement to earthy forest mushrooms. At the fromagerie I sampled an impressive display of artisanal Belgian cheeses and a quiche made with broodkaas, a heartier version of Gouda. Putting everything together—the mushrooms, cheese, quiche and beer—I returned home, and came up with this recipe. You can use any variety of mushrooms (the more the better), but even one kind will work.—RON

THREE CHEESE MUSHROOM TORTE
Young Oak Leaf Salad, Apple Beer Dressing

SERVES 6

TORTE

- **1 tablespoon** butter, softened
- **1 tablespoon** olive oil
- **2 tablespoons** minced shallots
- **¼ pound** cremini mushrooms
- **½ pound** oyster mushrooms
- **¼ pound** shiitake mushrooms
- **¼ pound** morel mushrooms
- **¼ cup** white port
- **4 large** eggs
- **1 cup** heavy cream
- **¼ cup** dried porcini mushrooms
- **1 tablespoon** chopped fresh parsley leaves
- **1 teaspoon** chopped fresh thyme leaves
- **¼ cup** grated Gruyère cheese
- **¼ cup** crumbled goat cheese
- **¼ cup** crumbled blue cheese
- **1 one-pound loaf** brioche
- **to taste** sea salt and freshly ground black pepper

Preheat oven to 350°F. Butter six 5-ounce baking dishes. Add dried porcinis to spice grinder. Process to a powder. Set aside. De-stem and thinly slice all mushrooms. Add olive oil to skillet over medium high heat. Add shallots and mushrooms. Cook without browning until all liquid evaporates, stirring often. Add cream. Bring to boil. Remove from heat. Stir in port. Season with salt and pepper. Beat eggs in large mixing bowl. Whisk in porcini powder, parsley, and thyme. Fold in Gruyère, goat cheese, blue cheese, and mushroom mixture. Trim crust from brioche. Cut brioche into 1-inch cubes. Fold into mushroom mixture, combining well. Divide among prepared baking dishes. Bake 30 minutes or until set and wooden skewer inserted in center comes out clean. Remove from oven. Rest 5 minutes.

SALAD

- **½ cup** Belgian dark beer
- **1 tablespoon** cider vinegar
- **1 teaspoon** brown mustard seeds
- **1 teaspoon** honey
- **3 tablespoons** safflower oil
- **to taste** sea salt and freshly ground black pepper
- **2 heads** baby green oak lettuce, trimmed, leaves separated
- **2 heads** baby red oak lettuce, trimmed, leaves separated
- **1 cup** watercress leaves
- **1** green apple, cored, cut into matchsticks

Add beer, vinegar, mustard seeds and honey to saucepan over medium heat. Reduce by half. Transfer to mixing bowl. Cool. Add oil in a slow steady stream, whisking vigorously to emulsify. Season with salt and pepper. Set aside one third of dressing in small bowl for plate presentation. Gently toss remaining dressing with greens and apples.

PRESENTATION

- **2 teaspoons** pure pumpkin seed oil
- **¼ cup** toasted walnuts
- **6 sprigs** dill

Unmold torte on center of serving plate. Drizzle with pumpkin seed oil. Mound salad atop. Garnish with walnuts and dill sprigs. Spoon dressing around torte.

BRAZIL

On my way to Belém, a city in the north of Brazil, I trekked through the Amazon jungle's maze of rivers, dense vegetation, and mosquitoes so big they looked like hummingbirds. I experienced a cuisine influenced by the Tupi tribe who live in houses built on stilts along the river bank. Freshly caught fish, accompanied by wild fruits and plants harvested in the Amazon basin, reflect the region's blend of Portuguese and indigenous ancestry. Throughout Brazil, social life revolves around the table. Every meal is a celebration of family, friends and life. A staple at dinner tables and marketplaces are *salada de bacalhau* and crispy *bolinhos*—cod fish fritters reminiscent of Portuguese heritage. I was addicted. —BERNARD

BELEM DO PARA BACALHAU
Pink Grapefruit, Hearts of Palm Salad

SERVES 6

SALTED COD

1 pound salted cod
1 stalk lemongrass, crushed
1 serrano pepper, halved, seeded

Add cod to 3 quarts cold water. Refrigerate overnight. Add 2 quarts water, lemongrass, and pepper to stock pot over medium-high heat. Simmer 5 minutes. Remove from heat. Cool. Refrigerate overnight. The next day, rinse cod under cold running water. Add lemongrass broth and cod to large stock pot over medium-high heat. Bring to simmer. Cook 10 minutes. Transfer cod to platter. When cool enough to handle, shred cod, discarding bones. Cover. Refrigerate until chilled.

BACALHAU

1 tablespoon unsalted butter
1 cup minced leeks, white part only, washed
¾ cup crème fraîche
1 large egg yolk
2 cloves garlic, minced
1 lemon, zested, juiced
⅛ teaspoon chile powder
½ cup olive oil
¼ cup plain yogurt
2 tablespoons chopped parsley leaves
1 tablespoon chopped mint leaves
to taste sea salt and freshly ground black pepper

Melt butter in saucepan over medium heat. Add leeks. Cook until liquid evaporates, stirring occasionally. Add crème fraîche. Bring to simmer. Remove from heat. Cool. In separate bowl, whisk egg yolk, garlic, lemon juice, and chile powder. Add oil in a slow steady stream, whisking vigorously to emulsify. Stir in yogurt, parsley, and mint. Fold in leeks and cod. Season with salt and pepper. Pack into plastic wrap-lined, 5-inch wide bowl. Cover. Refrigerate 1 hour.

PRESENTATION

1 head red leaf lettuce, washed, leaves separated, patted dry
3 pink grapefruits, peeled, segmented
4 hearts of palm, quartered lengthwise
4 radishes, thinly sliced
¼ cup toasted Brazil nuts
2 tablespoons seasoned rice vinegar
¼ cup olive oil
to taste sea salt and freshly ground black pepper

Line chilled serving platter with lettuce leaves. Unmold bacalhau in center. Arrange grapefruit, hearts of palm, radishes and brazil nuts around bacalhau. Add vinegar and olive oil to small mixing bowl. Whisk vigorously to emulsify. Season with salt and pepper. Drizzle over salad.

FRANCE

Chef Pierre Chambrin is one of 304 Maîtres Cuisiniers de France. I had the privilege of working as part of his kitchen brigade for three years at Maison Blanche in Washington D.C. I was the tournant cook, hopping from station to station and absorbing everything I could under his tutelage. My favorite station was the pantry where I prepared cured fish, terrines, and composed salads. This recipe truly reflects Pierre's passion for flavorful cuisine and in-season ingredients. In the kitchen we called him "Le Gros," and this was his favorite dish, so we named it "La Salade Gourmande du Gros." If artichokes are not in season, shaved fennel is a great substitute. —BERNARD

SALADE GOURMANDE DU GROS
Lobster, Artichoke Heart, Haricot Vert, Banyul Hazelnut Vinaigrette

SERVES 4

ARTICHOKES

1 quart cold water
¼ cup lemon juice
2 cloves garlic, crushed
2 sprigs thyme
½ teaspoon salt
1 teaspoon whole black peppercorns
4 large artichokes
2 lemons, halved
¼ cup flour
1 cup white wine

Add water, lemon juice, garlic, thyme, salt and pepper to large pot over medium high heat. Bring to simmer. Snap off and discard dark green outer leaves of artichokes until reaching tender light green leaves. Using pairing knife, remove remaining leaves. Trim fibrous green exterior from bottom and sides of the heart. Cut off stems near the base. Rub all cut surfaces immediately with lemon halves. In small bowl, mix flour and wine. Whisk into simmering liquid. Add artichoke hearts. Cook 15 minutes or until tender. Transfer to plate. Refrigerate until chilled. Using small spoon, scoop fuzzy choke and discard. Slice artichoke thinly crosswise.

LOBSTER AND HARICOT VERT

1 pound haricot vert (small green beans), trimmed
4 one-pound live Maine lobsters

Bring 2 gallons lightly salted water to boil in large stock pot. Add haricot vert. Cook 3 minutes or until al dente. Transfer to ice bath. Drain in colander. Return water to boil. Add lobsters. Cook 8 minutes. Transfer to ice bath to chill. Separate heads from tails. Remove tail, knuckle, and claw meat from shells. Set aside. Clean head by removing and discarding inner contents of head cavity. Wash head under running water. Cut bottom, thicker part of shell into V-shape, creating base for presentation. Leave antennae intact.

VINAIGRETTE

¼ cup hazelnut oil
2 tablespoons banyul sherry vinegar
1 teaspoon honey
1 teaspoon minced shallots
1 teaspoon finely chopped tarragon leaves
2 tablespoons toasted, chopped hazelnuts
to taste sea salt and freshly ground black pepper

Add all ingredients to mixing bowl. Whisk to emulsify. Season with salt and pepper.

PRESENTATION

2 tablespoons minced chives
to taste sea salt and freshly ground black pepper
1 loaf fig anise bread, sliced, toasted

Cut tail into medallions. Toss gently in large mixing bowl with artichokes, haricot vert, knuckle meat, claw meat, chives and vinaigrette. Arrange in center of chilled plate. Garnish with lobster head. Serve with fig anise bread.

November is prime hunting season in Virginia, where little Briery Creek Lake sits among beautiful rolling hills. This is the perfect habitat for rabbit, pheasant, quail, geese, duck, and wild turkey—a hunter's paradise. My friends would gather at dawn and work out a strategy to be back by sundown with their loot. The shots of the hunting rifles sounded like cannons to me and I loved the serenade of sleek hound dogs singing victory after each kill. But I am not a hunter, just a lover! Back at camp, I got ready to cook those delicacies over an open fire. Roasted, grilled, barbequed, or simply braised, quail are the perfect fare when winter is knocking at the door.—BERNARD

VIRGINIA BOBWHITE QUAIL SALAD

Bartlett Pear Dressing, Pistachios, Olives

SERVES 4

DRESSING

⅓ cup olive oil
2 tablespoons champagne vinegar
1 tablespoon minced shallots
2 tablespoons shelled, roasted, chopped pistachios
1 teaspoon chopped tarragon leaves
to taste sea salt and freshly ground black pepper

Add olive oil and vinegar to mixing bowl. Whisk to emulsify. Add remaining ingredients. Season with salt and pepper.

POTATOES

½ pound fingerling potatoes, washed
1 tablespoon extra virgin olive oil
to taste sea salt and freshly ground black pepper

Cook potatoes in simmering, salted water until tender. Drain in colander. Rinse with cold water. Cut into halves lengthwise. Pat dry. Transfer to mixing bowl. Toss with olive oil, salt and pepper.

QUAIL

4 5-ounce semi-boneless quail
4 chicken livers, cleaned
to taste sea salt and freshly ground black pepper
2 teaspoons thyme leaves
1 tablespoon peanut oil
1 teaspoon unsalted butter
¼ cup blood orange juice
1 teaspoon blood orange zest

Preheat oven to 375°F. Season quail and livers with salt, pepper, and thyme on all sides. Add peanut oil to heavy bottom skillet over medium high heat. Place quail into pan, breast side down. Cook until golden brown. Flip over. Place skillet in oven. Roast 8 minutes or until fully cooked. Transfer quail to plate. Cover loosely with foil to keep warm. Return skillet to stovetop over medium high heat. Add butter and chicken livers. Brown on all sides until pink in center. Add orange juice and zest, tossing to coat. Transfer to plate.

PRESENTATION

¼ pound organic young lettuce leaves, washed, patted dry
¼ cup Sultana golden raisins
8 sprigs chive
4 sprigs parsley
4 quail eggs
1 teaspoon peanut oil
to taste sea salt and freshly ground black pepper
½ cup finely diced Bartlett pear

Arrange potatoes in center of large serving plate. Carve quail legs from breast. Place legs besides potatoes and breast atop potatoes. Toss salad leaves with 2 tablespoons dressing. Arrange leaves behind breast. Season with salt and pepper. Garnish plate with chicken liver, raisins, chives and parsley. Crack quail eggs into 4 small ramekins. Add oil to non-stick skillet over low heat. Add eggs to skillet. Season with salt and pepper. Cook sunny side up. Place atop quail legs. Fold pears into remaining dressing. Spoon dressing onto plate.

My first encounter with wild ostrich was in the middle of Australia in the mountainous village of Hall's Gap, located between Melbourne and Adelaide. I was looking for an aboriginal site on my way to Mount Langhi Ghiran winery. Traveling through the bush on a dirt road under the baking sun, the ride was bumpy, slow, and dusty. Suddenly, out of nowhere, I caught sight of a flock of these beautiful creatures running by the side of the car. Focused, on a mission, one by one, they passed me with great speed and elegance, all legs and feathers. The show was over quickly, as the flock disappeared into the dense habitat beneath the forest canopy. Maybe they realized I was a chef. —BERNARD

WATTLESEED RUBBED OSTRICH FAN FILET

Beetroot Jam, Peppery Greens, Blackberry Grenache Reduction

SERVES 4

OSTRICH

2 tablespoons unsalted butter
4 5-ounce ostrich fan fillets
1 pint blackberries
2 tablespoons minced shallots
1 teaspoon brown sugar
½ teaspoon orange zest
½ cup Grenache wine
2 sprigs thyme
1 cup chicken stock
to taste sea salt and freshly ground black pepper

Add butter to large skillet over medium high heat. Season ostrich with salt and pepper on all sides. Place in skillet. Cook on all sides until medium rare. Transfer ostrich to wattleseed mixture. Roll to coat thoroughly. Set on wire rack. Discard excess butter from skillet and return to medium-high heat. Add blackberries, shallots, brown sugar, and orange zest. Cook 2 minutes, stirring often. Add Grenache and thyme. Bring to simmer. Reduce by two thirds. Add chicken stock. Reduce to syrupy consistency. Strain through fine sieve. Season with salt and pepper. Cool. Transfer to squeeze bottle.

WATTLESEED SPICE

¼ cup ground wattleseed
1 tablespoon cocoa nibs
¼ cup sliced toasted almonds
½ teaspoon fleur de sel
¼ teaspoon black pepper

Add all ingredients to coffee grinder. Process to coarse consistency. Transfer to shallow plate. Set aside.

PRESENTATION

1 cup arugula leaves
½ cup watercress leaves
¼ cup parsley leaves
1 tablespoon lemon juice
2 tablespoon extra virgin olive oil
1 bartlett pear, cored, cut in matchsticks
¼ cup crumbled blue cheese
to taste sea salt and freshly ground black pepper
4 sprigs marjoram
½ cup Beetroot Jam (recipe on page 230)

Gently toss arugula, watercress, parsley, lemon juice, olive oil, pear, and blue cheese in mixing bowl. Season with salt and pepper. Mound salad in center of warm serving plate. Slice ostrich fillets into 5 medallions. Fan around salad. Squeeze sauce onto plate. Garnish with marjoram and beetroot jam.

The truth is that neither of us has ever seen a dish like this in Italy, but it was so cute that we just had to share this recipe. One day, while working on the photo shoot for our Italian recipes, we decided to cook lunch for the crew. Using all the ingredients in front of us, we came up with this Italian version of a veggie burger. A splash from the bottles of carob vincotto and mosto olive oil brought a layer of sweet and citrus flavors. It was like magic. Everyone started to attack the platter when our photographer, Gregory, screamed, "Stop, I need to get a picture of this!" An aged balsamic would be a good substitute for carob vincotto. You can mimic the flavor of lemon mosto olive oil by infusing extra virgin olive oil with dried lemon peel. —RON

INSIDE-OUT PORTOBELLO BURGER
Carob Vincotto, Lemon Mosto Olive Oil

SERVES 4

POTATOES

- **1½ pounds** russet potatoes
- **1 teaspoon** minced garlic
- **½ cup** goat cheese
- **⅓ cup** mascarpone
- **2 tablespoons** unsalted butter
- **to taste** sea salt and freshly ground black pepper

Preheat oven to 375°F. Wrap potatoes individually in aluminum foil. Bake 1 hour, or until tender. Remove from oven. Discard foil. Cut in half. Holding each half cradled in a kitchen towel, scoop flesh into large mixing bowl. Mash until smooth. Fold in remaining ingredients. Cool. Form into patties, 3 inches in diameter.

MUSHROOMS

- **8** portobello mushrooms, 4-inch cap
- **¼ cup** maple syrup
- **⅓ cup** balsamic vinegar
- **3 tablespoons** olive oil
- **1 tablespoon** chopped lemon thyme leaves
- **to taste** sea salt and freshly ground black pepper

Brush mushroom caps with damp paper towel to clean. Discard stems. Remove gills with spoon and discard. Combine maple syrup, balsamic, olive oil and thyme in large mixing bowl to make marinade. Season with salt and pepper. Add mushrooms. Toss to coat. Transfer mushrooms and marinade to casserole dish. Place in oven. Cook 5 minutes. Flip mushrooms. Cook additional 5 minutes. Transfer mushrooms to plate, reserving marinade. Set both aside.

WILTED GREENS

- **1 large** red onion, peeled
- **2 tablespoons** olive oil
- **to taste** sea salt and freshly ground black pepper
- **½ pound** baby spinach leaves, washed, patted dry
- **½ pound** baby green chard leaves, washed, patted dry
- **1 tablespoon** lemon juice

Slice onion crosswise into ¼-inch thick wheels. Insert 3 toothpicks into each wheel to keep rings intact. Add oil to large skillet over medium high heat. Carefully place onion wheels in pan. Season with salt and pepper. Cook 3 minutes or until golden brown. Flip carefully using spatula. Cook additional 2 minutes. Transfer to platter. Immediately add spinach and chard to pan. Season with salt, pepper and lemon juice. Cook 1 minute or until wilted, stirring constantly. Transfer to colander to drain.

PRESENTATION

- **2 tablespoons** reserved marinade from mushrooms
- **2 tablespoons** lemon mosto olive oil
- **2 tablespoons** carob vincotto
- **to taste** flaky sea salt and freshly ground black pepper

Place 4 mushroom caps, gill side up, in casserole dish. Fill evenly with wilted greens. Top with red onion, potato, and mushroom cap, to form a sandwich. Drizzle reserved marinade atop. Bake 15 minutes or until 160°F in center. Remove from oven. Transfer to serving platter. Drizzle with oil and vincotto. Sprinkle with flaky sea salt and black pepper.

SEA FARE STARTERS

HONG KONG

The weather was cool and crisp on an early morning ferry ride from Kowloon Peninsula to Lantau Island. It is a one-hour journey through Hong Kong harbor. The ocean, as smooth as glass, reflected the glittering lights of the city. As the ferry glideed between the islands, the hustle and bustle of Hong Kong slowly disappeared and a peaceful serenity set in.

I met my friend Urs Besmer at the coastal town of Mui Wo. From there we took a bus to the 300-year-old Chinese fishing village of Tai O, a somewhat rocky ride snaking around the coast through areas of dense vegetation. Tai O is the home of the Ming dynasty's oldest temple and the Tanka people, skilled fishermen who reside in enchanting stilt houses called *pangwu*. These homes, boasting views of both the mountains and the sea, have been built above the tidal flats for generations.

A multicolored fleet of old wooden fishing boats gently rocks in the small harbor as egrets and herons eagerly look out for small fish to capture for lunch. So do the fishermen!

Walking through the narrow streets at the entrance of the village, the Tai O market emerged in a burst of vibrant color and the sounds of children playing. Fish were drying on bamboo slats and beechwood racks just off the walkway, under the harsh midday sun. Silver shrimp are in abundance during the summer. Proud villagers peeled and mixed the flesh with sea salt then dried it in the sun to make their famous shrimp paste, considered Tai O's gold.

Baskets of salted fish, dried seahorses, starfish, blowfish, shark fins, and smoked meats were displayed as symbols of the surrounding culture. We crossed paths with a stunning sixty-five-pound grouper hanging from a pole, balanced between the shoulders of two smiling fishermen.

We passed a stall selling bright bunches of green mint, lotus leaves, lemongrass stalks, herbs, and fragrant fruits. Street vendors steamed fish balls, simmered noodle soups, and lathered barbecued pork with homemade sauces of bean curd and chiles. The salted fish was steamed, then stir-fried with ginger, vegetables, and shrimp paste. We drank a couple of cold local beers to chase it down. My favorite dish was the preparation of dried scallops called *conpoy* prepared in a clay pot with rice, greens, black mushrooms, and Lee Kum Kee XO sauce. It is heaven on earth!

At my final stop, the tranquil village of Ngong Ping, a hundred-foot-tall bronze Buddha stood towering over the island. I felt intoxicated by the fragrance of incense burning inside the monastery's enclave, and delighted to spend a few precious moments reflecting on my special journey of enlightenment.

—BERNARD

PERU

All of my Peruvian friends claim their country's ceviche is the best and most original recipe. South of Lima, I arrived at a large sea port called Chimbote, where small fishing boats, anchored in soldier-like rows, bob in a windswept harbor. You couldn't paint a prettier scene. Throughout Peru, ceviche is fresh, diverse, and innovative, but on the shore of Chimbote, it's all about the seafood and the curious shot of ceviche juice called "Tiger's Milk." Here, ceviche is abundant and the cevicherias in the not-so-picturesque parts of town are hidden jewels waiting to be discovered. If you can find fresh key limes, they make the best and most authentic tasting ceviche. —RON

CHIMBOTE SEA BASS CEVICHE
Sweet Corn Potato Relish, Tiger Milk

SERVES 6

CEVICHE

2 cloves garlic, sliced paper thin
½ cup paper thin sliced red onion
¾ cup lime juice
½ cup lemon juice
1 hot chile pepper, seeded, sliced paper thin
1 teaspoon sea salt
¼ teaspoon freshly ground white pepper
2 tablespoons chopped parsley leaves
1 pound sea bass, skinless, boneless
9 large fresh oysters, washed

Combine garlic, onion, lime juice, lemon juice, chile pepper, salt, white pepper and parsley in large mixing bowl. Cut sea bass into ½-inch cubes. Add to marinade. Shuck oysters, discarding top shells. Remove oyster meat from bottom shell. Remove all shell fragments from meat. Cut oysters in half. Fold into sea bass. Cover. Refrigerate 6 hours. Using slotted spoon, transfer sea bass and oysters from marinade to chilled serving bowls.

TIGER MILK

¼ cup pisco brandy, chilled

Strain 1 cup marinade through coffee filter. Add pisco. Divide into 6 shot glasses.

SWEET CORN POTATO RELISH

2 cups ¼-inch diced peeled sweet potato
3 tablespoons olive oil
¼ teaspoon cumin seeds
1½ cups sweet corn kernels
to taste sea salt and freshly ground black pepper
2 oranges, peeled, cut into segments
¼ cup cilantro leaves
¼ cup chopped toasted almonds

Bring large pot of salted water to boil. Add sweet potatoes. Cook 3 minutes. Drain in colander. Rinse under cold running water. Pat dry with paper towels. Add oil and cumin seeds to large skillet over medium heat. Toast 30 seconds. Add corn and potatoes. Season with salt and pepper. Sauté until corn and potatoes are tender. Remove from heat. Transfer to cookie sheet, spreading evenly to cool quickly. Refrigerate until well chilled. Transfer to mixing bowl. Toss with orange and cilantro. Season with salt and pepper. Divide into chilled serving bowls. Sprinkle with almonds.

MEXICO

After a night of too much tequila and mariachi, Ron and I met for ceviche at the Mercado de Mariscos in Ensenada, one of our favorite escapes from San Diego. It's a great spot to check out our neighbors' cuisine and sample some of the best grub south of the border. The prized giant sea scallop, *Mano de León*, or "Lion's Paw," gets its name from the unique shape of its shell, which resembles a lion's paw. They are hand-harvested from the Baja sea floor and sold right on the docks. The sweet, succulent flesh of the scallop makes the ultimate ceviche. If you don't have any pumpkin seed oil, any nut oil will do. —BERNARD

MANO DE LEÓN SEA SCALLOP PETALS
Tequila Papaya Salsa, Manchego, Pumpkin Seed Oil

SERVES 6

PAPAYA SALSA

½ cup finely diced, peeled papaya

¼ cup finely diced, peeled jicama

¼ cup peeled, seeded, finely diced cucumber

2 teaspoons grated ginger

½ teaspoon seeded, minced red chile pepper

2 tablespoons chopped cilantro leaves

1 orange, zested, juiced

2 tablespoons gold tequila

to taste sea salt and freshly ground black pepper

Toss all ingredients in mixing bowl. Season with salt and pepper. Cover. Refrigerate 1 hour.

SEA SCALLOPS

12 large sea scallops, size u-10

Remove tendon from scallops. Wash scallops by dipping in ice water. Pat dry with paper towels. Cut scallops horizontally into 4 slices. Pack 2 tablespoons fruit relish into 1½-inch cookie cutter ring in center of chilled serving plate. Remove ring. Arrange 8 scallop "petals" around salsa to create a flower shape.

PRESENTATION

2 limes, halved

2 tablespoons pumpkin seed oil

to taste sea salt and freshly ground black pepper

1 tablespoons minced chives

2 tablespoons shaved Manchego cheese

6 edible flowers

12 chive stalks

2 tablespoons toasted pepitas

Squeeze lime juice over scallops. Drizzle with pumpkin seed oil. Season with salt and pepper. Sprinkle with chives. Shave Manchego cheese atop. Garnish with edible flower, chive stalks, and pepitas.

PUERTO RICO

Living in Orlando, I was surrounded by the tropical beat of Puerto Rican culture. With cheap mom-and-pop eateries all around, I rarely passed three days without fried plantains, sofrito, black beans, and roasted pork. Puerto Ricans always talk about their dishes with a gleam in their eye and mouth-watering anticipation for their next good meal. On a trip to the island I discovered a lighter and brighter side to the cuisine—reflected in the following dish, like stars reflecting on the luminescent bay in Isla de Vieques. By the way, if you are ever in need of one magical night, here is the place. —RON

ISLA DE VIEQUES VANILLA SPICED SHRIMP
Chickpea Salad, Annatto Pineapple Emulsion

SERVES 6

PINEAPPLE EMULSION

2 tablespoons honey
3 tablespoons dark rum
¼ cup canola oil
½ teaspoon annatto powder
½ cup cored, diced pineapple
1 tablespoon lime juice
pinch cayenne pepper
to taste sea salt and freshly ground black pepper

Combine all ingredients in blender. Purée at medium speed to emulsify. Season with salt and pepper. Set aside.

SHRIMP

½ vanilla bean, finely chopped
¼ cup sliced almonds
½ teaspoon fennel seeds
½ teaspoon chile flakes
¼ teaspoon coarse sea salt
2 tablespoons peanut oil
12 large shrimp, size u-15, shell-on

Add vanilla, almonds, fennel seeds, chile flakes, and sea salt to large skillet over low heat. Cook until almonds are toasted, stirring often. Transfer mixture to spice grinder. Process to coarse meal. Set aside. Add oil to large skillet over medium-high heat. Add shrimp. Roast 2 minutes on each side or until slightly underdone. Transfer to platter. Place in freezer 5 minutes to cool quickly. Remove shell, leaving tail intact. Devein. Transfer to large mixing bowl. Toss with ¼ cup pineapple emulsion. Sprinkle with almond spice blend.

SALAD

1 cup cooked chickpeas
2 tomatoes, seeded, diced
½ cup diced peeled jicama
½ cup seeded, thinly sliced yellow bell pepper
⅓ cup cilantro leaves
to taste sea salt and freshly ground black pepper

Combine all ingredients in mixing bowl. Toss with ¼ cup pineapple emulsion. Season with salt and pepper.

PRESENTATION

3 avocados
¼ cup lemon juice

Cut avocado in half lengthwise. Remove seed. Peel carefully using small paring knife. Brush entire surface of avocados with lemon juice. Transfer avocado halves to chilled serving plates. Wrap 2 shrimp around base of each avocado. Fill with chickpea salad. Spoon remaining dressing atop.

In Barcelona, classic and contemporary co-exist in a seamless flow. My wife and I walked alongside medieval stone walls frilled with neon signs, noting the striking juxtaposition of old and new worlds. Maitre D' Marc Martinez invited us to his restaurant, Comerç 24, where Chef Arnau Muñío injected modern inspiration into the best ingredients from the local land and sea. This recipe is a tribute to that experience. Raw artichoke and white asparagus give a crisp, fresh complement to sushi-grade tuna. If you can't find white asparagus, use hearts of palm. —RON

SPANISH TUNA CRUDO
Artichoke Asparagus Salad, Orange Gastrique, Pecorino

SERVES 4

GASTRIQUE

1 cup blood orange juice
¼ cup sherry vinegar
¼ teaspoon Spanish paprika
¼ cup light brown sugar
2 tablespoons almond oil
to taste sea salt and freshly ground black pepper

Add orange juice, sherry vinegar, paprika, and brown sugar to small saucepan over medium heat. Reduce to half cup. Add almond oil in slow steady stream, whisking vigorously to emulsify. Season with salt and pepper. Cool. Transfer to squeeze bottle.

SALAD

2 large artichokes
1 lemon, halved
2 tablespoons lemon juice
4 extra large white asparagus, peeled
4 yellow teardrop tomatoes, halved
4 red teardrop tomatoes, halved
2 tablespoons extra virgin olive oil
12 sprigs chervil
1 teaspoon honey
to taste sea salt and freshly ground black pepper

Cut off artichoke stems. Snap off all leaves from the artichoke heart. Trim off fibrous green exterior around bottom of heart. Using melon baller, scoop fuzzy choke and discard. Rub all cut surfaces immediately with lemon halves. Cut into thin slices using sharp knife or mandoline slicer. Transfer to mixing bowl. Toss with lemon juice. Using vegetable peeler, shave white asparagus lengthwise to form ribbons. Add to artichokes. Combine with remaining ingredients. Season with salt and pepper.

TUNA

1 pound ahi tuna, sushi-grade #1
2 tablespoons almond oil
1 tablespoon mustard seeds
to taste flaky sea salt and freshly ground black pepper
4 fresh figs, halved
4 caper berries
2 ounces Pecorino Romano cheese, shaved

Thinly slice tuna against the grain. Arrange slices side by side on chilled serving plates. Drizzle with almond oil. Sprinkle with mustard seeds, sea salt and pepper. Place artichoke salad in center of plate. Garnish with figs, caper berries, and Pecorino. Squeeze gastrique in thin line around tuna.

ECUADOR

My friend Lauralee took me on a journey to the highest market in the Andes in Otavalo, surrounded by mountain peaks and volcanoes. At dawn, the native Indians descended the mountain trails, bringing colorful weavings of textiles, leather, and live animals for auction, energizing the market while Incan music played vibrantly in the background. A group of indigenous children were eating a teardrop-shaped yellow- and purple-streaked fruit called "pepino." Laughing at my strange appearance, the kids ran toward me to share their treat, which tastes like a blend of honeydew and Asian pear. If you can't find pepinos, avocados will work great in this recipe. —BERNARD

SALINAS MAHI MAHI ESCABECHE
Pepino Melon, Jicama Salad, Sesame Sea Salt Popped Corn

SERVES 4

ESCABECHE

1 cup orange juice
¼ cup lemon juice
¼ cup white wine vinegar
1 tablespoon black peppercorns
2 cloves garlic, chopped
1 tablespoon celery seeds
2 bags chamomile tea
1 pound center cut mahi mahi fillet, skinless, boneless
½ teaspoon sea salt

Combine orange juice, lemon juice, vinegar, peppercorns, garlic, celery seeds, and tea in medium saucepan. Bring to simmer. Remove from heat. Cool to room temperature. Strain through fine sieve into shallow baking dish, pressing on solids. Cut mahi mahi crosswise into ¼-inch thick slices. Place mahi mahi slices in marinade. Cover. Refrigerate 2 hours.

JICAMA SALAD

½ cup matchstick-cut jicama
¼ cup thinly sliced red onion
2 tablespoons chopped cilantro leaves
¼ cup finely diced yellow bell pepper
1 jalapeño pepper, seeded, sliced paper thin
2 tablespoons olive oil
to taste sea salt and freshly ground white pepper

Combine all ingredients in mixing bowl. Season with salt and pepper. Cover. Refrigerate 30 minutes.

POPPED CORN

1½ tablespoons light sesame oil
¼ cup popcorn kernels
¼ teaspoon flaky sea salt

Add 1 tablespoon oil and popcorn kernels to heavy bottom pot over medium heat. Cover. Cook, shaking pot often, until popping slows down. Turn off heat. Let sit 30 seconds. Uncover. Add sea salt and remaining sesame oil. Toss to coat.

PRESENTATION

4 pepino melons
12 leaves cilantro

Cut pepino melons in half lengthwise. Slice enough off the bottom to create a flat surface to prevent toppling. Use a melon baller to remove seeds. Discard. Scoop out half of the pulp from each melon. Coarsely chop pulp. Combine with jicama salad. Adjust seasoning. Fill each melon with salad. Top with mahi mahi slices. Spoon 1 teaspoon marinade atop. Garnish with cilantro leaves and popped corn.

I strolled through the ancient village of Garmouth, following the banks of the river Spey, where Scottish families were out for the Maggie Fair. Handicrafts, pies, and multicolored fishing lures were being sold for a bargain. Men lined the banks of the river, fishing for migratory sea trout and Atlantic salmon. The peacefulness of the surrounding countryside was broken by the excitement and struggle of hooking "the big one." Back at the fair, a woman wearing a black lace shawl poured batter into a cast iron skillet to make Scottish crumpets served with butter, jam, and clotted cream. Standing in line and observing the production, I imagined a crumpet with the cream and slices of cured salmon. —RON

WHISKY SMOKED SCOTTISH SALMON
Horseradish Chive Crumpets, Green Pea Cream

SERVES 6 FAMILY STYLE

SALMON

1 cup brown sugar
⅔ cup coarse sea salt
1 tablespoon cracked black pepper
1 teaspoon allspice
½ cup chopped fresh dill
2 pounds salmon fillet, center cut, skinless, boneless
1 tablespoon liquid smoke
½ cup whisky
1 tablespoon orange bitters

In a mixing bowl, combine brown sugar, sea salt, pepper, allspice, and dill. Spread one third of mixture in nonreactive dish to cover bottom. Place salmon atop. Cover salmon evenly with remaining mixture. In separate bowl, combine liquid smoke, whisky, and orange bitters. Ladle mixture over salmon. Cover. Refrigerate 12 hours. Turn salmon over. Cover. Refrigerate an additional 6 hours. Remove salmon from dish. Discard liquid. Scrape excess spice mixture from surface of salmon. Using very sharp knife, thinly slice salmon across the grain.

SAUCE

1 cup green peas
1 cup watercress leaves
¼ cup chopped scallions
18 leaves mint
¼ cup parsley leaves
1 lemon, zested, juiced
½ cup crème fraîche
to taste sea salt and freshly ground black pepper
1 sprig parsley

Bring 1 quart lightly salted water to boil. Add peas. Cook 30 seconds. Transfer to ice bath. Drain. Add to blender with remaining ingredients. Blend until smooth. Strain through fine sieve. Season with salt and pepper. Transfer to sauce dish. Garnish with parsley sprig.

GREEN APPLE SALAD

6 walnut halves
2 tablespoons walnut oil
1 large green apple, cored, cut into matchsticks
1 tablespoon lemon juice
½ cup watercress leaves
to taste sea salt and freshly ground black pepper

Combine all ingredients in mixing bowl. Season with salt and pepper. Arrange on top of crumpets.

CRUMPETS

1½ cups self-rising flour
2 tablespoons granulated sugar
½ teaspoon baking powder
½ teaspoon sea salt
1⅓ cups whole milk
2 extra large eggs
1 tablespoon freshly grated horseradish
2 tablespoons chopped chives
2 tablespoons unsalted butter, melted

Sift flour, sugar, baking powder, and salt into medium bowl. Set aside. Add milk, eggs, horseradish, and chives to blender. Blend until smooth. Add flour mixture. Pulse to combine. Add oil to large non-stick pan over low heat. Brush inside of three 2-inch cookie cutter rings with butter. Place into pan. Pour 3 tablespoons batter into each ring. Cook 10 minutes, or until center is set and top is full of bubbles. Remove rings. Flip crumpets. Cook 1 more minute. Repeat process with remaining batter.

HAWAII

While visiting Hawaii for the first time as a young teenager, I was captivated by the clear warm tropical waters. I remember the feeling of ditching my snorkel in order to delve as far as possible into the underwater realm. I was alone in a world where fish circled by like flocks of swimming parrots. Larger marine strangers, alone like me, came in and out of view with a flash of fin or tail. The fish of Hawaii, like their habitat, are clean and vibrant, inviting us to enjoy them in the raw state. Some fish, like the Kona kampachi, are sustainably farm-raised in the same waters. If you can't find kampachi, hamachi or ahi tuna work as well. —RON

BIG ISLAND KONA KAMPACHI TARTARE
Daikon, Quail Eggs, Tobiko Caviar

SERVES 4

KONA KAMPACHI TARTARE

1 tablespoon minced shallots
1 tablespoon avocado oil
1 tablespoon lemon juice
1 tangerine, zested, juiced
6 drops Tabasco® sauce
8 ounces Kona kampachi fillet, skinless, boneless
1 tablespoon chopped parsley leaves
1 teaspoon roasted sesame seeds
2 roma tomatoes, peeled, seeded, diced
1 tablespoon finely chopped Thai basil
to taste sea salt and freshly ground black pepper

Whisk shallots, avocado oil, lemon juice, tangerine juice, zest, and Tabasco® in small mixing bowl. Finely dice Kona kampachi. Add to bowl. Combine well. Fold in remaining ingredients. Season with salt and pepper. Cover. Refrigerate 30 minutes.

PRESENTATION

2 tablespoons seasoned rice vinegar
1 teaspoon honey
¼ teaspoon sea salt
1 medium daikon radish, peeled
12 leaves watercress
2 quail eggs, hard boiled, peeled, halved
4 chives stalks, cut 2 inches long on bias
2 tablespoons avocado oil
2 tablespoons red tobiko caviar

Whisk rice vinegar, honey, and sea salt in large mixing bowl. Using sharp knife or vegetable slicer, cut daikon into forty eight ⅛-inch thick slices. Add to vinegar mixture. Toss to coat. Marinate 5 minutes. Drain in colander. Overlap 12 slices daikon in flower pattern on chilled serving plate. Pack kampachi tartare in 2-inch ring in center of plate. Remove ring. Garnish with watercress, quail egg, and chive stalks. Add avocado oil to small bowl. Stir in tobiko. Spoon onto plate around daikon.

PERU

In the town of Chorrillos, a large hill with a huge white cross marks the spot where the Peruvian army made its last stand, defending Lima against Chilean invaders in 1879. It bears an uncanny resemblance to Mt. Soledad back home, a cross-topped hill above the city and shores of La Jolla, two minutes from The Marine Room. Chorrillos, like so many coastal towns in Peru, is a seafood paradise. The style of cooking here, called *Chorrillana,* is heavily based on tomatoes and chiles. In this recipe we substituted peaches for the tomatoes, combining the sweetness of the fruit with sour tamarind for a tasty glaze. —RON

TAMARIND PEACH GLAZED SHRIMP
Pisco Criolla Salad, Hearts of Palm

SERVES 6

PISCO CRIOLLA SALAD

1 cup thinly sliced red onion
⅓ cup thinly sliced seeded Anaheim pepper
⅓ cup thinly sliced seeded yellow bell pepper
½ teaspoon toasted cumin seeds
2 tablespoons minced cilantro leaves
¼ cup key lime juice
2 tablespoons Pisco brandy
2 tablespoons hazelnut oil
½ teaspoon ground red chile flakes
to taste sea salt and freshly ground white pepper

Soak onion in cold water for 10 minutes. Drain. Squeeze out water. Transfer to mixing bowl. Toss with remaining ingredients. Season with salt and pepper.

SHRIMP

2 cups diced ripe peaches
2 tablespoons seedless tamarind paste
1 orange, zested, juiced
1 tablespoon brown sugar
1 tablespoon safflower oil
12 large shrimp, size u-10, peeled, deveined, tail-on
to taste sea salt and freshly ground white pepper

Preheat broiler to high. Combine peach, tamarind, orange, and brown sugar in small saucepan over medium heat. Simmer 10 minutes. Puree in blender. Strain through fine sieve. Add oil to large, ovenproof skillet over high heat. Sear shrimp 30 seconds on each side. Remove skillet from heat. Brush shrimp generously with glaze on both sides. Place skillet under broiler. Cook 1 minute or until slightly under done.

PRESENTATION

3 large hearts of palm, sliced on bias
¼ cup opal basil leaves
1 teaspoon extra virgin olive oil
to taste sea salt and freshly ground white pepper

Place criolla salad in center of warm serving plate. Arrange shrimp on top. Garnish with hearts of palm and opal basil. Drizzle with olive oil. Sprinkle with sea salt.

VIETNAM

Ben Thanh Market, the biggest indoor market in Saigon, is along a river next to the citadel. Its huge clock tower entrance is a major city landmark. Outside, empty baskets hang on motor scooters awaiting their owner's purchases. Once inside, I perused stalls of souvenirs, candies, spices, textiles, clothing, and, of course, kitchenware, under the high metal roof. Products were neatly grouped into sections, making it easy for tourists to wander while locals did the serious shopping. In the food court, the cooking was Vietnamese to the core—fresh, aromatic, and spicy ingredients were seared, simmered, rolled, stuffed, and fried right before my eyes. Spring rolls are a common theme among the eateries and cheap enough to make a whole day's meal. This recipe has a bit of a modern twist. —RON

LOBSTER SPRING ROLL
Guava Soy Dipping Sauce

SERVES 6

GUAVA SOY DIPPING SAUCE

1 hot red chile, seeded
2 cloves garlic
⅓ cup roasted cashews
¼ cup cilantro leaves
1 tablespoon brown sugar
1 tablespoon soy sauce
2 tablespoons lime juice
½ cup guava puree
1 tablespoon fish sauce
1 teaspoon sesame oil

Add chile and garlic to mortar. Pound to a paste. Add cashews and cilantro leaves. Mash until smooth. Transfer to mixing bowl. Whisk in remaining ingredients. Divide between six sauce dishes.

SPRING ROLL

2 1¼-pound live Maine lobsters
¼ cup seasoned rice vinegar
1 teaspoon honey
1 tangerine, zested, juiced
½ teaspoon sambal chile sauce
1 small cucumber, peeled, seeded, cut into strips
1 large carrot, peeled, cut into matchsticks
12 8-inch round rice paper sheets

1 teaspoon black sesame seeds
1 head green leaf lettuce, washed, spun dry
12 leaves Thai basil
24 sprigs cilantro
1 mango, peeled, seeded, cut into strips
24 leaves mint
½ cup bean sprouts

Bring 1 gallon lightly salted water to boil in large stock pot. Add lobsters. Cook 8 minutes. Transfer to ice bath to chill. Separate heads from tails. Remove tail, knuckle, and claw meat from shells. Cut tail and claw meat into strips. Combine seasoned rice vinegar, honey, tangerine juice, zest, and sambal in mixing bowl. Add cucumber and carrot. Toss to coat. Set aside. Add 1 quart hot water to shallow baking dish. Soak one sheet rice paper in water for 30 seconds, or until softened. Transfer to cutting board. Sprinkle with sesame seeds. Create roll by placing following ingredients on rice paper in this order: lettuce leaf, basil, cilantro, mango, mint, lobster meat, bean sprouts, carrots, and cucumbers. Tightly roll bottom edge of rice paper just to enclose filling. Fold up sides. Continue to roll to top to seal. Transfer to plate. Cover with lightly damp cloth. Set aside in refrigerator. Repeat method to form 12 rolls. Cut spring rolls crosswise on bias. Arrange on chilled serving platter. Serve with dipping sauce.

FRANCE

On a bus ride through the back country of Provence, I followed the lower Corniche road that skirts the coastline of the Baie des Anges. Jumping off the bus at St. Jean Cap-Ferrat, I could see the beautiful beaches of Plage des Fourmis and the open air market close to the harbor. From the terrace of a small café, a colony of seagulls hovered above fish monger stalls where baskets of sardines and dorade were displayed. A rogue bird dove for a sardine and victoriously flew away with its prize. At that moment, I enjoyed the specialty of the house, made with local aromatic vegetables and just-caught sardines. If you can't find fresh sardines, use either Spanish or Japanese mackerel.—BERNARD

ST. JEAN CAP-FERRAT SARDINE CHARTREUSE
Pine Nut Crumble, Prosciutto Cider Vinaigrette

SERVES 6 FAMILY STYLE

CHARTREUSE

12 large fresh sardines, scaled, gutted, cleaned
4 tablespoons extra virgin olive oil
4 large tomatoes, thinly sliced
2 red onions, thinly sliced
1 large bulb fennel, thinly sliced crosswise
1 tablespoon thyme leaves
8 cloves garlic, sliced paper thin

½ pound stemmed, washed, spoon spinach leaves
2 cups stemmed, washed, chopped sorrel
2 tablespoons Pernod® liquor
1 large lemon, halved
to taste sea salt and freshly ground black pepper

Divide vegetables in half. Preheat oven to 350°F. Rinse sardines under cold running water. Cut tails from two sardines 2-inches in length on the bias. Reserve in refrigerator for garnish. Fillet all sardines. Place 2 fillets together, skin side out, to reform the shape of sardine. Brush 9-inch square baking dish with 1 tablespoon olive oil. Layer one half of vegetables and herbs in dish in the following order: tomato, onion, fennel, thyme, garlic, spinach, and sorrel. Lay sardines side by side atop. Drizzle with Pernod and 1 tablespoon olive oil. Squeeze half of lemon over top. Season with salt and pepper. Cover evenly with remaining sorrel, spinach, thyme, garlic, fennel, red onion, and tomato in that order. Squeeze other half of lemon over top. Drizzle with 1½ tablespoons olive oil. Season with salt and pepper. Transfer to oven. Cook 40 minutes. Top with pine nut crumble in even layer. Toss reserved tails with salt, pepper, and remaining olive oil. Place atop crumble. Cook 15 minutes or until center of chartreuse reaches at least 140°F. Cool to room temperature. Cover. Refrigerate overnight. Invert chartreuse onto serving platter. Garnish with sardine tails.

PINE NUT CRUMBLE

½ cup pine nuts
¼ cup bread crumbs
¼ teaspoon freshly ground black pepper
2 tablespoons chopped parsley leaves
½ cup grated Emmental cheese

Add pine nuts to skillet over medium heat. Toast, stirring often, until golden brown. Transfer to food processor. Add bread crumbs and black pepper. Pulse until coarsely ground. Spread evenly on plate to cool. Transfer to mixing bowl. Mix with parsley and cheese. Set aside.

VINAIGRETTE

¼ cup finely diced prosciutto
⅓ cup extra virgin olive oil
1 teaspoon whole grain mustard
12 green olives, pitted, finely chopped
3 tablespoons apple cider vinegar
2 tablespoons minced shallots
1 tablespoon minced chives
to taste sea salt and cayenne pepper

Add all ingredients to mixing bowl. Whisk to emulsify. Season with sea salt and cayenne. Spoon around chartreuse. Transfer remaining vinaigrette to sauce dish.

I took the ferry to Kusu Island to escape the constant hubbub of mainland Singapore and recharge my spiritual battery at the Tua Pek Kong temple. During my week-long culinary promotion at the Tower Club, I explored the early morning markets, reveling in the Asian, Hindi and Middle Eastern ingredients and spices. On Clark Quay, relaxing late at night with friends, we enjoyed a feast of local chile crabs and noodles. This dish includes ingredients I discovered on this journey. My other favorite crabs for this dish are Peekytoe, Dungeness, or stone crab. —BERNARD

BLUE CRAB EGGPLANT CAKES
Radish Salad, Turmeric Tangerine Butter

SERVES 6

CRAB CAKES

1 one-pound eggplant
2 large eggs, beaten
½ cup crème fraîche
2 tablespoons minced chives
⅛ teaspoon cayenne
⅛ teaspoon ground cumin
1 pound blue crabmeat, jumbo lump, shelled
½ cup almond meal

to taste sea salt and freshly ground black pepper
¾ cup breadcrumbs
¼ cup cornmeal
¼ cup finely chopped parsley leaves
2 tablespoons olive oil
** olive oil spray

Preheat oven to 350°F. Puncture eggplant 10 times with tip of knife. Bake in microwave 6 minutes or until tender. Cool. Cut off stem end. Peel off skin. Chop flesh. Transfer to colander to drain. In mixing bowl, combine eggs, cream, chives, cayenne, and cumin. Gently fold in crabmeat, eggplant, and almond meal. Season with salt and pepper. Divide mixture into 6 portions. Combine breadcrumbs, cornmeal, parsley, and olive oil in mixing bowl. Grease baking sheet with olive oil spray. Place 3-inch round cookie cutter on baking sheet. Evenly spread 1 heaping tablespoon breadcrumb mixture in ring. Tightly pack crabmeat into ring. Spread 1 heaping tablespoon breadcrumbs atop. Remove ring. Repeat process, leaving 2 inches between each cake. Spray top of cakes with olive oil spray. Bake ten minutes or until hot in the center. Transfer crab cake to warm serving plate. Arrange radish salad atop. Spoon tangerine butter around.

TANGERINE BUTTER

¼ cup chopped shallots
¼ teaspoon ground turmeric
3 tangerines, zested, juiced
1 tablespoon white vinegar
2 sprigs fresh thyme

2 tablespoons heavy cream
½ cup unsalted butter, cut into six pieces
to taste sea salt and freshly ground black pepper

Add shallots, turmeric, tangerine zest, tangerine juice, vinegar, and thyme to saucepan over medium heat. Reduce by two thirds. Swirl in cream. Bring to boil. Reduce heat to simmer. Vigorously whisk in butter, one piece at a time, until fully incorporated. Do not let boil. Season with salt and pepper. Strain through fine sieve. Set aside. Keep warm.

RADISH SALAD

1 cucumber
1 green apple, cored
6 large radishes
1 tablespoon lemon juice
¼ cup julienned mint leaves

¼ cup cilantro leaves
1 tablespoon sesame oil
to taste sea salt and freshly ground black pepper

Peel, seed and thinly slice cucumber. Cut apple and radishes into ⅛-inch thick slices. Cut slices into matchsticks. Transfer to mixing bowl. Toss with sliced cucumber and remaining ingredients. Season with salt and pepper.

After a photo safari through Salim Ali Bird Sanctuary, a network of water channels led me to the harbor where I embarked on a moonlight cruise from Goa to Mumbai. I discovered a multi-cultural melting pot of Indian cuisine, layered with spices, curries, and to my surprise, fantastic wines. I learned that *garam* means "hot" or "heating" and *masala* means "spice blend." The "hot" is not referring to the kind of heat found in hot chiles but to the fact that the spices are toasted before grinding. Cooking with *garam masala* will fill your house with a wonderful aroma that gets your family's appetite going! —BERNARD

GARAM MASALA SQUID SALAD
Cool Red Lentils, Globe Zucchini, Tamarind Nectarine Dressing

SERVES 6

RED LENTILS

1 cup red lentils
½ cup finely diced peeled carrots
½ cup peeled, seeded, finely diced cucumber
½ cup finely diced seeded tomato
1 lemon, zested, juiced
2 tablespoons peanut oil
2 tablespoons chopped mint leaves
1 tablespoon chopped chives
to taste sea salt and freshly ground black pepper

Bring 3 cups water to boil in large pot. Stir in red lentils. Simmer approximately 6 minutes, or until al dente. Drain in colander. Rinse under cold water. Let sit in colander 5 minutes. Transfer lentils to large mixing bowl. Combine with remaining ingredients. Season with salt and pepper.

GLOBE ZUCCHINI

6 medium globe zucchini
3 tablespoons olive oil
¼ teaspoon ground cumin
¼ teaspoon freshly ground black pepper
½ teaspoon sea salt

Preheat oven to 300°F. Cut small slice from the bottom of zucchini so that they sit flat. Remove top by cutting 1 inch from stem. Reserve top. Using melon baller, scoop and discard pulp. In small bowl, whisk oil, cumin, pepper, and sea salt. Rub onto zucchini inside and out. Transfer zucchini and tops to baking sheet lined with wax paper. Cook 15 minutes or until tender. Invert onto paper towel to drain excess liquid. Fill cavity with lentil mixture. Cover with top.

DRESSING

¼ cup tamarind pulp
1 cup water
3 ripe nectarines, pitted, chopped
2 tablespoons honey
3 tablespoons lime juice
3 tablespoons peanut oil
2 cloves garlic, minced
1 tablespoon peeled, minced ginger
2 tablespoons chopped cilantro leaves
1 teaspoon sambal chile paste
to taste sea salt and freshly ground black pepper

Add tamarind, water, nectarines, and honey to sauce pot over medium heat. Simmer 20 minutes, whisking occasionally. Strain through coarse sieve into mixing bowl. Whisk in remaining ingredients. Season with salt and pepper.

SQUID

2 pounds squid tubes and tentacles, cleaned
¼ cup peanut oil
½ cup garbanzo bean flour
1 teaspoon garam masala
to taste sea salt and freshly ground pepper to taste
¼ cup chopped roasted peanuts
4 sprigs cilantro

Cut tubes into ¼-inch thick rings. Add to large mixing bowl with tentacles, pat dry thoroughly. Add oil to skillet over medium-high heat. Sift flour and garam masala together. Sprinkle over squid. Toss to coat. Add squid to skillet. Sauté 1 minute or until squid just starts to turn opaque. Using slotted spoon, transfer squid to paper towel-lined mixing bowl to drain excess oil. Discard paper towel. Add ⅓ cup dressing. Toss to coat. Pile squid onto center of warm serving plate. Place zucchini beside. Spoon remaining dressing onto plate. Garnish with peanuts and cilantro sprig.

I first saw a pomelo when I was working as a cook in central Florida. I was in charge of the grill station and creating daily specials. In moving from South Carolina to Florida, I was introduced to an abundance of tropical ingredients. Barbecue is big in the South, shrimp is big in Florida, and the sweetness of tropical fruits makes a great complement to grilled seafood. This trinity of thoughts led me to create many different combinations of tropical fruit-glazed fish and shellfish—cooking native Floridian ingredients with a Caribbean flair. I was particularly intrigued by the pomelo, the largest of all citrus fruits, which tastes like a sweet grapefruit. Pomelos are in season November through March. During the other months you can use grapefruit with equal success. —RON

POMELO GLAZED JUMBO SHRIMP
Grilled Eggplant, Rum Spiced Mango

SERVES 6

POMELO GLAZE

1 cup freshly squeezed pomelo juice
¼ cup soy sauce
⅓ cup packed brown sugar
¼ teaspoon Tabasco® sauce
1 teaspoon freshly grated ginger
2 tablespoons white wine vinegar
1 teaspoon finely chopped garlic
⅓ cup minced scallions
2 tablespoons finely chopped cilantro leaves

Add all ingredients to saucepan over medium heat. Bring to simmer. Reduce by half or until syrupy. Strain through fine sieve. Cool.

EGGPLANT

3 Japanese eggplants
½ cup olive oil
½ teaspoon chile powder
1 tablespoon chopped lemon thyme leaves
¼ teaspoon sea salt flakes
⅛ teaspoon freshly ground black pepper

Preheat grill to medium high. Cut eggplants in half lengthwise. Whisk remaining ingredients in large mixing bowl. Add eggplant. Coat thoroughly. Place on grill, flesh side down. Cook 2 minutes on each side or until golden brown and tender.

SHRIMP

12 jumbo shrimp, size u-10, shell-on
2 tablespoons grapeseed oil
to taste sea salt and freshly ground black pepper

Using sharp serrated knife, butterfly shrimp by cutting lengthwise through the upper shell down to, but not through, the bottom shell. Remove the vein and discard. Brush flesh side with grapeseed oil. Season with salt and pepper. Place shrimp on hot grill, flesh side down. Cook 30 seconds. Flip over. Generously brush flesh side with pomelo glaze. Cook two minutes or until slightly underdone.

PRESENTATION

1 mango, peeled, diced
1 tablespoon chopped cilantro
1 tablespoon spiced rum
6 sprigs lemon thyme

Toss mango, cilantro, and rum in small mixing bowl. Place 1 eggplant on warm serving plate. Lean 2 shrimp against eggplant, flesh side up. Brush with glaze. Garnish with mango and lemon thyme.

AUSTRALIA

While vacationing in South Australia, I met my friend Chef Andrew Davies at the prestigious D'Arenberg Winery, located in the heart of the small township of McLaren Vale. We shopped the Adelaide fish market for spiny lobsters, scallops, king prawns, and oysters to create a menu showcasing the best ingredients of the region. It was a grand gala dinner to celebrate the last day of a successful harvest. We cooked all day, sharing stories, recipes, and glasses of wine. The deep-fried oysters, that Andrew learned to make as an apprentice in London were the hit of the night, paired with Chester's Last Ditch Viognier! —BERNARD

COFFIN BAY DEEP FRIED OYSTERS
Olive Oil Hollandaise, Shiraz Reduction

SERVES 6

OLIVE OIL HOLLANDAISE

½ cup white wine vinegar
2 sprigs thyme
¼ cup chopped shallots
1 clove garlic, crushed
½ cup extra virgin olive oil
3 large egg yolks
2 tablespoons apple juice
to taste sea salt and freshly ground black pepper

Add vinegar, thyme, shallots, and garlic to saucepan over medium heat. Reduce by two thirds. Strain through fine sieve into blender. Heat olive oil in small saucepan over low heat to 160°F. Add egg yolks and apple juice to blender. Blend at high speed until thick and frothy. With blender running at medium speed, slowly pour in warm olive oil. Blend 20 seconds or until thick and smooth. Season with salt and pepper. Transfer to sauce dish. Keep warm.

SHIRAZ REDUCTION

2 cups shiraz wine
2 sprigs thyme
2 tablespoons chopped shallots
2 tablespoons brown sugar
1 cup chicken stock

Add shiraz, thyme, shallots, and sugar to medium saucepan over medium heat. Reduce to ¼ cup. Add chicken stock. Reduce to ¼ cup or until syrupy. Strain through fine sieve. Transfer to squeeze bottle. Set aside.

ZUCCHINI

6 medium zucchini, split lengthwise
2 tablespoons olive oil
2 teaspoons paprika
1 teaspoon coarse sea salt

Preheat oven to 375°F. Place zucchini, cut side up, on baking sheet. Drizzle with olive oil. Sprinkle with paprika and salt. Bake 10 minutes or until tender.

OYSTERS

1 quart canola oil for frying
36 large fresh oysters, washed
4 large eggs
¼ cup milk
1 cup flour, sifted
1 cup seasoned fine bread crumbs
to taste sea salt and freshly ground black pepper
1 lemon, halved

In deep, 4-quart sauce pot, preheat oil to 375°F. Shuck oysters, discarding top shells. Remove oyster meat from bottom shell. Discard bottom shells and all shell fragments from meat. Transfer oyster meat to paper towel-lined plate. Whisk eggs and milk in small bowl. Dredge oysters in flour. Dip in egg mixture. Roll in bread crumbs. Deep fry 10 seconds until golden brown. Transfer to paper towel-lined plate. Sprinkle with salt and pepper. Place two zucchini halves on center of warm serving plate, overlapping one end. Arrange fried oysters atop one half. Squeeze lemon over oysters. Dot shiraz reduction onto plate. Serve with hollandaise sauce.

BELGIUM

Down the Galerie de la Reine under a misty sky, I made my way to the landmark brasserie Chez Leon. Walking through the door, one can feel the footprints of the souls who have eaten there since the mid 1800s. *Moules frites* are the house specialty, with a side of fries and Leon's brew, a delicate beer with sweet-and-sour orange peel aroma. Dunking my bread into the broth of a pot of steaming mussels, I was transported back to a simpler time when you could hear the clattering of horse hooves on the cobblestone and the clinking of beer glasses in celebration of friendship. —BERNARD

DARK BEER STEAMED BLACK MUSSELS
Apple Wood Smoked Bacon

SERVES 6 FAMILY STYLE

4 pounds black mussels, scrubbed, beard removed

1 loaf sourdough bread

¼ cup extra virgin olive oil

to taste sea salt and freshly ground black pepper

2 tablespoons olive oil

½ cup diced applewood smoked bacon

1 cup diced eggplant

¼ cup chopped shallots

2 portobello mushrooms, stemmed, gills removed, diced

1 cup diced leeks, white part only, washed

12 ounces dark beer

½ teaspoon fennel seeds

1 lemon, zested

¼ teaspoon freshly ground black pepper

¾ cup heavy cream

¼ cup chopped flat leaf parsley

Soak mussels in cold water for 30 minutes to purge sand. Preheat broiler to medium-high. Cut bread into 1-inch thick slices. Drizzle with extra virgin olive oil. Sprinkle with sea salt and pepper. Toast under broiler on both sides until golden. Transfer to bread basket. Keep warm. Transfer mussels to colander. Add 2 tablespoons olive oil to large stock pot over medium heat. Add bacon, eggplant, shallots, mushrooms, and leeks. Cook 5 minutes without browning, stirring often. Add mussels, beer, fennel seed, lemon zest, and black pepper. Raise heat to high. Cover. Cook 5 minutes or until liquid starts to boil. Uncover. Using slotted spoon, rotate mussels from bottom to top to ensure even cooking. Add cream. Cover. Cook additional 5 minutes or until shells open. Sprinkle mussels with parsley. Serve with toasted sourdough bread.

THAILAND

The beach of Patong, under a full moon in early November is magical. With hundreds of illuminated paper lanterns floating into the night sky, I searched for a restaurant packed with locals. Thai meals are very social and bring people together from all different backgrounds, including a French guy on vacation. Eating Thai style means sharing lots of dishes with friends. So we did. Sweet, sour, salty, and spicy are the characteristics of this cuisine. Steamed clams, freshly raked from the beach and served in clay pots with chile peppers were to die for. My taste buds were dancing. What better place to discover culinary treasures than Thailand? —BERNARD

PHUKET STYLE CLAM HOT POT
Coconut Milk, Red Curry

SERVES 6 FAMILY STYLE

⅓ cup sea salt

¼ cup cornmeal

6 pounds Manila clams, cleaned

2 tablespoons peanut oil

½ cup sliced shallots

4 cloves garlic, minced

12 medium shiitake mushrooms, stemmed, quartered

2 links andouille sausage, sliced ¼-inch thick

1 tablespoon brown sugar

1 teaspoon red curry paste

1 tablespoon Thai fish sauce

¾ cup white wine

1 stalk lemongrass, crushed

1½ cups coconut milk

5 small Thai red chiles

⅓ cup minced cilantro leaves

⅓ cup sliced scallions

⅓ cup chopped honey roasted peanuts

Add 1 gallon cold water to large pot. Stir in salt and cornmeal. Add clams. Soak 45 minutes to purge sand. Remove clams from water. Transfer to colander. Add peanut oil to large skillet over medium heat. Add shallots, garlic, mushrooms, and sausage. Cook 2 minutes without browning, stirring often. Add sugar, curry paste, fish sauce, white wine, and lemongrass. Bring to simmer. Add clams, coconut milk, and chiles. Cover. Increase heat to high. Bring to boil. Uncover. Using slotted spoon, rotate clams from bottom to top to ensure even cooking. Cover. Cook until shells open. Add cilantro, scallions, and honey roasted peanuts. Toss and serve.

CANADA

On Canada's eastern coast, the green land meets the blue sea for hundreds of jagged miles. My family and I spent a week driving from the U.S. border to Nova Scotia. We passed the time watching for elk and eagles, cherishing the opportunity to be together. In New Brunswick, we enjoyed sweet scallops seared in brown butter, allowing their rich flavor to capture the spotlight. The most important part of cooking scallops is buying good ones. Look for scallops with a clean, sweet aroma that is reminiscent of sweet corn, and firm meat that is ivory to light yellow in color. Good quality scallops will brown easily and not exude liquid when cooked. —RON

BROWN BUTTER ROASTED DIVER SCALLOPS
Vanilla Kabocha Squash Tian, Icewine Vinaigrette

SERVES 4

KABOCHA

1 3-pound kabocha squash
2 tablespoons grapeseed oil
2 tablespoons softened unsalted butter
2 tablespoons maple syrup
⅛ teaspoon chile powder
½ teaspoon sea salt
1 vanilla pod, (half lengthwise, scrape seeds, reserve pod for garnish)
1 tablespoon mascarpone
to taste sea salt and freshly ground black pepper

Preheat oven to 350°F. Cut squash in half. Remove seeds. Brush entire surface of flesh with oil. Place squash on baking sheet, cut side down. Bake 45 minutes or until tender. Remove from oven. Cool. Scoop flesh from shell and transfer to food processor. Add butter, maple syrup, chile powder, sea salt, and vanilla seeds. Purée until smooth. Transfer purée to saucepan over medium heat. Cook until thickened to the consistency of mashed potatoes, stirring constantly. Remove from heat. Fold in mascarpone. Season with salt and pepper. Set aside. Keep warm.

ICEWINE VINAIGRETTE

½ cup icewine
¼ cup white balsamic vinegar
¼ cup chicken stock
2 black plums, pitted, diced
¼ cup hazelnut oil
1 tablespoon finely chopped tarragon leaves
to taste sea salt and freshly ground black pepper

Add icewine and vinegar to skillet over medium heat. Reduce by half. Add chicken stock. Reduce by half. Add plums, simmer 2 minutes, stirring often. Transfer to blender. Add hazelnut oil and tarragon. Blend to emulsify. Strain through fine sieve. Season with salt and pepper. Cool. Transfer to squeeze bottle.

SCALLOPS

12 large sea scallops, size u-10, tendon removed
to taste sea salt and freshly ground black pepper
2 tablespoons unsalted butter
2 tablespoons grapeseed oil

Season scallops on both sides with salt and pepper. Melt 1 tablespoon butter with 1 tablespoon grapeseed oil in large skillet over high heat until foamy. Add 6 scallops, spaced evenly in pan. Cook 1 minute on each side. Remove from heat. Keep warm. Repeat process with remaining ingredients.

PRESENTATION

2 halves reserved vanilla pod
¼ cup chopped toasted hazelnuts
¼ cup watercress leaves

Cut vanilla pods in half lengthwise to create 4 equally sized strips. Spoon kabocha into 2-inch ring in center of large serving plate. Top with hazelnuts. Remove ring. Place scallops beside. Squeeze vinaigrette onto plate. Garnish with watercress and vanilla bean.

STOCK OPTIONS

"Cooking slowly on the back of the stove, a liquid draws flavor and nutrients from fish, meat, or poultry bones. The perpetual motion of a steady simmer provides a zen-like backdrop to the ever-changing kitchen scenery. Vegetables add a second layer of taste as their aroma floats inward and upward, enriching the stock. A bouquet garni, made of fragrant herbs, infuses the final touch. As time passes, evaporation leads to reduction, intensifying the elixir. This is the art of cooking. From great sauciers, great chefs are born."

CHICKEN

YIELDS 4 QUARTS

5 pounds chicken legs, washed
1 pound carrots, peeled, halved
4 ribs celery, halved crosswise
3 white onions, halved
12 cloves garlic
2 leeks, white part only, washed, halved lengthwise
8 sprigs thyme
½ bunch parsley with stems, washed
2 bay leaves
1 teaspoon whole black peppercorns
4 cloves
6 quarts cold water
1 bottle sauvignon blanc

Place chicken in 14-quart stock pot with vegetables and spices. Add water and sauvignon blanc. Turn heat to high. Bring to boil. Lower to simmer. Cook 4 hours, skimming foam occasionally. Carefully strain stock through fine mesh sieve into a clean pot. Discard solids. Chill stock in ice bath to 55°F Refrigerate immediately. Remove hardened fat from surface before using. Store stock refrigerated for up to 3 days, or freeze in airtight containers for up to 3 months.

BEEF

YIELDS 3 QUARTS

4 pounds oxtail, fat trimmed, cut into 2-inch pieces
4 pounds bone-in beef short ribs
1 pound carrots, trimmed, peeled, chopped
5 stalks celery, chopped
1 pound brown mushrooms, halved
1 head garlic, cut in half crosswise
2 bay leaves
1 bunch curly parsley, with stems, washed
10 sprigs thyme
1 teaspoon whole black peppercorns
2 tablespoons grapeseed oil
** canola oil spray
3 red onions, peeled, halved
6 large ripe tomatoes, cored, halved
6 quarts cold water
1 bottle cabernet sauvignon

Preheat oven to 450°F. Place oxtail and beef short ribs in large roasting pan. Roast 45 minutes or until well browned, turning bones occasionally. Toss carrots, celery, mushrooms, garlic, bay leaf, parsley, thyme, and peppercorns with grapeseed oil in large mixing bowl. Add to roasting pan. Toss with bones. Roast 30 minutes, turning bones and vegetables every 10 minutes. Meanwhile, place grill pan over high heat. Spray with canola oil. Grill onions and tomatoes, cut side down, until charred. Transfer bones, vegetables, onions, and tomatoes to 14-quart stock pot. Remove excess fat from roasting pan. Place pan on stove top over medium-high heat. Add 1 quart water and the wine. Bring to simmer, scraping bottom of pan with wooden spoon. Cook 5 minutes. Transfer to stock pot. Add remaining 5 quarts water to stock pot. Turn heat to high. Bring to boil. Reduce to simmer. Cook 6 hours, skimming foam as it comes to surface. Carefully strain stock through fine mesh sieve into a clean pot. Discard solids. Chill stock in ice bath to 55°F. Refrigerate immediately. Remove hardened fat from surface before using. Store stock refrigerated for up to 3 days, or freeze in airtight containers for up to 3 months.

SHELLFISH

YIELDS 4 QUARTS

1½ gallons water
2 leeks, white part only, halved lengthwise, washed
1 stalk lemongrass, split lengthwise
4 sprigs thyme
1 teaspoon whole white peppercorns
3 1½ pound live Maine lobsters
¼ cup grapeseed oil
2 pounds whole, head-on shrimp, medium size
4 carrots, trimmed, peeled, halved
6 ribs celery, halved
2 Spanish onions, peeled, halved
6 cloves garlic, smashed
4 pods green cardamom
2 cups vermouth

Add water, leeks, lemongrass, thyme, and peppercorns to 14-quart stock pot over medium heat. Bring to boil. Simmer 15 minutes. Add lobsters. Cover. Cook 8 minutes. Transfer lobsters to ice bath to cool. Separate heads from tails. Remove tail, knuckle, and claw meat from shells. Reserve meat for another use. Set aside heads and shells. Strain broth through fine sieve. Set aside. Add oil to stock pot over high heat. Add shrimp, lobster heads and lobster shells. Cook 5 minutes, stirring often, until well-roasted. Lower heat to medium high. Add carrots, celery, onion, garlic, and cardamom. Cook 5 minutes, stirring often. Add vermouth and reserved broth. Bring to simmer. Cook 1 hour, skimming foam occasionally. Carefully strain stock through fine mesh sieve into a clean pot. Discard solids. Chill stock in ice bath to 55°F. Refrigerate immediately. Store stock refrigerated for up to 3 days, or freeze in airtight containers for up to 3 months.

VEGETABLE

YIELDS 4 QUARTS

2 tablespoons grapeseed oil
3 Spanish onions, peeled, halved
1 pound carrots, trimmed, peeled, halved
1 bulb fennel, quartered
1 small bulb celery root, peeled, quartered
1 pound button mushrooms, wiped clean
8 sprigs thyme
1 teaspoon whole black peppercorns
6 cloves garlic, halved
2 leeks, white part only, halved lengthwise, washed
2 ears corn, shucked, sliced into 2-inch wheels
1 small ginger root, peeled, halved
1 bunch parsley with stems, washed
2 bay leaves
1 teaspoon sea salt
5 quarts water

Add oil to 14-quart stock pot over medium heat. Add onions, carrots, fennel, celery root, mushrooms, thyme, and black peppercorns. Cook 10 minutes without browning, stirring often. Add remaining ingredients. Turn heat to high. Bring to boil. Lower to simmer. Cook 1 hour, skimming foam occasionally. Carefully strain stock through fine mesh sieve into a clean pot. Discard solids. Chill stock in ice bath to 55°F Refrigerate immediately. Store stock refrigerated for up to 3 days, or freeze in airtight containers for up to 3 months.

SEA FARE ENTRÉES

BOLIVIA

Legend has it that many moons ago, on the shores of Lake Titicaca in Bolivia, the Incan king Huayna Capac abandoned power by his own will and sailed beyond the water's horizon toward the setting sun. Before departing, he promised to return one day with new ideas and technologies that would return the Incan Empire to prosperity.

That's what my friend Fernando told me, before switching the topic to Bolivia's exotic springtime produce. I sat cross-legged in his living room, beneath a poster of Andean wind instruments. Fernando's spirited stories together with my fascination for his native country inspired me to experience the land for myself.

Traveling to the "Altiplano," a 14,000 foot high plateau, was like arriving at a place of haven within the Andes mountain range. Snow white peaks, posed like geographical bodyguards, encircle the plateau, providing an imaginary sense of protection. That feeling is fortified by the local tale that the grandest mountain of them all, El Ilimani, gives eternal security to the people of the region. The mystical nature of this geography climaxes at the deep blue shores of Lake Titicaca. For someone like me, who's lived his entire life at sea level, it is magical to realize that a lake exists where sky should be.

Beatriz, a local tour guide, invited me on a trip across the lake. We took a taxi to the water's edge where we picnicked on roasted chicken and a variety of boiled potatoes sprinkled with salt. After lunch, we took turns standing lookout for any vessels headed toward shore. Near sunset, a small fishing boat approached, skippered by a short man whose dark skin revealed the harsh elements of the Altiplano. We negotiated a fee. He unloaded his day's catch and helped us aboard, together with Beatriz's mom, her infant son, and of course, Mr. Taxi Driver. We cruised until the stars came out, staring across the sparkling water and contemplating the ancient mysteries that still permeate the thin mountain air.

Lake Titicaca holds three culinary treasures—kingfish, giant frogs and the renowned Titicaca trout. I couldn't travel this far without discovering the trout that Fernando described with such mouth-watering commentary. Almost every eatery in the vicinity specializes in cooking the trout in one style or another. Most of the dishes are simply prepared with respect for the trout's inherent delicate texture and earthy flavor. I distinctly remember one parsley crusted fillet with garlic butter and a hot bowl of quinoa soup. It remains one of my most memorable food experiences. As simple as that preparation is to duplicate, I know I could never truly recreate it. The ambience was just as much a part of that experience and I will never be in that place for the very first time again. To me, the beauty of culinary travel lies in the inimitability of certain captivating moments.

—RON

SPAIN

The Coast of Catalonia is dotted with traditional fishing towns and villages. Fishermen deliver their harvest early each morning to Arenys de Mar's fourteenth-century fisherman's quarter. The town awakens to gleaming fish, lobsters, squid, and other fruits from the sea. Locals and visitors participate in the deep-rooted custom of gathering the freshest ingredients for traditional dishes, such as paella. Rice is the key ingredient in making great paella. Most Catalonians take pride in their own version of the dish, but all agree on the following tips: 1) Use paella rice. Other types don't absorb the wonderful aromas. 2) Do not wash the rice before cooking. 3) Stir the rice once upon adding the liquid, then do not stir again. —RON

ARENYS DE MAR SEAFOOD PAELLA
Saffron Rice, Chorizo, Peas

SERVES 4 FAMILY STYLE

⅓ **cup** sea salt
¼ **cup** cornmeal
12 littleneck clams, scrubbed
2 pounds large black mussels, beard removed, scrubbed
½ **teaspoon** saffron threads
3 cups vegetable broth
½ **pound** calamari tubes and tentacles
1 red bell pepper
1 yellow bell pepper
1 green bell pepper
1 tablespoon olive oil

½ **cup** diced Spanish chorizo sausage
½ **cup** diced onion
3 cloves garlic, minced
2 cups paella rice or arborio rice
½ **cup** white wine
2 8-ounce lobster tails, halved lengthwise
8 large shrimp, size u-15, peeled, deveined
½ **cup** green peas
1 lemon, halved
2 tablespoons extra virgin olive oil

Add 1 gallon cold water to large pot. Stir in salt and cornmeal. Add clams, then mussels. Soak 45 minutes to purge sand. Remove mussels and clams from water. Transfer to colander. Bring saffron and broth to low simmer in saucepan. Clean calamari. Cut tubes into ¼-inch rings. Set aside. Cut all peppers into ¼-inch thick rings, discarding seeds. Heat olive oil in large deep skillet or paella pan over medium-high heat. Add chorizo, onion, and garlic. Cook 2 minutes, or until lightly brown. Add rice. Cook 1 minute, stirring continuously. Add wine. Bring to boil. Add saffron broth. Bring to simmer. Reduce heat to low. Stir once. Cover. Cook for 10 minutes. Add mussels, clams, lobster, and shrimp, nestling them into rice mixture. Place bell peppers atop. Cover. Cook 7 minutes. Add calamari and peas. Cover. Cook 3 minutes or until all seafood is cooked. Remove from heat. Squeeze lemon juice atop. Drizzle with extra virgin olive oil.

Sankaty Lighthouse stands guard over the long shoreline of Sconset Beach on Nantucket Island. Wearing my waders on a cold windy day, fighting to keep my hat on, I followed Pam, my "American mom," and a group of her friends to harvest bay scallops. Combing the beach with push rakes, the beautiful orange-blue ridged shells appeared from beneath the sand like an invitation to lunch. These delicate creatures should be cooked very quickly with browned butter to enhance their sweet, nutty flavor. — BERNARD

CARAMELIZED NANTUCKET BAY SCALLOPS
Navy Beans, Mâche, Truffle Vinaigrette

SERVES 4 FAMILY STYLE

NAVY BEANS

¾ cup navy beans
1 quart vegetable stock
2 tablespoons olive oil
½ cup diced onion
¼ cup diced apple smoked bacon
2 cloves garlic, minced
3 leaves sage
1 tablespoon maple syrup
½ cup sherry wine
to taste sea salt and freshly ground white pepper
2 tablespoons mascarpone
2 tablespoons almond meal
2 tablespoons bread crumbs
2 tablespoons chopped parsley leaves
4 slices black truffle

Soak beans in water overnight. Drain beans. Bring vegetable stock to boil. Add beans. Simmer 30–45 minutes or until tender. Drain in colander, reserving stock for another use. Preheat oven to 375°F. Add 1 tablespoon olive oil to large saucepan over medium heat. Add onions, bacon, garlic, and sage. Cook 5 minutes without browning, stirring often. Add maple syrup, sherry, and beans. Season with salt and pepper. Simmer 10 minutes, stirring occasionally. Remove from heat. Fold in mascarpone. Season with salt and pepper. Transfer to ovenproof serving bowl. Combine almond meal, bread crumbs and parsley in small bowl. Sprinkle over beans. Drizzle with 2 tablespoons truffle vinaigrette from mâche salad. Bake 15 minutes or until piping hot. Top with black truffle slices.

MÂCHE SALAD

1 tablespoon aged sherry vinegar
2 tablespoons minced shallots
1 tablespoon finely chopped parsley leaves
2 tablespoons chopped smoked almonds
2 tablespoons almond oil
1 tablespoon truffle oil
to taste sea salt and freshly ground black pepper
¼ pound mâche lettuce, washed, patted dry

Add sherry vinegar, shallots, parsley, and smoked almonds to large mixing bowl. Add oils in slow stream, whisking vigorously to emulsify. Season with salt and pepper. Reserve 2 tablespoons vinaigrette for beans. Toss remaining vinaigrette with mâche. Transfer to serving bowl.

BAY SCALLOPS

1½ pounds Nantucket Bay scallops, tendon removed
to taste sea salt and freshly ground black pepper
2 tablespoons safflower oil
2 teaspoons unsalted butter
½ teaspoon lemon thyme leaves

To cook scallops in two batches. Season scallops with salt and pepper. Add 1 tablespoon safflower oil to large skillet over high heat. Add half the scallops to skillet in single layer. Cook 30 seconds or until caramelized without disturbing. Shake skillet to turn scallops. Add 1 teaspoon butter. Sprinkle scallops with ¼ teaspoon lemon thyme. Sauté 30 seconds longer. Transfer to serving bowl. Repeat process with remaining ingredients.

VIETNAM

The old quarter of central Hanoi, flooded with throngs of people and 2000 years of history, represents the eternal soul of the city. The aroma of curry and fried shrimp led me through a labyrinth of streets where merchants produced and sold their wares on site. Farmers carried just-picked vegetables in baskets balanced on shoulder poles while motor bikes and cyclos weaved through the crowd. One morning, I bought live shrimp at 4 A.M. at the overnight market for breakfast after a night on the town. Stir-frying quickly at high heat in a wok enhances the bright flavors of all your ingredients. —BERNARD

INDOCHINE STIR FRIED PRAWNS
Coconut and Lemongrass

SERVES 4

PRAWNS

1 stalk lemongrass
2 cloves garlic, slivered
¼ cup cilantro leaves
2 teaspoons brown sugar
1 tablespoon lime juice
2 tablespoons Thai fish sauce
to taste sea salt and freshly ground black pepper
3 tablespoons peanut oil
20 large prawns, size u-15, peeled, deveined, tail-on
1 large bulb fennel, trimmed, cut into thin wedges
1 tablespoon grated fresh ginger
1 hot red chile, seeded, thinly sliced
½ cup green onions, thinly sliced on bias
2 cups sugar snap peas, cut in half on bias
½ cup coconut milk
¼ teaspoon Chinese five spice powder

Cut root end of lemongrass. Peel off outer green layers of lemongrass stalk. Cut layers lengthwise into 8 sticks. Reserve for garnish. Slice tender inner part thinly crosswise. Measure ¼ cup. Add to mortar with garlic, cilantro, and sugar. Pound to paste. Stir in lime juice and fish sauce. Season with salt and pepper. Set aside. Add 2 tablespoons peanut oil to wok over high heat. Add prawns and fennel. Stir fry 1 minute. Remove prawns and transfer to plate. Add 1 tablespoon peanut oil, ginger, chiles, green onions, and snap peas to fennel. Stir fry 1 minute. Add lemongrass paste and coconut milk. Bring to simmer. Cook 1 minute. Add prawns and five spice. Cook 1 minute or until prawns are slightly underdone. Adjust seasoning.

CRISPY SHALLOTS

½ cup peanut oil
½ cup thinly sliced shallots

Add oil to small saucepan over medium heat. When hot, add shallots. Cook, stirring occasionally, until golden and crisp. Using perforated spoon, transfer shallots to paper towel-lined plate, spreading evenly.

PRESENTATION

8 leaves mint, thinly sliced
2 scallions, green part only, thinly sliced on bias
8 sticks lemongrass, reserved from prawns

Arrange prawns and vegetables in center of large serving bowl. Ladle sauce into bowl. Sprinkle with mint, scallions, and crispy shallots. Garnish with lemongrass.

One evening off the mesmerizing island of Capri, I watched a local fisherman catch cuttlefish from a boat by the light of the setting sun, keeping in balance with the gentle rolling of the waves. This is how many locals spend their summer nights in Capri. Stuffed cuttlefish is a signature preparation on the island as a *piatto principale*, or main course. That night I enjoyed it with sweet peppers grown at the base of the local mountains, and a chilled glass of Capri Bianco. In the United States, squid is commonly available and makes a great substitute for cuttlefish. —BERNARD

CREMINI STUFFED SQUID TORPEDO
Red Pepper Coulis, Pancetta, Arugula Salad

SERVES 4 FAMILY STYLE

RED PEPPER COULIS

2 tablespoons olive oil
¼ cup minced white onion
3 cloves garlic, minced
2 cups seeded, diced red bell pepper
1 cup diced tomatoes
½ cup V-8® juice
1 teaspoon hot chile sauce
to taste sea salt and freshly ground black pepper

Add oil to saucepan over medium heat. Add onion, garlic and peppers. Cook 5 minutes without browning, stirring often. Add tomatoes, V-8® juice and chile sauce. Simmer 20 minutes. Season with salt and pepper. Transfer mixture to blender. Puree until smooth. Strain through fine sieve. Keep warm.

ARUGULA SALAD

2 tablespoons grapeseed oil
½ cup diced pancetta
¼ cup walnut halves
2 tablespoons lemon juice
½ pound arugula leaves, washed, spun dry
to taste sea salt and freshly ground black pepper

Add oil and pancetta to skillet over medium-high heat. Cook until pancetta is golden brown, stirring often. Add walnuts. Cook 1 minute. Transfer to large mixing bowl. Cool. Stir in lemon juice. Toss in arugula. Season with salt and pepper.

SQUID

1 tablespoon unsalted butter
½ cup chopped shallots
2 pounds cremini mushrooms, stemmed, diced
2 tablespoons lemon juice
½ cup chopped basil leaves
⅛ teaspoon ground nutmeg
3 tablespoons balsamic vinegar
⅓ cup mascarpone
⅓ cup grated parmesan
8 large squid tubes
2 tablespoons extra virgin olive oil
to taste sea salt and freshly ground black pepper

Preheat oven to 375°F. Melt butter in large skillet over medium heat. Add shallots and mushrooms. Cook 5 minutes, stirring often. Add lemon juice, basil, nutmeg, and vinegar. Season with salt and pepper. Cook until all liquid evaporates, stirring occasionally. Turn off heat. Fold in mascarpone and parmesan. Adjust seasoning. Cool. Stuff squid with mushroom mixture. Close opening with 2 toothpicks. Add bell pepper coulis to large baking dish. Place squid atop. Bake 15 minutes or until center of stuffing is hot. Remove toothpicks. Ladle sauce onto large serving platter. Place squid atop. Garnish with arugula salad. Drizzle with olive oil.

PORTUGAL

In the hilly region of Alentejo, the bread basket of Portugal, freshwater rivers flow through medieval towns. Castles sit between lush green fields of coriander, garlic, and cork-oak plantations. River clams, prized for their sweet, plump meat, are traditionally cooked with pork, creating Portugal's unique version of "surf-and-turf." If you can't find linguiça sausage, use andouille. It will bring a subtle heat and smokey flavor to the dish. —RON

LITTLENECK CLAM AND MUSSEL RAGOUT
Oven-Dried Tomatoes, Linguiça, Leeks

SERVES 4 FAMILY STYLE

TOMATOES

4 plum tomatoes, cored
2 tablespoons extra virgin olive oil
1 tablespoon honey
1 teaspoon finely chopped sage
1 tablespoon red wine vinegar
to taste sea salt and freshly ground black pepper

Preheat oven to 200°F. Quarter tomatoes lengthwise. Whisk olive oil, honey, sage, and vinegar in mixing bowl. Dip tomatoes one at a time into marinade, coating all sides. Transfer, skin side down, to wire rack set over sheet pan. Season with salt and pepper. Cook 2 hours, or until edges start to dry.

PRESENTATION

4 teaspoons extra virgin olive oil
4 sprigs basil

Transfer mixture to large casserole dish or serve directly in skillet. Garnish with oven-dried tomatoes and basil springs. Drizzle with olive oil.

RAGOUT

⅓ cup sea salt
¼ cup cornmeal
20 littleneck clams, scrubbed
3 pounds large black mussels, beard removed, scrubbed
1 pound red new potatoes, washed
1 tablespoon olive oil
1 large leek, white part only, julienned, washed
3 cloves garlic, thinly sliced

½ cup finely diced linguiça sausage
¼ cup finely sliced shallots
1 cup white port
¼ cup unsalted butter
1 lemon, zested, juiced
¼ pound spinach leaves, washed, chopped
to taste sea salt and freshly ground black pepper

Add 1 gallon cold water to large pot. Stir in salt and cornmeal. Add clams then mussels. Soak 45 minutes to purge sand. Remove mussels and clams from water. Transfer to colander. Add potatoes to large pot. Cover with lightly salted cold water. Bring to simmer over medium high heat. Cook until tender. Drain. Transfer to ice bath until well chilled. Cut potatoes in half lengthwise. Add olive oil to large deep skillet over medium heat. Add leeks, garlic, linguiça, and shallots. Cook 3 minutes without browning, stirring occasionally. Add white port, clams, mussels, butter, lemon juice, and zest. Toss to distribute ingredients evenly. Raise heat to high. Cover. Cook 5 minutes or until liquid starts to boil. Uncover. Add potatoes and spinach. Using slotted spoon, rotate all ingredients from bottom to top to ensure even cooking. Season with salt and pepper. Cover. Cook 5 minutes or until shells open.

Rock lobster is called crayfish in Australia. In the quiet fishing town of Mindarie, the opening of "cray" season is celebrated at the marina with the annual blessing-of-the-fleet ceremony. I watched the best-dressed boat competition, browsed the outdoor market, jumped in with the oyster shuckers, and saw the rope coiling contest, where the girls demonstrated some serious skills. I couldn't wait until morning to pick up a lobster and a bottle of Margaret River Chardonnay for the beach barbecue. When choosing a lobster, look for a lively one. The tail should curl under when picked up. Lobsters will live about 36 hours if kept in cool, damp conditions. Do not overcook lobsters or they will become tough and rubbery. —BERNARD

OVEN ROASTED WEST AUSTRALIA LOBSTER TAIL
Pistachio Stuffed Peach, Seven Spice Barbecue Sauce

SERVES 6 FAMILY STYLE

BARBECUE SAUCE

1 cup diced red onion
¾ cup brown sugar
¾ cup red wine vinegar
¼ cup diced ginger
8 cloves garlic
½ teaspoon hot red chile flakes
1 tablespoon mustard seeds
1 teaspoon Chinese five spice
12 medium peaches, pitted, quartered
3 large tomatoes, chopped
⅓ cup soy sauce
to taste sea salt and freshly ground black pepper

Add onions, brown sugar, and vinegar to large sauce pot over medium-high heat. Cook 5 minutes or until thick and syrupy, stirring occasionally. Add ginger, garlic, chile flakes, mustard seeds, and five spice. Cook 2 minutes. Fold in peaches and tomatoes. Bring to simmer. Cook 35 minutes, stirring often. Transfer to blender. Add soy sauce. Purée until smooth. Season with salt and pepper. Set aside.

LOBSTER

6 8-ounce spiny lobster tails
⅓ cup melted unsalted butter
to taste sea salt and freshly ground black pepper

Preheat oven to 450°F. Make a lengthwise cut through the top of each lobster shell using kitchen shears, cutting to, but not through, the base of tail. Press shell on both sides to open. Pull out meat and place on top of shell, leaving meat attached at the base of tail. Devein. Place lobster tails, meat side up, onto baking sheet. Brush with melted butter. Season with sea salt and pepper. Bake 5 minutes. Brush generously with barbecue sauce. Bake 5 more minutes or until meat is opaque throughout and firm to the touch. Transfer to serving platter. Transfer remaining sauce to sauce boat.

PEACHES

½ cup raw pistachios
⅓ cup tawny port
¼ teaspoon anise seed
½ cup finely diced cooked andouille sausage
2 tablespoons unsalted butter, softened
2 tablespoons chopped parsley leaves
to taste sea salt and freshly ground black pepper
6 medium peaches
2 tablespoons maple syrup
2 tablespoons hazelnut oil
¼ teaspoon sea salt
pinch cayenne pepper

Preheat oven to 350°F. Add pistachios, port and anise seed to saucepan over medium heat. Bring to simmer. Remove from heat. Cover tightly with plastic wrap. Steep 30 minutes. Transfer mixture to food processor. Add andouille, butter and parsley. Purée until coarsely ground. Season with salt and pepper. Cut small slice from stem end of peaches so that they sit flat. Cut 1 inch from bottom of peach to create the top. Remove pit. Add maple syrup, hazelnut oil, sea salt, and cayenne pepper to mixing bowl. Whisk to emulsify. Rub onto entire surface of peaches, including tops. Stuff peaches with pistachio mixture, mounded above surface. Cover with tops. Transfer to wax paper-lined baking sheet. Bake 15 minutes or until heated through. Transfer to serving dish.

FRANCE

I traveled the rugged edges of Brittany's windswept coast, from Lorient to the medieval town of Vannes. Every Saturday morning, the open-air market invites the sunrise with galettes, café au lait and buttered croissants, just out of the oven. At one stand I met Loic, a local lobster fisherman selling the Brittany lobster—a noble crustacean with a shell color that mimics Brittany's emerald ocean. The vanilla in this recipe enhances the lobster's dense, sweet flesh. When buying lobster it is helpful to bring an ice chest to keep them alive until cooking time. —RON

HOMARD BRETON VALENTIN
Meli Melo Cauliflower, Vanilla Absinthe Sauce

SERVES 4

SAUCE

1 tablespoon unsalted butter
¼ cup minced shallots
½ cup diced bosc pear
2 tablespoons champagne vinegar
1 cup vermouth
¼ cup absinthe liquor
½ vanilla bean, chopped
⅓ cup crème fraîche
½ cup packed watercress leaves
¼ cup chervil leaves
to taste sea salt and freshly ground white pepper

Melt butter in sauce pan over medium heat. Add shallots and pear. Cook 2 minutes, stirring often. Add vinegar, vermouth, absinthe, and vanilla. Reduce by half. Transfer to blender. Add crème fraîche, watercress, and chervil. Blend until smooth. Strain through coarse sieve into sauce pan. Bring to simmer over medium heat. Season with salt and pepper. Keep warm.

CAULIFLOWER

1 large leek, white part only
3 tablespoons unsalted butter
2 cups cauliflower florets
½ cup finely sliced celery, inner stalk
½ cup dry vermouth wine
½ teaspoon finely chopped thyme leaves
to taste sea salt and freshly ground white pepper

Cut leeks in half lengthwise, then slice crosswise ¼-inch thick. Wash thoroughly. Transfer to colander to drain. Melt butter in large skillet over medium heat. Add cauliflower, leeks and celery. Cook 2 minutes without browning, stirring occasionally. Add vermouth and thyme. Cover. Cook additional 3 minutes until cauliflower is tender and liquid evaporates. Remove from heat. Season with salt and pepper. Keep warm.

LOBSTER

4 1½-pound live Maine lobsters

Bring 3 gallons salted water to boil in large stock pot. Add lobsters. Cook 5 minutes. Transfer to ice bath. Separate heads from tails. Remove meat from claws, knuckles, and tails. Set aside claw and knuckle meat. Cut tails in half lengthwise. Devein. Set aside.

PRESENTATION

3 tablespoons unsalted butter
to taste sea salt and freshly ground white pepper
¼ cup vermouth
½ cup diced bosc pear
4 sprigs chervil

Melt butter in large skillet over medium heat until foamy. Add lobster tails, claws, and knuckles. Season with salt and pepper. Cook 30 seconds. Flip lobster. Add vermouth and pears. Cook one minute or until hot. Tightly pack cauliflower mixture into 4-inch ring in center of large warm serving plate. Arrange two tail halves, two claws, and knuckle meat atop. Remove ring. Spoon sauce around. Garnish with pears and chervil.

GERMANY

I took a six-mile train ride from Germany's mainland to the island of Sylt, located right below Denmark on the North Sea Coast. With ocean lapping at both sides of the entire manmade path, I knew I was in for a seafood adventure. Fish stands and restaurants dot the narrow island. I felt like a kid in an oceanic candy shop! But with only 24 hours to spend, my plan was to dine smorgasbord-style, tasting as many different dishes and preparations as possible. This dish combines Germany's traditional sauerkraut with the northern island's seafood culture. Feel free to use any type of fish you like, following the same preparation described in this recipe. —RON

NORTH SEA SAUERKRAUT
Sea Catch, Caviar Butter Sauce

SERVES 4

SAUERKRAUT

2½ tablespoons olive oil
2 pounds green cabbage, cored, thinly sliced
1 bay leaf
¼ cup white wine vinegar
¾ cup lager beer
6 juniper berries
¼ cup chopped bacon
½ cup minced white onion
1 clove garlic, minced
to taste sea salt and freshly ground black pepper

Add 2 tablespoons olive oil to large stock pot over medium heat. Stir in cabbage. Cook 5 minutes without browning, stirring often. Add bay leaf, vinegar, beer, and juniper berries. Bring to simmer. Cook 30 minutes, stirring occasionally. Transfer to colander to drain excess liquid. Add remaining oil to large, deep skillet over medium heat. Add bacon, onion, and garlic. Cook 3 minutes without browning, stirring often. Fold in cabbage. Season with salt and pepper. Cover. Simmer 5 minutes. Keep warm.

SAUCE

4 jumbo shrimp, size u-10
2 tablespoons grapeseed oil
3 sprigs thyme
2 tablespoons minced shallots
½ cup white wine
1 lemon, zested, juiced
1 cup shellfish stock
¼ cup crème fraîche
2 tablespoons unsalted butter
to taste sea salt and freshly ground black pepper

Remove shells from shrimp, leaving tail on. Place shrimp in refrigerator. Add oil to skillet over medium-high heat. Add shrimp shells. Cook 3 minutes, stirring often. Add thyme, shallots, wine, lemon juice, and zest. Reduce by half. Add shellfish stock. Reduce by half. Stir in crème fraîche. Bring to boil. Turn off heat. Cover. Steep 10 minutes to infuse. Strain through fine sieve into saucepan, pressing on solids to extract maximum flavor. Bring sauce to simmer over medium heat. Reduce by half. Add butter, 1 tablespoon at a time, whisking vigorously to incorporate. Remove from heat. Season with salt and pepper. Keep warm.

SEA CATCH

4 reserved jumbo shrimp (from sauce)
½ pound sea bass fillet, boneless, skinless
4 large sea scallops, size u-10, tendon removed
½ pound salmon fillet, boneless, skinless
½ pound monkfish, boneless, skinless
to taste sea salt and freshly ground black pepper
¼ cup chopped parsley leaves
5 teaspoons grapeseed oil
1 tablespoon sturgeon caviar
4 sprigs parsley

Preheat oven to 400°F. Devein shrimp. Cut each fish into 4 equal pieces. Season bass, scallops, salmon, monkfish, and shrimp with salt, pepper, and parsley. Add 1 teaspoon grapeseed oil to large skillet over high heat. Sear bass 1 minute on each side. Transfer to parchment-lined baking sheet. Repeat process with remaining grapeseed oil, scallops, salmon, monkfish, and shrimp. Bake 2 minutes or until slightly underdone. Place sauerkraut in center of warm serving plate. Arrange fish and shellfish around sauerkraut. Stir caviar into sauce. Spoon sauce onto plate. Garnish with parsley.

TURKEY

My first time in Turkey, I stepped off a cruise ship in the port city of Kuşadasi. A popular port for tourists, I was not hoping for much. Sometimes the best travel experiences come when you least expect them. Wasn't I surprised when the Kuşadasi fish market became the object of my intrigue! Rows of fish, stacked vertically as if standing on their tails, were illuminated by bare incandescent light bulbs hanging from low rafters. The place felt like a bootleg gambling hall where squid, shrimp, little crabs, big crabs, and scallops vied for position among the rows of fish. The palm tree- and tourist-lined streets outside suddenly seemed miles away. These little discoveries are the essence of foreign travel. This recipe takes me back to my Turkish grandfather's dining table where eggplant, pomegranates, bulgur, and feta cheese were never absent. —RON

ZAATAR SPICED SWORDFISH KEBAB
Bulgur Salad, Eggplant Tahini

SERVES 6

TAHINI

1 one-pound eggplant
2 tablespoons extra virgin olive oil
½ cup tahini
¼ cup plain yogurt
2 cloves garlic, crushed
1 tablespoon chopped parsley leaves
2 tablespoons lemon juice
½ teaspoon sea salt
⅛ teaspoon cayenne pepper

Preheat oven to 350°F. Puncture eggplant 10 times with tip of knife. Bake in microwave 6 minutes or until tender. Cool. Cut off stem end. Peel off skin. Chop flesh. Transfer to colander to drain. Place flesh in food processor. Add remaining ingredients. Blend until smooth. Transfer to six sauce dishes.

SWORDFISH

2 pounds swordfish loin, boneless, skinless
1 lemon, zested
¼ cup olive oil
6 cherry tomatoes
6 brown mushrooms
6 pearl onions, peeled
3 tablespoons zaatar
6 8-inch bamboo skewers, soaked in water 2 hours
** canola oil spray
to taste sea salt and freshly ground black pepper

Cut swordfish into 6 rectangular pieces. Mix lemon zest and oil in large mixing bowl. Add swordfish, tomatoes, mushrooms, and pearl onions. Toss to coat. Season with salt and pepper. Sprinkle with zaatar. Thread swordfish, tomatoes, mushrooms, and onions onto skewers. Heat grill pan to medium high. Spray with canola oil. Cook skewers 1 minute on each side or until fish is slightly underdone.

BULGUR SALAD

2 cups vegetable stock
2 teaspoons dried orange peel
1 cup bulgur or cracked wheat
½ cup crumbled feta cheese
2 tablespoons minced scallions, white part only
¼ cup minced mint leaves
¼ cup minced Italian parsley leaves
3 tablespoons lemon juice
1½ tablespoons extra virgin olive oil
to taste sea salt and freshly ground black pepper

Bring vegetable stock and orange peel to boil in medium saucepan. Turn off heat. Stir in bulgur. Cover 20 minutes. Fluff with fork. Fold in remaining ingredients. Season with salt and pepper.

ZAATAR

2 tablespoons sesame seeds
½ cup slivered almonds
2 tablespoons ground sumac
⅓ teaspoon sea salt
1 tablespoon dried savory leaves
1 tablespoon dried thyme leaves

Toast sesame seeds and almonds in skillet over medium heat until golden. Transfer to spice grinder. Add remaining ingredients. Pulse to lightly coarse texture.

PRESENTATION

4 sprigs parsley
1 tablespoon extra virgin olive oil
1 pomegranate, seeded

Mound bulgur in center of warm serving plate. Lean kebab atop. Place eggplant tahini beside. Garnish with parsley sprig and pomegranate seeds. Drizzle olive oil onto plate.

SEA FARE ENTRÉES | **153**

I stayed with friends and family on the Kenai Peninsula in Alaska for a week of nature. We launched our boat from the city of Seward for a day of halibut fishing. My reward for catching an 82-pound halibut was to make it back to shore safely after we were engulfed by a quick moving gale. Even the puffins sitting on the rock that we nearly crashed into looked nervous. I was soaked like a French Gilligan. Shivering from the cold, I was taken to The Salty Dog pub where the waitress administered whiskey-spiked coffee to warm me up. Cooking halibut to medium rare with a resting time of two minutes will retain optimum moisture and enhance its light, delicate and sweet flavor. —BERNARD

POTATO ROSEMARY CRUSTED HALIBUT
Aromatic Pepper Sauce

SERVES 4

HALIBUT

4 medium Yukon gold potatoes, peeled
4 six-ounce Northern halibut fillets, skinless and boneless
to taste sea salt and freshly ground black pepper
½ teaspoon finely chopped rosemary leaves
2 tablespoons grapeseed oil
3 tablespoons butter

Using mandoline or vegetable slicer, cut potatoes crosswise into very thin slices, almost transparent. Do not wash. Season halibut on both sides with salt and pepper. Cover fish with potato slices, overlapping to create a scale pattern. Sprinkle with rosemary. Cover with plastic wrap. Using palm of hand, press on potatoes to adhere them to halibut. Discard plastic wrap. Place in freezer 15 minutes. Add grapeseed oil and butter to large nonstick skillet over medium heat. When butter is foamy, lay halibut in skillet, potato side down. Cook 3 minutes or until golden. Carefully slide spatula under potatoes. Flip over. Cook 3 minutes or until firm but slightly underdone.

AROMATIC PEPPER SAUCE

2 tablespoons grapeseed oil
4 cloves garlic, sliced
½ cup thinly sliced shallots
½ cup seeded, diced red bell peppers
½ cup seeded, diced yellow bell peppers
½ cup seeded, diced vine-ripened tomatoes
2 lemons, peeled, seeded, flesh diced
16 black olives, pitted, chopped
2 tablespoons extra virgin olive oil
to taste sea salt and freshly ground white pepper

Add grapeseed oil to saucepan over medium heat. Add garlic, shallots, and bell peppers. Season with salt and pepper. Cook 10 minutes without browning, stirring often. Add tomatoes. Cook 2 minutes. Fold in lemon and olives. Remove from heat. Let stand 10 minutes. Add extra virgin olive oil. Adjust seasoning.

PRESENTATION

4 sprigs rosemary

Spoon sauce onto center of warm serving plate. Top with halibut. Garnish with rosemary sprigs.

BALI

On a trip to Komodo National Park, a spectacle of raw beauty unfolded. Jumping off the boat, I was greeted by an 8-foot Komodo dragon. This beast loves to feast on local wild boar, temor deer, and unfortunate chickens. I fished offshore with the local islanders in a narrow wooden boat fitted with nets, hooks, and traditional rods. We caught snapper, giant trevally, and wahoo near the reef. Back on shore, village women waited with banana leaves, hoisin, and chile paste to wrap the fish and hot-smoke it over palm wood. This recipe is my version. Mahi-mahi, swordfish, or yellowtail suit this dish as a perfect alternative to wahoo. —BERNARD

HOISIN MACADAMIA CRUSTED WAHOO
Napa Cabbage Slaw, Taro Root Chips

SERVES 4

NAPA CABBAGE SLAW

1 Asian pear
1 teaspoon honey crystals
2 tablespoons light sesame oil
½ teaspoon red chile paste
1 teaspoon grated ginger
2 tablespoons seasoned rice vinegar
2 cups thinly sliced napa cabbage
¼ cup toasted coconut flakes
2 tablespoons nori flakes
to taste sea salt and freshly ground black pepper

Peel and core Asian pear. Cut into ⅛-inch thick slices. Cut slices into match sticks. Whisk honey, sesame oil, chile paste, ginger, and vinegar in mixing bowl. Add Asian pear, cabbage, coconut flakes, and nori flakes. Season with salt and pepper. Toss thoroughly.

WAHOO

¼ cup hoisin sauce
1 tablespoon teriyaki sauce
¼ teaspoon ground star anise
1 tablespoon orange juice
¼ teaspoon orange zest
2 tablespoons peanut oil
4 six-ounce wahoo fillets, skinless, boneless
to taste sea salt and freshly ground black pepper
¾ cup chopped macadamia nuts

Preheat oven to 375°F. Whisk hoisin sauce, teriyaki sauce, star anise, orange juice, and zest in mixing bowl. Add oil to skillet over medium high heat. Season wahoo with salt and pepper. Sear 1 minute on each side. Remove from heat. Spoon hoisin mixture atop of fish. Coat evenly with macadamia nuts. Place in oven. Cook 5 minutes or until slightly under done.

TARO ROOT CHIPS

1 quart peanut oil
2 pounds taro root
to taste sea salt flakes
¼ teaspoon togarashi

Heat oil in heavy sauce pot to 325°F. Peel taro root. Using mandoline or vegetable slicer, cut taro root crosswise into 1/16-inch thick slices. Rinse under cold running water. Pat dry. Add to oil in small batches. Fry until golden and crisp. Transfer to paper towel-lined plate. Sprinkle with salt and togarashi.

PRESENTATION

1 tablespoon macadamia oil
¼ cup diced peeled pineapple

Place slaw in center of serving plates. Top with wahoo. Drizzle with macadamia oil. Garnish with taro root chips and diced pineapple.

Walking through the Newton Circus Hawker Centre, I experienced the true heart and soul of Singapore, a hub for culinary thrill seekers like me. I was surrounded by authentic varieties of Chinese, Malay, and Indian treats cooked in woks, grilled on barbecues, and steamed in bamboo trays. Fried noodles, fish ball soup, clay pot chicken, and a multitude of seafood dishes were ready for locals and travelers alike. Food bridges the language barrier. I watched an elderly woman teach her grandson the tradition of making spicy sauces using crushed chiles, tomatoes, and secret spices. She then prepared local mud crabs, shrimp, and the prized line-caught sea bass. Savoring these delicacies to the last bit, I looked forward to sharing this memory with my friends and family. —BERNARD

ALMOND TATSOI CRUSTED SEA BASS
Plum Tomato Sambal, Sweet Soy

SERVES 4

SAMBAL

2 tablespoons sesame oil
½ cup diced smoked bacon
¾ cup thinly sliced red onion
4 cloves garlic, thinly sliced
1 Thai chile, seeded, thinly sliced
⅓ cup honey
2 cups diced plum tomatoes
1 lemon, zested, juiced
3 tablespoons red wine vinegar
3 tablespoons finely chopped Thai basil leaves
to taste sea salt and freshly ground black pepper

Add sesame oil and bacon to large skillet over medium-high heat. Cook 2 minutes, stirring often, to render bacon fat. Add onion, garlic, and chile. Raise heat to medium-high. Cook 1 minute, stirring constantly. Add honey. Cook 30 seconds. Fold in tomatoes, lemon zest, juice, and vinegar. Cook 20 minutes or until jam consistency, stirring often. Fold in basil. Season with salt and pepper. Keep warm.

SEA BASS

½ cup packed, julienned tatsoi leaves
⅓ cup toasted sliced almonds
¼ teaspoon ground star anise
3 tablespoons peanut oil
4 six-ounce sea bass fillets, boneless, skinless
to taste sea salt and freshly ground black pepper

Preheat oven to 375°F. Add tatsoi, almonds, star anise, and 2 tablespoons peanut oil to mixing bowl. Toss thoroughly. Set aside. Season sea bass with salt and pepper. Add remaining peanut oil to nonstick skillet over medium heat. Sear bass 1 minute on each side. Transfer to baking sheet. Coat evenly with tatsoi mixture. Bake 5 minutes or until slightly underdone.

PRESENTATION

¼ cup kecap manis sweet soy

Place sweet soy in squeeze bottle. Spoon sambal onto center of warm serving plate. Place fish atop. Squeeze sweet soy around.

Tahiti has been creating Asian-fusion cuisine for much longer than the term has existed. The cooking displays an unusual blend of French, Asian, and Polynesian influence. Chinese immigrants arrived in the islands in the 1860s to work the cotton fields. They intermarried with the locals and the French, fusing the cultures and cuisines of the three groups. This dish captures the spirit of Tahiti's intercultural unity—Asian and island ingredients prepared using French techniques. At the market look for ahi with a vibrant color and tightly bound flesh with no brown spots. If buying steaks, ask your butcher for the center cut. —RON

SESAME PEPPERED RUBY RED AHI TUNA
Fennel Mango Salad, Avocado Fritter, Hibiscus Essence

SERVES 4

SALAD

1 small bulb fennel
1 mango
1 teaspoon chopped cilantro
1 tablespoon shaved, toasted coconut
2 tablespoons hazelnut oil
1 tablespoon white rum
2 tablespoons seasoned rice vinegar
dash tabasco
to taste sea salt and freshly ground black pepper

Trim fennel bulb, reserving fronds for presentation. Cut bulb in half. Remove core. Slice thinly crosswise. Peel mango. Cut flesh from inner seed. Slice thin. Transfer fennel and mango slices to mixing bowl. Add remaining ingredients. Season with salt and pepper. Toss gently.

HIBISCUS

⅓ cup white wine
¼ cup guava juice
2 tablespoons chopped shallots
10 dried hibiscus flowers
2 tablespoons heavy cream
½ cup unsalted butter, cut into 4 cubes
to taste sea salt and finely ground white pepper

Add wine, guava juice, shallots, and hibiscus flowers to saucepan over medium heat. Reduce liquid by two thirds. Stir in cream. Bring to boil. Turn heat to low. Whisk in butter, 1 cube at a time. Strain through fine sieve. Season with salt and pepper. Keep warm.

TUNA

½ cup white sesame seeds
½ cup black sesame seeds
4 six-ounce center cut sushi grade #1 ahi tuna steaks, 1-inch thick
2 tablespoons grapeseed oil
to taste sea salt and freshly ground black pepper

Place sesame seeds into two separate shallow bowls. Season fish on both sides with salt and pepper. Press one side of tuna into white sesame seeds and the other side into black sesame seeds. Add oil to heavy skillet over high heat. Sear tuna one minute on each side. Transfer to cutting board. Cut in half on bias.

PRESENTATION

1 teaspoon black sesame seeds
1 teaspoon white sesame seeds
1 teaspoon pink peppercorns, chopped
½ teaspoon togarashi pepper
1 teaspoon dried parsley leaves
4 spring roll wrappers, 7-inch square
** canola oil spray
4 fronds fennel top
8 Avocado Fritters (recipe on page 224)

Preheat oven to 300°F. Combine sesame seeds, peppercorns, togarashi, and parsley in small bowl. Fold spring roll wrapper accordion-style in ½-inch increments. Fold one inch of one end onto itself. Secure with toothpick. Open fan. Lay on baking sheet. Spray with canola oil. Sprinkle with spice mixture. Bake 20 minutes, or until brittle. Remove toothpick. Arrange tuna on center of warm serving plate, leaning one slice against the other. Mound salad behind and atop tuna. Spoon sauce onto plate. Secure fan with avocado fritters behind tuna. Garnish with fennel tops.

AUSTRALIA

Fly fishing in Tasmania is a skilled sport best performed under a blanket of clouds and mist. The salmon come up to the surface in a flurry looking for food. On the shores of the Derwent Estuary, with colorful flies in my hands and a net hooked on the side of my waders, I went on a mission. After many casts, I suddenly felt the incredible power of a salmon running away, somersaulting over the water, fighting hook and line. Fishing is a game of give and take. My friend, Chef Benjamin Christie, likes to cook his salmon on charred cedar planks to give the fish a delicate, smokey, barbecued flavor. For me, the exotic fragrance of curry with an apricot glaze and pistachios just rocks my world. —BERNARD

APRICOT GINGER GLAZED TASMANIAN SALMON
Corn Fennel Relish, Avocado Oil

SERVES 4

GLAZE

1 pound apricots
2 tablespoons brandy
1 tablespoon white wine vinegar
3 tablespoons brown sugar
2 tablespoons grated ginger
2 tablespoons chopped shallots
to taste sea salt and freshly ground black pepper

Chop apricots, discarding pits. Add to saucepan with remaining ingredients over medium heat. Bring to simmer. Cook 15 minutes or until thick and syrupy, stirring often. Transfer to blender. Purée until smooth. Strain through coarse sieve. Season with salt and pepper. Set aside.

SALMON

½ cup shelled raw pistachios
¼ cup sliced almonds
1 teaspoon Madras curry
1 tablespoon minced chives
1 tablespoon toasted white sesame seeds
2 tablespoons grapeseed oil
4 6-ounce wild king salmon fillets, boneless
to taste sea salt and freshly ground black pepper

Preheat oven to 375°F. Add pistachios, almonds, curry, chives, and sesame seeds to food processor. Pulse until coarsely chopped. Transfer to bowl. Set aside. Add oil to large oven-proof skillet over medium-high heat. Season salmon with salt and pepper. Lay in skillet, flesh side down. Sear 2 minutes or until golden brown. Flip over. Generously coat top of each salmon with apricot glaze. Sprinkle with pistachio mixture. Transfer to oven. Cook 3 minutes or until slightly underdone.

RELISH

2 tablespoons avocado oil
2 ears sweet corn, shaved
½ cup thinly sliced fennel
½ cup quartered gold gooseberries
1 green apple, peeled, diced
1 teaspoon honey
1 tablespoon chopped scallions
1 tangerine, juiced, zested
1 teaspoon finely chopped mint leaves
to taste sea salt and freshly ground black pepper

Add oil to skillet over medium heat. Add corn and fennel. Cook 3 minutes, stirring often. Transfer to mixing bowl. Combine with remaining ingredients. Season with salt and pepper.

PRESENTATION

2 teaspoons avocado oil
4 gooseberries, with husk

Spoon relish onto center of large serving plate. Lean salmon atop. Drizzle with avocado oil. Garnish with gooseberry.

BOLIVIA

Not all of my travels have been glamorous. One time, my father and I were attacked in the town of Copacabana, Bolivia, and robbed of the most precious thing one needs at 14,000 feet elevation—oxygen. I awoke first to find my Dad sprawled in the middle of the dusty road with an Aymara woman crying at his side. We both survived and celebrated our good fortune in an eatery on the bank of Lake Titicaca, a place where every restaurant specializes in locally caught trout. The fillets are seared in brown butter, stuffed, or slathered in garlic and served with quinoa soup, quinoa salad, or just plain steamed quinoa. When buying trout, look for resilient flesh, moist, slippery skin and a clean aroma. —RON

INCAN SPICED SWEETWATER TROUT
Quinoa Heart of Palm Salad

SERVES 2 ROMANTIC STYLE

QUINOA HEART OF PALM SALAD

1 cup quinoa
2 cups vegetable stock
½ teaspoon sea salt
2 cloves garlic, minced
½ cup diced peeled tomato
½ cup diced peeled cucumber
½ cup julienned red onion
2 tangerines, peeled, seeded, diced
4 hearts of palm, sliced thinly crosswise
¼ cup chopped basil leaves
2 tablespoons lime juice
¼ cup extra virgin olive oil
to taste salt and fresh ground black pepper

Rinse quinoa thoroughly in colander under running cold water. Add stock and salt to sauce pot over medium-high heat. Bring to simmer. Stir quinoa into stock. Cover. Return to simmer. Cook 10 minutes or until stock is absorbed. Spread quinoa onto baking sheet to cool. Combine remaining ingredients in large mixing bowl. Fold in quinoa. Season with salt and pepper. Transfer to serving bowl.

INCAN SPICED SWEETWATER TROUT

¼ cup blue corn flakes cereal
¼ cup toasted pumpkin seeds
¼ teaspoon pasilla chile powder
¼ teaspoon achiote powder (annatto)
¼ teaspoon sea salt
⅛ teaspoon freshly ground black pepper
1 18-ounce lake trout, headless, butterflied, boneless
2 tablespoons butter
1 lemon, halved
½ tablespoon chopped parsley leaves

Preheat oven to 375°F. Process blue corn flakes, pumpkin seeds, chile powder, achiote powder, salt and pepper to a coarse meal in food processor. Add butter to large cast iron skillet. Place skillet over medium-high heat until butter is foamy. Lay trout in skillet skin side down. Sprinkle trout generously with corn flake mixture. Cook 1 minute. Transfer to oven. Bake 5 minutes or until flesh is firm and flaky. Remove from oven. Squeeze half lemon over trout. Sprinkle with parsley. Serve with quinoa.

NEW ZEALAND

In the Bay of Islands lies the port city of Paihia. Crystal clear waters are inhabited by eagle rays alongside schools of mackerel, John Dory, and multicolored reef fish. A gentleman seated on the dock with a friendly black lab was jigging small live bait on a rod. Two John Dory swam blissfully in his yellow bucket, the dog occasionally poking his nose in to take a peek. The man told me that John Dory is his wife's favorite catch for making the best fish and chips. Walking down the wharf, I stopped at a fish shack to indulge in this local tradition. If you cannot find John Dory, use your local flounder or striped bass. —BERNARD

THYME SCENTED JOHN DORY FRITTER
Kiwano Relish, Wasabi Dip

SERVES 6

KIWANO RELISH

6 medium kiwano melons
1 cup cored, diced Asian pear
1 avocado, peeled, pitted, diced
⅓ cup thinly sliced shallots
2 tablespoons chopped cilantro
1 lime, juiced
1 small Thai chile pepper, seeded, minced
to taste sea salt and freshly ground black pepper
6 springs cilantro

Slice one inch from one end of kiwano melon crosswise. Scoop out pulp. Pass pulp through coarse sieve into large mixing bowl. Discard seeds. Gently toss remaining ingredients with kiwano pulp. Season with salt and pepper. Slice ¼-inch from other end of kiwano to create base. Stand up. Fill kiwano with relish. Garnish with cilantro springs. Set aside.

JOHN DORY

1 quart grapeseed oil
6 6-ounce John Dory fillets, boneless, skinless
2 large eggs
1 tablespoon lemon thyme leaves
1 tablespoon lemon zest
⅔ cup cold lager beer
½ cup all purpose flour
½ cup cornstarch
1 teaspoon baking soda
1 teaspoon baking powder
1 teaspoon sugar
½ teaspoon salt
¼ teaspoon freshly ground black pepper

Heat oil in heavy sauce pot to 365°F. Cut John Dory into 18 strips of equal size. Whisk eggs in large mixing bowl with lemon thyme and lemon zest. Stir in beer. Combine dry ingredients in small bowl. Sift over egg mixture. Mix gently, just to incorporate. Dip John Dory into batter. Fry 1 minute or until golden, crisp and slightly underdone. Transfer to paper towel-lined platter. Season with salt and pepper.

WASABI DIP

1 large egg yolk
1 teaspoon Dijon mustard
3 tablespoons sake wine
3 cloves garlic, minced
1 tablespoon prepared wasabi
2 tablespoons lemon juice
¾ cup avocado oil
to taste sea salt and freshly ground black pepper

Whisk egg yolk, mustard, sake, garlic, wasabi, and lemon juice in large mixing bowl. Add avocado oil in a slow steady stream, whisking vigorously to mayonnaise consistency. Season with salt and pepper. Transfer to 6 sauce dishes.

PRESENTATION

3 sheets parchment paper
to taste flaky sea salt

Cut parchment paper into six 9x12-inch triangles. Roll into cone shapes. Fill with fritters. Transfer to large, warm serving plate. Sprinkle with sea salt. Serve with kiwano and wasabi dip.

On the rugged coast of Brittany lies the regional port of Cancale where fishermen unload their catch into baskets on the pier. Lobster, loup de mer, langoustine, mullet, and monkfish are available to the locals at the crisp, early hour of five A.M. My friend Didier spoke the Breton language and was eager to strike a bargain. He quickly scored a monkfish tail and a bushel of Belon oysters for the Sunday family feast, and away we went. His partner, Gilberte, along with her daughters and grandkids, prepared the monkfish using homemade cider from their orchard and vegetables from the garden. It was quite a family affair—slow food style. Meanwhile, the boys invited me to the cellar to toast with local Chouchen honey wine. —RON

MONKFISH BRETONNE
Wilted Vegetables, Apple Cider Sauce

SERVES 4

WILTED VEGETABLES

1 large leek, white part only
2 carrots, washed, peeled
½ pound fingerling potatoes, washed
2 tablespoons unsalted butter
⅓ cup sauvignon blanc
3 tablespoons crème fraîche
16 medium asparagus, peeled, trimmed
to taste sea salt and freshly ground black pepper

Cut leek and carrots into 3-inch long matchsticks. Wash leeks. Transfer to colander. Quarter potatoes lengthwise. Melt butter in nonstick skillet over medium heat. Add potatoes. Season with salt and pepper. Cook 3 minutes, turning occasionally. Add leeks and carrots. Cook 1 minute. Add sauvignon blanc and crème fraîche. Bring to simmer. Place asparagus on top. Cover. Cook 2 minutes or until asparagus are al dente. Turn off heat. Adjust seasoning.

PRESENTATION

4 slices apple wood smoked bacon, cooked crisp, warm
4 sprigs thyme

Arrange vegetables in center of warm serving plate. Top with monkfish. Spoon apple cider sauce around. Garnish with bacon and thyme sprig.

MONKFISH

4 6-ounce monkfish fillets, boneless, skinless
to taste sea salt and freshly ground black pepper
1 teaspoon thyme leaves
2 tablespoons unsalted butter
¼ cup cider vinegar
½ cup apple cider
¼ cup minced shallots
2 sprigs thyme
1 bay leaf
½ tablespoon cracked black pepper
1 cup chicken stock
½ cup heavy cream
2 gala apples, cored, diced
2 tablespoons apple brandy

Preheat oven to 400°F. Season monkfish with salt, pepper, and thyme. Melt butter in deep skillet over medium-high heat until golden brown. Roast monkfish 2 minutes on each side. Place skillet in oven. Cook 3 minutes or until monkfish is opaque in center and slightly underdone. Transfer monkfish to platter. Tent loosely with foil to keep warm. Return skillet to medium heat. Add vinegar, apple cider, shallots, thyme sprig, bay leaf, and cracked pepper. Reduce liquid to syrupy consistency. Add chicken stock, cream, and apples. Bring to simmer. Reduce by half. Transfer to blender. Purée until smooth. Strain through fine sieve. Stir in brandy. Season with salt and pepper. Keep warm.

WINGS

MEXICO

Standing in the middle of a corn field in Central Mexico, the September sun heated my neck while a corn stalk hung from my lips like a huge cigar. That field was no different than thousands of others that line the outskirts of Mexican pueblos, but at that moment it was very special to me. I came there to choose the sweetest nectar-filled ears of corn for my mother-in-law Doña Luz's fresh corn tamales.

Doña's specific instructions, and much practice, have made me an expert at selecting the perfect ears while maneuvering between six-foot-high stalks. Still, an occasional stumble over low-lying thicket or a wild-growing pumpkin gave me a chance to pause and contemplate for a moment. The field's warm sweet air is a treat to inhale. I thought about corn's long role in the evolution of Mexican culture. An imaginary Aztec corn-harvest ritual started to dance in my mind as I continued filling the burlap bag.

Everyone in Doña's household took part in preparing the feast. Raul milked the neighbor's cow before sun-up so that the cream had time to rise. Liliana picked long green chiles from aunt Chucha's garden for roasting. Everyone else gathered to shuck the corn for the regional tamale called *uchepo*. Doña's husband, Salvador, showed us how to remove the husks in one piece, so they could be used to wrap the fresh corn masa. I appointed myself as director. "Remember people, every husk torn is one uchepo lost." Their chuckles implied that my Spanish has progressed since last year's visit.

In Doña Luz's house, multiple rooms surround an open-air courtyard that is divided into sections. One area is overgrown with citrus and fig trees, edible and ornamental foliage, culinary plants, herbs, and a huge assortment of brightly colored flowers. The other is designated for raising small animals like geese, turkeys, quails, chicken, and ducks in spacious tranquility. Not knowing which of the fowl are considered pets and which are destined for the dinner table, I am careful not to get too emotionally attached to any of them.

On the morning of the feast, I awoke to find brilliant orange squash blossoms neatly arranged in a pail on the kitchen table. Sitting in the sunbeams that highlighted the dust-speckled air, the flowers were displayed in a decorative bouquet. Before noon they would be cooked into squash blossom quesadillas to hold everyone over until the feast. While I was admiring the delicate, silky texture of the flowers, Doña Luz was in the poultry pen sacrificing the feast's main attraction—a turkey she has raised since its birth.

Early that evening, the house overflowed with guests and the table was filled with nature's edible gifts. Toasts were made, conversations were struck and life was truly celebrated. I learned many things on this journey, especially how grand Mexican Septembers can be. After the feast, Doña Luz promised me that if I return for next year's harvest she will teach me how to make more of the regional dishes she is so proud of. I assured her that I and my notepad would be there, come the first sign of September.

—RON

ITALY

The rolling hills of the Sicilian province of Trapani are blanketed with patchwork fields of flowers, lucerne, maize, frumento, and vineyards that lead the way to Segesta. After visiting the ancient ruins of a Doric temple, I bicycled to a local winery in Alghero. I received the warmest reception from Mama Lucia and her husband Francesco. We toured the vineyard and garden behind the house where magnificent, tall fava beans soaked in the sun. Our lunch that day reminded me of supper at my grandmother's house when friends and family would drop by. For this recipe, you should prepare the fava beans a day ahead as they are more flavorful when reheated. —BERNARD

CHICKEN SEGESTA

Aromatic Fava Beans, Arugula Salad, Parmesan

SERVES 4 FAMILY STYLE

FAVA BEANS

1 pound shucked fava beans
1 tablespoon olive oil
¼ cup diced pancetta
2 bay leaves
½ cup diced carrots
1 cup diced celery root
3 cloves garlic, minced
2 tablespoons chopped oregano leaves
to taste sea salt and freshly ground black pepper

Bring lightly salted water to boil in large pot. Add fava beans. Cook 3 minutes. Drain. Transfer beans to ice bath. Peel beans, discarding skins. Add olive oil to large skillet over medium heat. Add pancetta, bay leaf, carrots, celery, garlic, and oregano. Cook 5 minutes, stirring often. Fold in beans. Remove from heat. Discard bay leaves. Season with salt and pepper.

ARUGULA SALAD

1 tablespoon lemon juice
2 tablespoons extra virgin olive oil
1 teaspoon minced shallots
to taste sea salt and freshly ground black pepper
2 cups arugula leaves, washed, patted dry
2 ounces shaved parmesan cheese

Whisk lemon juice, olive oil, shallots, salt and pepper in large serving bowl. Add arugula. Toss. Garnish with parmesan.

CHICKEN BREAST

1 tablespoon olive oil
4 eight-ounce chicken breasts, with wing bone
to taste sea salt and freshly ground black pepper
1 cup sliced leeks, white part only, washed
½ cup diced vine ripened tomatoes
12 Kalamata olives, pitted, chopped
⅓ cup Marsala wine
¼ cup chicken stock
pinch saffron threads
1 tablespoon chopped oregano leaves
1 tablespoon extra virgin olive oil
4 sprigs oregano

Add olive oil to large skillet over medium-high heat. Season chicken with salt and pepper. Sear, skin side down, until golden brown. Turn. Cook 2 minutes. Add leeks, tomatoes, olives, and Marsala to skillet. Lower heat to medium. Cook 1 minute. Add chicken stock and saffron. Sprinkle chicken with oregano. Cover. Cook 5 minutes or until chicken is cooked through. Remove chicken from pan. Keep warm. Fold fava bean mixture into skillet. Bring to simmer. Season with salt and pepper. Transfer to serving dish. Arrange chicken atop. Drizzle with extra virgin olive oil. Garnish with oregano sprigs.

"Every Georgian dish is a poem," said the renowned Russian poet, Alexander Pushkin. At the central market in the heart of Tblisi, my friend Koko and I visited the "spice girls." Stall after stall of smiling women displayed stacks of pungent colorful spices in small clay vats. With the focus of a chemist, the spice lady blended powdered marigold petals with other herbs and spices gathered from throughout the Middle East for the traditional khmeli suneli spice mixture. We grabbed the bag and returned to the house where Koko's mom Lali roasted a whole piglet, a leg of lamb, and a chicken seasoned with the aromatic blend. Her stuffed eggplant was Koko's father's favorite dish. —BERNARD

WALNUT SUNELI SPICED CHICKEN BREAST
Telavi Eggplant, White Wine Raisin Jus

SERVES 4 FAMILY STYLE

EGGPLANT

2 one-pound eggplants
1 cup diced seeded red bell pepper
½ cup diced red onion
6 cloves garlic, slivered
1 hot chile pepper, seeded, sliced
2 cups diced vine ripened tomato
1 cup sliced stemmed oyster mushrooms
1 lemon, zested, juiced
½ cup julienned basil leaves
to taste sea salt and freshly ground black pepper
¼ cup extra virgin olive oil

Heat oven to 350°F. Cut eggplants in half lengthwise. Hollow center of each half by scooping out flesh. Chop flesh. Transfer to mixing bowl. Combine with remaining ingredients. Place eggplant halves in large ovenproof dish. Pack mixture into each eggplant. Tent with foil. Bake 30 minutes. Remove foil. Bake until eggplant is tender, about 20 minutes more.

KASHA

2 large egg whites
1 cup whole grain kasha (buckwheat grouts)
2 cups chicken stock
1 tablespoon olive oil
1 tablespoon walnut oil
to taste sea salt and freshly ground black pepper

Beat egg whites in mixing bowl until frothy. Stir in kasha. Refrigerate 1 hour. Bring chicken stock to simmer in saucepan. Keep hot. Add oil to large nonstick skillet over medium heat. Add kasha. Cook 3 minutes, stirring constantly. Stir in stock. Bring to simmer. Cook 10 minutes or until liquid is absorbed. Fluff with fork. Fold in walnut oil, sea salt and pepper. Spread evenly in bottom of ovenproof serving dish, large enough to hold the chicken.

CHICKEN

2 tablespoons olive oil
1 four-pound chicken, quartered
to taste sea salt and freshly ground black pepper
⅓ cup walnut suneli
1 tablespoon unsalted butter
¼ cup chopped shallots
⅓ cup dark raisins
½ cup syrah wine
2 cups chicken stock
1 bouquet sage sprigs

Preheat oven to 350°F. Add oil to ovenproof skillet over medium-high heat. Season chicken with salt and pepper. Cook, skin side down, 5 minutes or until golden brown. Turn over. Sear 2 minutes. Arrange chicken, skin side up, on top of kasha. Sprinkle chicken generously with walnut suneli. Bake 10 minutes or until chicken is fully cooked. Meanwhile, return skillet to medium heat. Add butter, shallots, and raisins. Cook 1 minute. Add wine. Reduce by half. Add stock. Reduce to sauce consistency. Season with salt and pepper. Spoon sauce around chicken. Garnish with sage sprigs.

WALNUT SUNELI

¼ pound walnut halves
½ teaspoon marigold or cumin powder
1 tablespoon dried dill
½ tablespoon sea salt
¼ cup dried parsley
1 teaspoon dried mint
1 teaspoon ground coriander

Heat oven to 350°F. Spread walnuts in single layer on baking sheet. Toast until golden brown. While hot, transfer to food processor. Add remaining ingredients. Grind to coarse meal. Spread on cookie sheet to cool.

CZECH REPUBLIC

Cesky Krumlov may be the most beautiful little-known town in Europe. I spent half a day there, but wouldn't have minded if it had been half my life. The visit was a detour on a trip through Germany and Austria. This is the real magic of Bavaria. Ancient streets, pubs, gypsy music, and plenty of ghost stories liven this town whose medieval architecture is overseen by a thirteenth-century castle. In a restaurant on the banks of the Vltava river, which runs through the center of town, I tried Sekana, a Czech-style meatloaf with smokey bacon. This recipe is a version that captures the aromatic spice and complex flavors of Czech cuisine. —RON

CHICKEN PISTACHIO MEAT LOAF
Gingered Tomato Jam, Pear Frisée Salad

SERVES 6 FAMILY STYLE

MEAT LOAF

½ tablespoon olive oil

2 pounds ground chicken, preferably thigh meat

1 cup finely chopped sweet onion

½ cup grated peeled carrot

½ cup breadcrumbs

½ cup chicken stock

3 large eggs, lightly beaten

3 juniper berries, finely chopped

2 tablespoons brandy

1 teaspoon freshly ground black pepper

1½ teaspoons sea salt

¼ teaspoon sweet paprika

¼ teaspoon ground cumin

¼ teaspoon ground star anise

¾ cup chopped sun dried apricots

½ cup toasted pistachio nuts

2 tablespoons chopped parsley leaves

12 slices turkey bacon

Preheat oven to 350°F. Coat loaf pan or Le Creuset pâté terrine dish with olive oil. Combine all ingredients, except bacon, in large mixing bowl. Line loaf pan with bacon. Pack chicken mixture into dish. Fold overhanging bacon atop. Cover tightly with plastic wrap, then foil. Bake 45 minutes. Remove foil and plastic. Cook additional 10 minutes or until internal temperature reaches 160°F. Remove from oven. Let stand 5 minutes. Invert meat loaf on serving platter.

TOMATO JAM

3 pounds vine ripened tomatoes

3 tablespoons extra virgin olive oil

¼ cup finely julienned peeled ginger root

2 tablespoons balsamic vinegar

1 lemon, zested, juiced

2 tablespoons brown sugar

1 tablespoon thyme leaves

1 teaspoon sambal chile sauce

1 teaspoon sea salt

½ teaspoon freshly ground black pepper

Peel, seed, and dice tomatoes. Place in large sauce pot over medium heat. Add remaining ingredients. Bring to simmer. Cook 1 hour or until jam consistency, stirring occasionally with wooden spoon. Adjust seasoning. Transfer to serving dish.

FRISÉE SALAD

½ pound frisée lettuce, inner leaves only, washed, spun dry

1 pear, cored, sliced

4 ounces aged cheddar cheese, shaved

1 tablespoon extra virgin olive oil

½ tablespoon red wine vinegar

to taste sea salt and freshly ground black pepper

Gently toss all ingredients in serving bowl. Season with salt and pepper.

IRELAND

"A cabin with plenty of food is better than a hungry castle." This is one of my favorite Irish sayings. Time spent with good food lovingly shared with good company can turn any dwelling into a wonderful place. In Ireland I saw a love of the earth in the local gastronomy. An Irish woman held a bunch of freshly picked potatoes by the stems, moist dirt still crumbling from the roots. I thought she wanted to sell them to me, but then realized they were a gift. In the next town, I asked a local chef to prepare them for me. Twenty minutes later he presented them in the form of a rustic pie w th caramelized onions. At home with the kids, I also like to make this dish using quail. —RON

ROCK CORNISH GAME HEN
Rustic Potato Onion Pie, Rhubarb Sauce

SERVES 4 FAMILY STYLE

CORNISH HEN

1½ cups finely diced rhubarb
½ cup dried currants
¼ cup grape juice
2 oranges, zested, juiced
½ teaspoon finely chopped rosemary leaves
⅛ teaspoon ground allspice
⅓ cup Drambuie liqueur
¼ cup unsalted butter, softened
4 one-pound cornish hens, dressed, rinsed, patted dry
to taste sea salt and freshly ground black pepper
1 cup chicken stock
2 tablespoons Irish whisky
4 sprigs sage

Preheat oven to 425°F. Combine rhubarb, currants, grape juice, orange juice, zest, rosemary, allspice, and Drambuie in mixing bowl. Set aside. Rub entire surface of hens with butter. Season with salt and pepper. Transfer to roasting pan. Place in oven. Roast 15 minutes. Reduce heat to 350°F. Transfer rhubarb mixture to roasting pan, spreading evenly around hens. Add chicken stock. Cook 30 minutes or until temperature at thickest part of thigh reaches 160°F and juices run clear. Turn off oven. Transfer hens to ceramic serving platter. Place in oven to keep warm. Place roasting pan on stovetop over medium heat. Bring pan juices to simmer. Stir in whisky. Reduce to sauce consistency. Season with salt and pepper. Spoon sauce around hens. Garnish each hen with sage sprig.

RUSTIC POTATO ONION PIE

2 tablespoons unsalted butter
2 cups thinly sliced yellow onions
¾ cup peeled, seeded, diced, roasted red bell pepper
to taste sea salt and freshly ground black pepper
5 medium Yukon gold potatoes, peeled
1 teaspoon finely chopped fresh thyme leaves
1 tablespoon canola oil

Preheat oven to 350°F. Melt 1 tablespoon butter in skillet over medium heat. Add onions. Cook 5 minutes until caramelized, stirring often. Fold in roasted peppers. Season with salt and pepper. Remove from heat. Slice potatoes ⅛-inch thick with mandoline slicer. Toss in bowl with thyme, salt and pepper. Add oil to 8-inch nonstick sauté pan. Place single layer of potatoes in pan, overlapping to form a flower-like design. Spread half of onion mixture evenly over potatoes. Top with second layer of potatoes and onions. Cover with final layer of potatoes. Dot with remaining butter. Cover pan tightly with plastic wrap, then foil. Bake 50 minutes or until potatoes are tender throughout. Remove from oven. Let stand 15 minutes. Place over high heat 1 minute or until loosened from pan. Invert potato pie onto serving plate. Cut into quarters.

AUSTRIA

I took a cruise down the river Danube during the winter market season in Bavaria. Being a Southern Californian and summer traveler, I had never seen anyone celebrate the winter holidays like they do in the Austrian town of Salzburg. As if being the birthplace of Mozart weren't enough, this town's market plaza exudes a festive spirit. We followed the scent of roasting chestnuts to a red cart where we huddled in the line of people while candlelight carolers sang. That night we dined in a converted monastery on juniper spiced duck confit and the housemade *grüner veltliner*, a complex, food-friendly white wine made from the noble Austrian grape of the same name. A Napa Valley viognier would be tasty, too. —RON

JUNIPER SPICED DUCK LEG CONFIT
Honey Liquor Shallot Marmalade, Tomato Vinaigrette

SERVES 4

WARM TOMATO VINAIGRETTE

2 tablespoons grapeseed oil
¼ cup finely diced red onion
2 tablespoons sherry wine
2 tangerines, zested, juiced
1 tablespoon turbinado sugar
1 tablespoon apple cider vinegar
2 cups peeled, seeded, diced tomatoes
½ teaspoon chopped tarragon leaves
½ tablespoon thyme leaves
2 tablespoons extra virgin olive oil
to taste sea salt and freshly ground black pepper

Add grapeseed oil to large skillet over medium-high heat. Add onion. Cook 2 minutes without browning, stirring often. Add sherry, tangerine juice, zest, sugar, and vinegar. Reduce liquid to syrupy consistency. Add tomatoes, tarragon, and thyme. Season with salt and pepper. Simmer 15 minutes. Adjust seasoning. Transfer to colander set over mixing bowl to separate pulp from juice. Transfer pulp to small saucepan to keep warm. Whisk olive oil into tomato juice to create vinaigrette. Adjust seasoning.

DUCK LEG CONFIT

2 tablespoons crushed juniper berries
8 cloves garlic, halved
4 bay leaves, chopped
12 sprigs thyme
2 tablespoons brown sugar
3 tablespoons rock salt
4 eight-ounce duck legs, trimmed
1 quart grapeseed oil
8 medium red bliss potatoes, sliced ¼-inch thick
to taste sea salt and freshly ground black pepper

Combine juniper berries, garlic, bay leaves, thyme, sugar, and salt in mixing bowl. Add duck legs. Toss to coat. Cover. Refrigerate 12 hours. Preheat oven to 250°F. Set garlic and thyme aside. Rinse duck legs under cold running water. Pat dry. Transfer, skin side up, to casserole dish. Add garlic and thyme. Add oil. Cover. Bake 4 hours, or until meat pulls away from bone. Transfer duck leg, skin side up, to oven-proof baking dish. Transfer 1 cup oil to large, deep skillet over medium heat. Fry potatoes in batches until golden and tender. Transfer to paper towel-lined plate. Season with salt and pepper. Switch oven to broiler. Place duck under broiler until skin is golden crisp.

PRESENTATION

1 tablespoon unsalted butter
¼ cup vegetable stock
8 green asparagus, peeled, trimmed
¼ cup green peas
to taste sea salt and freshly ground black pepper
6 sprigs thyme
**Honey Liquor Shallot Marmalade (recipe on page 230)

Add butter and vegetable stock to skillet. Bring to simmer. Add asparagus and green peas. Season with salt and pepper. Cover. Cook 1 minute or until asparagus are al dente. Overlap potatoes in semi-circle pattern in center of warm serving plate. Spoon tomato pulp in center. Place duck atop. Garnish with asparagus, green peas, thyme, and shallot marmalade. Spoon tomato vinaigrette around.

Three days after I started cooking with Bernard at The Marine Room, I joined him at a cooking event. It was an art auction at a private residence in the upscale Rancho Santa Fe section of San Diego. This was my first experience witnessing Bernard in action. This crazy Frenchman was kissing all the women twice on each cheek "as is done in Brittany so that one cheek won't get jealous." *What did I get myself into?* I wondered. But his passion for the public eye spills over in a serious way into his cooking. This is the exact recipe Bernard showcased that day. It was an autumn theme and when I saw him basting a turkey with blood orange juice I knew we were gastronomically compatible. —RON

BLOOD ORANGE LAVENDER GLAZED TURKEY
Winter Root Vegetables, Black Muscat Gravy

SERVES 8 FAMILY STYLE

TURKEY

2 heads garlic

3 tablespoons olive oil

¼ cup chopped sun dried apricots

2 tablespoons chopped lemon thyme leaves

1 tablespoon chopped sage leaves

1 18-pound free range turkey

to taste sea salt and freshly ground black pepper

1 cup peeled cipollini onions

30 small new red potatoes, halved

20 baby carrots, peeled

20 baby beets, peeled

3 medium parsnips, peeled, cut into ½-inch pieces

½ cup unsalted butter

1 bouquet fresh herbs

Preheat oven to 350°F. Cut garlic heads in half crosswise. Place cut side down in casserole dish. Drizzle with 1 tablespoon olive oil. Cover. Cook 30 minutes or until soft. Squeeze pulp into mixing bowl. Mix with sun dried apricots, thyme, and sage. Rinse turkey under cold water inside and out, reserving neck and giblets for sauce. Pat dry. Carefully insert fingers between skin and flesh of turkey to loosen. Evenly spread garlic mixture under skin of breasts and legs. Rub remaining olive oil over entire turkey. Season inside and out with salt and pepper. Bake in roasting pan, breast side up, brushing with glaze every 30 minutes. After 2½ hours, surround turkey with vegetables. Dot vegetables with butter. Season with salt and pepper. Cook 1 hour or until internal temperature reaches 160°F at thickest part of thigh. Transfer turkey to ceramic serving platter. Surround with root vegetables. Garnish with herb bouquet before serving.

BLACK MUSCAT SAUCE

** reserved neck and giblets

2 tablespoons grapeseed oil

¾ cup diced red onions

½ cup diced celery

4 sprigs thyme

½ cup raisins

3 tablespoons unsalted butter

3 tablespoons flour

¼ cup sherry vinegar

1 cup black muscat wine

3 quarts chicken stock

to taste sea salt and freshly ground black pepper

Reduce chicken stock to 1 quart in large sauce pot. Set aside. Cut neck into 2-inch pieces using cleaver. Add oil to large sauce pot over medium-high heat. Add neck and giblets. Brown on all sides. Reduce heat to medium. Add onions, celery, thyme, raisins, and butter. Cook 5 minutes, stirring often. Stir in flour. Cook 1 minute. Add vinegar, black muscat, and chicken stock. Bring to simmer. Cook 15 minutes or until sauce consistency, stirring often. Season with salt and pepper. Strain through fine sieve. Transfer to sauce boat.

GLAZE

1 cup blood orange juice

½ cup pomegranate molasses

¼ cup maple syrup

¼ cup seasoned rice vinegar

¼ cup Cointreau liqueur

1 teaspoon dried lavender flowers

¼ teaspoon star anise powder

Combine all ingredients in small saucepan over medium heat. Bring to simmer. Reduce to syrupy consistency. Strain through fine sieve. Set aside.

FRANCE

My sister Sylvie lives in a remote village close to the Mont St. Michel castle. Her historic stone manor is a treasure, with walls so thick that they trap all the aromas of the food being prepared in the kitchen. She grows her own vegetables and raises chickens, ducks, turkeys, rabbits, and sheep. There is no need to go to the market when you have such a boon in your backyard! Harvesting turkeys at Christmas time is a family tradition and what grows in the garden determines what goes in the stuffing. Her tip for keeping this dish moist is to baste the turkey with a lot of butter during roasting. —BERNARD

SYLVIE'S TURKEY BREAST BALLOTINE
Croissant Sausage Stuffing, Glazed Carrots, Cipollinis, Apple Cider Gravy

SERVES 6

STUFFING

- **1 tablespoon** olive oil
- **1 cup** stemmed, diced oyster mushrooms
- **2 cups** minced leeks, white part only, washed
- **¼ cup** chopped roasted hazelnuts
- **½ cup** sun dried tart cherries
- **1 teaspoon** chopped sage
- **½ cup** chopped parsley leaves
- **1 cup** chicken stock

- **6 links** hot Italian sausages, casings removed
- **8 large** croissants, cubed
- **to taste** sea salt and freshly ground pepper
- **1 four-pound** boneless, free range turkey breast
- **3 tablespoons** unsalted butter, diced
- **2 teaspoons** chopped thyme leaves

APPLE CIDER SAUCE

- **2 tablespoons** unsalted butter
- **½ cup** chopped shallots
- **2** green apples, cored, chopped
- **4 leaves** sage
- **2 tablespoons** sifted flour
- **2 tablespoons** balsamic vinegar
- **1 cup** sparkling apple cider
- **2 cups** chicken stock
- **to taste** sea salt and freshly ground pepper

PRESENTATION

- **½ cup** verjus
- **½ pound** young carrots, peeled, trimmed
- **½ pound** cipollinis, peeled
- **2 tablespoons** butter
- **2 tablespoons** honey
- **1 tablespoon** minced mint leaves
- **to taste** sea salt and freshly ground black pepper
- ****Cranberry Relish** (recipe on page 231)

Preheat oven to 375°F. Add oil to large skillet over medium heat. Add mushrooms, leeks, hazelnuts, cherries, sage, and parsley. Season with salt and pepper. Cook 5 minutes without browning, stirring often. Transfer mixture to large mixing bowl. Add chicken stock. Fold in sausage and croissants. Place turkey breast on cutting board. Butterfly breast lengthwise. Place between two layers of plastic wrap. Pound lightly with mallet to flatten. Remove plastic. Place two thirds of stuffing in center. Roll. Tie with butcher twine. Transfer remaining stuffing to baking dish. Cover. Place turkey in roasting pan, skin side up. Dot with butter. Season with thyme, salt and pepper. Bake 1 hour or until center of stuffing reaches 160°F., basting often. Bake reserved stuffing during last 30 minutes of cooking turkey. Transfer turkey to cutting board. Place roasting pan on stovetop over medium heat to make sauce.

Add butter, shallots, apples, and sage to roasting pan. Cook 5 minutes, stirring often. Stir in flour. Cook 1 minute, stirring constantly. Whisk in balsamic, apple cider, and chicken stock. Bring to simmer. Reduce to sauce consistency. Strain through fine sieve. Season with salt and pepper.

Add butter, verjus, honey, cipollinis, and carrots to large skillet over medium heat. Bring to simmer. Season with salt and pepper. Cover. Cook 2 minutes. Uncover. Cook until liquid is syrupy. Add mint. Toss. Adjust seasoning. Set aside. Cut turkey breast into 1-inch thick slices. Place in center of warm serving plate. Garnish with carrots and cipollinis. Spoon sauce onto plate. Serve with cranberry relish.

HOOVES

RACK OF LAMB RENAISSANCE 192

MARRAKECH SPICED LAMB TAGINE 195

JERSEY ISLAND PISTACHIO CRUSTED LAMB 196

GARLIC STUDDED ROAST LEG OF LAMB 198

BAROLO BRAISED LAMB SHANK 200

KUROBUTA BARBECUE PORK TENDERLOIN 202

MUSTARD PEACH GLAZED PORK RIB ROAST 205

POMEGRANATE BRINED PORK CHOP 206

CAPE GOOSEBERRY GLAZED VENISON LOIN 209

FREE RANGE VEAL TENDERLOIN 210

ROASTED VEAL RIBEYE CHOP 212

MAPLE CHILE SMOKED NEW YORK STEAK 214

FILET MIGNON TIERRA Y MAR 217

KALBI GLAZED TRI TIP 218

STOUT BEER BRAISED BEEF SHORT RIBS 221

REPUBLIC OF GEORGIA

After a week visiting my friend Koko in Tbilisi, the capital of the Republic of Georgia, I had learned two very important words: *gamarjobat,* which means "hello" and *gaumarjous,* meaning "cheers." Touched by the beauty of the city and the warmth of the people, I felt as though I had lived there in another life. The cuisine reflects Georgia's location—sandwiched between Russia, Turkey, Armenia, and Azerbaijan. The dishes meld the best culinary traditions of the people of Transcaucasia.

Awake before sunrise, I could hear the tribulation of the big city. The echo of the neighbor's rooster was overshadowed by the horns of passing cars. Koko's parents, Lali and Temuraze, joined me on my way to the bizzari, where people bartered and bargained for their daily purchases.

Lali, who has been shopping here with her grandmother since she was a little girl, knew everyone. She smelled and touched all the ingredients before buying; only accepting the very best, and bargaining fiercely for the lowest price. We tasted dry-smoked Surghuni cheeses, cured meats, pickled beets, and mahogany chestnut honey. At the fishmonger's counter, line-caught Black Sea sturgeons were sitting on ice-covered concrete slabs. Siberian salmon, trout, river fish, and charcoal black Osetra caviar were the supporting cast.

Across the aisle, mounds of grains, flour, sugar, and cornmeal were being molded into large pyramids. Perched on an empty crate, a woman wearing a colored headscarf carefully weighed each item that I pointed to. Her genuine smile told me that I was getting a good price for the precious harvest. At the vegetable market, we bought fragrant herbs along with persimmons, walnuts, barberries, figs, potatoes, pomegranates, and wood mushrooms from an Azerbaijani farmer.

At the meat market, tables were stacked with chickens, ducks, quails, suckling pigs, lamb, and goat. Large slabs of beef hung from the rafters. A butcher, cleaver in hand, hacked a side of beef on an old oak block, reminding me of the Middle Ages. We bought rump roast, spleen, oxtails, liver, heart, and tongue and grabbed a couple of small suckling pigs for Sunday's feast, called a *supra*. We finely chopped the beef to fill the *khinkali*, small dumplings prized in the region. The liver, heart, and tongue were cooked in clay pots with butter and spices. The spleen was reserved for a special salad garnished with beets that were pickled in homemade vinegar. The rump was cut into mtsvadi shish kebabs and the suckling pigs slowly roasted in the wood burning oven until the skin became crispy.

That night, family and friends gathered to celebrate and honor life. As the man of the house, Temuraze performed the *tamada* ritual. Armed with the improvisation of a stand-up comedian and the wisdom of a philosopher, he took us on a journey between the past, present, and future. At least thirty heart-felt toasts were spoken by Temuraze, his level of emotion rising every time we all raised our glasses in cheers. After each round of clinking, the toast was made official with a sip of Telavi wine or my favorite moonshine drink, "Cha Cha." This is life in Georgia.

Gaumarjous!

—BERNARD

Spring in Athens brings festivities and gatherings. Many Athenians hold enormous outdoor picnics in the countryside or mountains for the entire family. I had the good fortune to celebrate an Easter barbecue with the Lumanis family along the banks of the Cephissus river. According to the grandfather, Spiro, such a festivity would not be complete without spit-roasted lamb, grilled sausages, and garden vegetables tossed in local olive oil with oregano and garlic. To kick off the celebration, we all gathered for a toast of chilled ouzo! After roasting whole cuts, rest the meat five to ten minutes before carving. It will make it more succulent and easier to carve. —BERNARD

RACK OF LAMB RENAISSANCE
Spring Vegetables, Ouzo Herb Sauce

SERVES 4 FAMILY STYLE

CRUST

½ cup sliced almonds
2 teaspoons sea salt flakes
¼ cup bread crumbs
2 tablespoons dried parsley flakes
¼ teaspoon garlic powder
½ teaspoon paprika
¼ teaspoon cracked black pepper
1 tablespoon melted butter

Add almonds to large skillet over low heat. Cook until toasted, stirring constantly. Transfer to spice grinder. Add remaining ingredients. Process to coarse meal. Transfer to small mixing bowl. Mix in melted butter. Set aside.

VEGETABLES

8 baby new potatoes, peeled
8 baby carrots, trimmed, peeled
8 baby turnips, trimmed, peeled
8 baby yellow beets, trimmed, peeled
12 peeled purple pearl onions
1 cup shelled green peas
1 cup cauliflower florets
to taste sea salt and freshly ground black pepper

Bring 4 quarts salted water to boil in large pot over high heat. Cook potatoes until tender. Transfer to plate. Cook each vegetable separately until al dente. Transfer to ice bath. Drain thoroughly.

LAMB

2 tablespoons safflower oil
2 1¼-pound lamb racks, 8 bones, frenched
1 cup diced vine ripened tomatoes
2 cloves garlic
¼ cup chopped shallots
½ cup white wine
1 cup beef stock
¼ cup oregano leaves
1 cup basil leaves
½ cup tarragon leaves
2 tablespoons ouzo liquor
1 tablespoon unsalted butter
to taste sea salt and freshly ground pepper

Preheat the oven to 400°F. Add oil to large roasting pan over medium-high heat. Season lamb with salt and pepper on all sides. Place in roasting pan fat side down. Sear 2 minutes or until golden brown. Flip. Sear 1 minute. Transfer lamb to platter. Discard excess fat from pan. Return to medium high heat. Add tomatoes, garlic, shallots, wine and stock. Bring to boil. Return lamb to pan, fat side up. Sprinkle evenly with crust. Bake in oven 10 minutes for medium rare, or until desired doneness. Transfer racks to serving platter, interlocking bones. Transfer pan juices to blender. Add herbs, ouzo, and butter. Purée until smooth. Season with salt and pepper. Transfer to sauce dish.

PRESENTATION

1 tablespoon olive oil
1 tablespoon unsalted butter
2 tablespoons honey
1½ tablespoons sherry vinegar
to taste sea salt and freshly ground pepper

Heat oil and butter in large skillet over medium-high heat until light brown and foamy. Add potatoes, carrots, turnips, beets, and pearl onions. Cook 2 minutes, stirring often. Add honey and vinegar. Season with salt and pepper. Cook additional 3 minutes or until glazed, stirring often. Fold in peas. Arrange vegetables around lamb.

MOROCCO

Shopping in the souks of Marrakech, we wandered down narrow paths carved between stacks of tagines that create the market's landscape. The air was energized by the movement of people, the constant bartering of shoppers and the aroma of smokey, grilled kabobs. Tagines are earthenware vessels used to cook or serve typical Moroccan stews. The conical shape of the lid is designed to trap steam and keep food moist and hot. For me, tagine means comfort— slowly cooked ingredients infused in harmony with complex local spices. If you don't care for lamb, you can also use pork shoulder or chicken thighs in this recipe. —BERNARD

MARRAKECH SPICED LAMB TAGINE
Preserved Fruits, Lemon Mint Couscous

SERVES 6 FAMILY STYLE

TAGINE

3 pounds lamb shoulder, boneless
3 tablespoons grapeseed oil
1 cup finely chopped white onion
1½ cups peeled, diced carrots
1 cup diced celery
8 cloves garlic, crushed
2 pinches saffron threads
¼ teaspoon turmeric
½ teaspoon ground cumin
1 teaspoon ground coriander
½ teaspoon ground ginger

2 cinnamon sticks
1 teaspoon sea salt
¼ teaspoon cayenne pepper
4 sprigs thyme
2 bay leaves
1 quart beef stock
½ cup golden raisins
½ cup dried figs, stemmed, quartered
1 tablespoon honey
½ teaspoon rose water

COUSCOUS

2 tablespoons dried parsley flakes
½ teaspoon curry powder
1 teaspoon sea salt
½ teaspoon freshly ground black pepper
2 cups vegetable stock
6 tablespoons extra virgin olive oil
1½ cups couscous
2 tablespoons lemon juice
½ cup chopped toasted almonds
½ cup quartered dried apricots
2 tablespoons chopped cilantro leaves
2 tablespoons chopped mint leaves

Cut lamb into 1-inch cubes. Season with salt and pepper. Add oil to large stock pot over high heat. Add one third of lamb to pot. Brown on all sides. Transfer to plate using slotted spoon. Repeat process with remaining lamb. Lower heat to medium. Add onion, carrot, celery, garlic, saffron, turmeric, cumin, coriander, ginger, cinnamon, salt, cayenne, thyme and bay leaf. Cook 3 minutes, stirring occasionally. Return lamb to pot. Add beef stock. Bring to simmer. Cover. Cook 1 hour. Stir in raisins and figs. Cover. Cook additional 30 minutes or until meat is very tender. Discard bay leaves and thyme. Stir in honey and rosewater. Adjust seasoning. Transfer to tagine bowl. Cover with top of tagine.

Add parsley flakes, curry, salt and pepper to coffee grinder. Process to powder. Add stock, 2 tablespoons olive oil, and spice mixture to sauce pot over medium high heat. Bring to boil. Stir in couscous. Cover. Turn off heat. Let stand five minutes. Fluff with fork. Fold in remaining ingredients. Adjust seasoning. Transfer to serving bowl.

ENGLAND

My parents ran a dairy farm in the township of Goray on the island of Jersey. I still have a picture of my father plowing potatoes in early fall, surrounded by fully grown vegetables waiting to be picked. Jersey Royal potatoes are highly prized for their distinctive buttery flavor and thin skin. My father loved them so much that he carried them back to Brittany where, to this day, we still enjoy the yearly harvest. When preparing your casserole, look for mushrooms and herbs in season to capture the best flavor. Fingerling potatoes mimic the prized characteristics of Jersey Royals. —BERNARD

JERSEY ISLAND PISTACHIO CRUSTED LAMB
Royal Potato Casserole, Ruby Port Wine Huckleberry Sauce

SERVES 6

POTATOES

1 pound fingerling potatoes, washed
½ pound baby zucchini, stems trimmed
½ pound baby yellow pattypan squash, stems trimmed
⅛ pound morel mushrooms
1 red onion, peeled, cut into 6 wedges
2 lemons, quartered
6 sprigs fresh thyme
¼ cup halved garlic cloves
¼ cup extra virgin olive oil
12 small cherry tomatoes
to taste sea salt and freshly ground black pepper

Preheat oven to 375°F. Cut potatoes in half lengthwise. Toss with zucchini, pattypans, morels, red onion, lemons, thyme, garlic, olive oil, salt and pepper in large casserole dish. Cover. Bake 30 minutes. Add tomatoes. Toss vegetables with large spoon. Cover. Bake additional 15 minutes or until vegetables are tender.

LAMB

3 1¼-pound lamb racks, trimmed, 8 bones, frenched
to taste sea salt and freshly ground black pepper
2 teaspoons finely chopped rosemary leaves
1 tablespoon grapeseed oil
½ cup chopped shallots
1 teaspoon black peppercorns
¾ cup ruby port wine
3 tablespoons sherry vinegar
1½ cups beef stock
½ cup sun dried huckleberries
1 teaspoon unsalted butter

Cut each lamb rack into 4 double chops. Remove 1 bone from each chop. Reserve bones for sauce. Season chops with salt, pepper, and rosemary. Add oil to large skillet over high heat. Sear chops 2 minutes on each side. Transfer to baking pan. Return skillet to medium heat. Add reserved bones, shallots, and peppercorns. Cook 3 minutes, stirring often. Add port wine, sherry vinegar, and beef stock. Bring to simmer. Reduce by two thirds. Strain through fine sieve into saucepan. Add huckleberries. Return to simmer. Reduce to sauce consistency. Swirl in butter. Season with salt and pepper. Keep warm.

PISTACHIO CRUST

¼ cup stone ground mustard
2 tablespoons honey
½ cup chopped pistachios
⅛ teaspoon ground cumin
½ teaspoon orange zest

In mixing bowl, blend stone ground mustard, honey, and orange zest. In separate bowl, combine pistachios and cumin. Set both aside.

PRESENTATION

6 sprigs sage

Preheat oven to 375°F. Spoon mustard mixture onto chops. Sprinkle with pistachio mixture. Place chops in oven. Cook 5 minutes for medium rare, or until desired doneness. Arrange vegetables on large warm serving plate. Place chops on plate, leaning against vegetables. Spoon sauce around. Garnish with sage sprigs.

ICELAND

On my arrival in Reyjavik, Iceland, I was surprised by the vibrant activity of the summer season. Staying out late seems to be the pastime, although I could never tell when it was day or night since the sun hardly ever goes down. As I stepped into my friend's apartment, my soul was warmed by the welcome aroma of roasted garlic, baking bread, and toasted spices. In the tiny kitchen, a country-style lamb roast was just out of the oven, ready for dinner. Before eating, Mishka surprised me with her homemade, caraway-infused aquavit to toast my arrival—my kind of people. —RON

GARLIC STUDDED ROAST LEG OF LAMB
Green Bean Salad, Cardamom Sauce

SERVES 8 FAMILY STYLE

LEG OF LAMB

1 eight-pound leg of lamb, bone-in, trimmed
12 cloves garlic, peeled, halved
3 tablespoons pumpkin seed oil
1 tablespoon chopped lemon thyme leaves
1 tablespoon chopped rosemary leaves
1 tablespoon flaky sea salt
1 teaspoon freshly ground black pepper
3 tablespoons unsalted butter

Preheat oven to 425°F. Make twelve ¼-inch wide by 1-inch deep slits in thicker part of lamb. Insert one garlic clove into each slit. Rub lamb with pumpkin seed oil, thyme, rosemary, sea salt and pepper. Transfer to roasting pan. Dot with butter. Place in oven. Cook 15 minutes. Reduce heat to 350°F. Cook 1 hour and 15 minutes or until meat thermometer inserted in thickest part of the roast registers 135°F for medium rare. Baste with pan juices every fifteen minutes during cooking process. Transfer lamb to carving board. Tent loosely with foil. Rest 15 minutes. Discard excess fat from roasting pan. Start sauce.

CARDAMOM SAUCE

1 cup chopped red onions
1 cup chopped peeled carrots
1 cup chopped celery
1 cup cranberry juice
1 cup aquavit liquor
½ teaspoon dried orange peel
8 pods cardamom
1 teaspoon black peppercorns
1 quart beef stock
to taste sea salt and freshly ground black pepper
1 tablespoon unsalted butter

Place roasting pan on stovetop over medium heat. Add onions, carrots, and celery. Cook 5 minutes, occasionally scraping bottom of pan with wooden spoon. Add cranberry juice, aquavit, orange peel, cardamom, and peppercorns. Reduce by two thirds. Add beef stock. Reduce by half. Strain through fine sieve, pressing on vegetables to extract maximum flavor. Transfer to saucepan over medium heat. Reduce to sauce consistency. Whisk in butter. Season with salt and pepper. Transfer to sauce dish.

GREEN BEAN SALAD

1 pound red new potatoes
½ teaspoon sea salt
1 pound green beans, trimmed
2 tablespoons aquavit liquor
2 large tomatoes, peeled, seeded
⅓ cup walnut oil
1 teaspoon honey
1 lemon, zested, juiced
1 teaspoon chopped tarragon leaves
to taste sea salt and freshly ground black pepper

Add potatoes to large pot. Cover with cold water. Add ½ teaspoon salt. Bring to simmer. Cook until potatoes are tender. Transfer to ice bath. Return water to boil. Add beans. Cook 3 minutes or until al dente. Transfer to ice bath. Drain in colander. Cut potatoes into slices. Cut tomatoes into thin wedges. Whisk aquavit, walnut oil, honey, lemon zest and juice in large mixing bowl until emulsified. Season with salt and pepper. Add potatoes, beans, tomatoes, and tarragon. Toss gently. Adjust seasoning. Transfer to serving bowl.

ITALY

Braising is a tried-and-true cooking method from Northern Italy, where Veal Osso Bucco a la Milanese is a traditional preparation. Humble, versatile, and easy to prepare, you can add your favorite ingredients to jazz up this regional specialty. Bicycling through the rolling hills, I saw vast fields of maize being hand-harvested. This new crop of golden grain would be stoneground into cornmeal for polenta. Back at the farmhouse, we cooked polenta in a copper pot over a wood fire and blended it with local cheese and orchard fruits. Lamb shank can be prepared a few days in advance, and is even better when reheated. —BERNARD

BAROLO BRAISED LAMB SHANK
Stone Fruit Polenta, Hazelnut Gremolata

SERVES 4

LAMB SHANK

2 tablespoons grapeseed oil
4 1¼-pound lamb shanks
to taste sea salt and freshly ground black pepper
2 cups peeled, diced carrots
2 cups peeled, diced celery root
1 cup peeled, sliced parsnips
½ cup peeled, diced rutabaga

1 cup chopped red onions
3 cups diced tomatoes
6 sprigs thyme
3 bay leaves
6 cloves garlic, crushed
1 bottle Barolo wine
1 quart beef stock

Preheat oven to 350°F. Add oil to large Dutch oven over high heat. Season shanks thoroughly with salt and pepper. Sear on all sides to golden brown. Remove shanks. Reduce heat to medium. Add carrots, celery, parsnips, rutabaga, and onions. Cook 5 minutes, stirring occasionally. Add tomatoes, thyme, bay leaves, and garlic. Cook 5 minutes. Return shanks to Dutch oven. Pour in wine. Raise heat to medium-high. Simmer 5 minutes. Add beef stock. Return to simmer. Cover. Place in oven. Cook 2½ hours or until meat is tender and separates slightly from bone. Using slotted spoon, carefully transfer shanks to baking dish large enough to hold them all. Transfer vegetables from broth to small skillet. Cover to keep warm. Place Dutch oven on stove top over medium heat. Reduce broth by two thirds. Skim and discard fat from sauce. Adjust seasoning. Strain through fine sieve into baking dish with shanks. Sprinkle shanks with gremolata. Bake shanks and vegetables 10 minutes.

POLENTA

½ cup diced sun dried plums
¼ cup dried cherries
¼ cup diced dried apricots
½ cup apple juice
3 cups vegetable stock
pinch saffron threads
1 cup fine cornmeal
½ cup goat cheese
to taste sea salt and freshly ground black pepper

Toss plums, cherries, and apricots with apple juice in small bowl. Set aside. Add stock and saffron to sauce pot over medium heat. Bring to simmer. Slowly stir in cornmeal. Return to simmer. Cook, stirring constantly, until thickened to the consistency of mashed potatoes. Thin with more vegetable stock if necessary. Fold in goat cheese and fruit mixture. Season with salt and pepper.

GREMOLATA

2 tablespoons olive oil
2 tablespoons minced parsley leaves
2 tablespoons hazelnut meal
2 cloves garlic, minced
1 lemon, zested

Combine all ingredients in small mixing bowl. Set aside.

PRESENTATION

1 tablespoon truffle oil
4 sprigs thyme

Scoop polenta in center of warm shallow pasta plate. Place shank beside polenta. Arrange vegetables around shank. Spoon sauce onto plate. Drizzle with truffle oil. Garnish with thyme.

English royals gifted a black Berkshire pig, famous for its taste and tenderness, to the empire of Japan in the 1800s. Driving around the volcanic island of Kyushu, I passed by rice fields, plots of vegetables, and tall reeds that border the Rokakku river. Local farmers grow tea, sweet potatoes, soy beans and ancient varieties of rice. I stopped at a family farm and saw a pen of little black pigs mingling with a half-dozen chooks and feasting on grains mixed with beer. What a life! My favorite cut of pork is the tenderloin for its texture and versatility. When barbecuing, try using different types of wood to experience different flavor accents. —BERNARD

KUROBUTA BARBECUE PORK TENDERLOIN
Baby Bok Choy, Daikon Radish, Mirin Sauce

SERVES 4

MIRIN SAUCE

½ cup mirin
3 bags hojicha green tea
2 tablespoons honey
1 stalk lemongrass, sliced
1 pod star anise
2 tablespoons brown rice vinegar
1 cup chicken stock
1 teaspoon corn starch
2 tablespoons soy sauce
to taste togarashi chile pepper

Combine mirin, hojicha tea, honey, lemongrass, star anise, and vinegar in saucepan over medium heat. Bring to simmer. Reduce by half. Add chicken stock. Return to simmer. Reduce by half. Mix corn starch with soy sauce. Whisk into sauce. Bring to simmer, whisking constantly. Strain through fine sieve. Season with togarashi.

PORK

½ cup minced green onions
¼ cup soy sauce
3 tablespoons brown sugar
3 tablespoons minced garlic
2 tablespoons sesame oil
1 teaspoon wasabi paste
1 tablespoon minced ginger root
3 tangerines, zested, juiced
2 pounds pork tenderloin, trimmed
¼ cup honey
½ cup toasted sesame seeds
** high-heat canola oil spray

Combine green onions, soy sauce, sugar, garlic, sesame oil, wasabi, ginger, tangerine juice, and zest in mixing bowl. Whisk to dissolve sugar. Transfer to large resealable bag. Add pork. Seal. Refrigerate 6 hours. Heat grill to medium high. Position grates 4 inches above heat source. Remove pork from bag. Reserve marinade for basting. Lightly coat grates with canola oil spray. Grill pork on all sides, turning and basting often to caramelize evenly. Cook to 140°F internal temperature. Remove from heat. Rest 5 minutes. Add sesame seeds to large platter. Brush entire surface of pork with honey. Roll in sesame seeds to coat. Discard excess marinade.

PRESENTATION

½ pound Japanese daikon radish
1 red chile pepper
2 oranges
1 tablespoon seasoned rice vinegar
⅛ teaspoon sea salt
pinch freshly ground black pepper
4 pods star anise
8 baby bok choy, trimmed, washed
4 sprigs amaranth flowers
to taste sea salt and freshly ground black pepper

Peel daikon. Cut into thin matchsticks. Cut chile pepper into thin strips, discarding seeds. Peel oranges. Cut into segments. Toss daikon with rice vinegar, sea salt, chile pepper, and black pepper. Set aside. Bring 1 quart lightly salted water to boil with star anise. Add bok choy. Cook 2 minutes or until tender. Drain in colander. Reserve star anise for garnish. Slice pork loin into ¼-inch thick slices. Transfer to warm serving plates. Garnish with bok choy, daikon salad, orange segments, amaranth flower, and star anise. Spoon sauce at base of pork.

ENGLAND

Three hours outside of London, rolling hills and green fields turned to flat walls of grey rock as we entered a narrow gorge heading towards the town of Cheddar. Generations of thriving dairies, deep local caves, and a spirit of craftsmanship came together to make the town of Cheddar the heart of England's love for cheese. "Cheddaring" refers to the innovative method of kneading the curd with salt then slicing into cubes to drain. It is best to use a six-month-aged cheddar for melting. It is young enough to melt easily but aged enough to give a sharp, pronounced cheddar taste. —RON

BERKSHIRE PORK RIB ROAST
Cheddar Grits, Butter Steamed Asparagus, Mustard Peach Glaze

SERVES 6 FAMILY STYLE

PEACH GLAZE

- **2 tablespoons** unsalted butter
- **½ cup** chopped shallots
- **2 cloves** garlic, crushed
- **½ teaspoon** diced seeded Serrano chile
- **4 cups** diced pitted peaches
- **1 tablespoon** grated ginger
- **1 teaspoon** dry mustard
- **½ cup** sherry vinegar
- **2 tablespoons** brown sugar
- **1 cup** port wine
- **1 cup** peach nectar
- **to taste** sea salt and freshly ground black pepper

Melt butter in large saucepan over medium heat. Add shallots, garlic, chile, peaches, and ginger. Cook 5 minutes without browning, stirring often. Stir in remaining ingredients. Simmer 20 minutes or until syrupy, stirring often. Transfer to blender. Purée until smooth. Strain through fine sieve. Season with salt and pepper. Transfer to small saucepan. Keep warm.

PORK RIBEYE

- **1 4-pound** pork rack, frenched, preferably Berkshire
- **1 tablespoon** olive oil
- ****** mustard peach glaze
- **6 sprigs** rosemary
- **to taste** sea salt and freshly ground black pepper

Preheat oven to 450°F. Wrap bones with foil. Rub pork with olive oil. Season thoroughly with salt and pepper. Place rosemary on wire rack set in roasting pan. Place pork atop. Roast 15 minutes. Reduce heat to 350°F. Brush ½ cup peach glaze onto entire surface of pork. Cook 1 hour or until temperature reaches 150°F in center of roast. Baste pork with peach glaze every 15 minutes during the cooking process. Remove from oven. Rest 10 minutes. Transfer to warm serving platter. Return remaining glaze to stovetop over medium heat. Bring to boil. Transfer to sauce dish.

CHEDDAR GRITS

- **1 tablespoon** olive oil
- **¼ cup** diced red onion
- **¼ teaspoon** sea salt
- **¼ teaspoon** paprika
- **3 cups** vegetable stock
- **¾ cup** white stone-ground grits
- **½ cup** grated 6-month aged cheddar cheese
- **1 tablespoon** chopped parsley leaves
- **to taste** sea salt and freshly ground black pepper

Add oil to small saucepan over medium heat. Add onions, salt, and paprika. Cook 1 minute, stirring often. Add stock. Bring to simmer. Whisk in grits. Return to simmer. Cook 5 minutes or until thickened. Remove from heat. Whisk in cheese. Season with salt and pepper. Transfer to serving bowl. Sprinkle with parsley.

ASPARAGUS

- **18** jumbo green asparagus
- **2 tablespoons** unsalted butter
- **¼ cup** vegetable stock
- **to taste** sea salt and freshly ground black pepper

Peel asparagus stalks starting 2 inches from tip. Cut into six-inch spears, discarding bottom. Place in skillet with butter and stock. Season with salt and pepper. Cover. Place over medium-high heat. Bring to boil. Cook 2 minutes or until al dente. Transfer to serving bowl. Spoon cooking liquid atop.

Why brine? It is a great way to allow the flavors of your marinade to penetrate into large cuts of meat or poultry. Using discreet amounts of salt in your brine will result in meat that is succulent, tender, and moist. Pomegranate trees have thrived under the hot sun of the San Joaquin Valley since the 1700s. I picked a dozen on the way to Yosemite. We peeled and seeded the pomegranates by a stream in our bathing suits for easy clean up. Crushing the seeds for the brine was as fun as cooking the pork over the campfire. At home, submerge your pomegranates in water when seeding to avoid stains. —BERNARD

POMEGRANATE BRINED ORGANIC PORK CHOP
Cumin Gouda Mushroom Stuffing, Braised Endive, Red Onion Honey Sauce

SERVES 4

PORK

2 pomegranates, seeded
½ cup apple juice
2 tablespoons sea salt
1 teaspoon cracked black pepper
2 tablespoons honey
4 sprigs marjoram
4 ten-ounce pork chops, 2 inches thick

Combine pomegranate seeds, apple juice, salt, pepper, honey, and marjoram in blender. Puree until smooth. Pour mixture into large resealable bag. Add pork chops. Seal. Refrigerate 6 hours.

STUFFING

4 slices diced smoked bacon
½ pound oyster mushrooms, stemmed, sliced
½ pound baby red Swiss chard leaves
4 ounces cumin Gouda cheese, cut into ¼-inch cubes
¼ cup chopped pecans
2 tablespoons bourbon
1 tablespoon chopped parsley leaves
to taste sea salt and freshly ground black pepper

Render bacon in large skillet over medium-high heat. Add mushrooms. Cook 3 minutes, stirring often. Add Swiss chard. Cook until wilted. Drain in colander. Transfer to mixing bowl. Refrigerate until chilled. Add gouda, pecans, and bourbon. Season with salt and pepper. Remove pork chops from brine. Pat dry. Using a boning knife, make a horizontal cut, 3-inches into center of each chop to form a pocket. Stuff mushroom mixture into pocket. Secure with toothpick. Add grapeseed oil to large skillet over medium-high heat. Sear chops 2 minutes on each side. Transfer to baking sheet. Reserve skillet for sauce. Drizzle chops with remaining grapeseed oil. Sprinkle with parsley.

RED ONION HONEY SAUCE

¼ cup honey
1 cup diced red onions
1 teaspoon marjoram leaves
¼ cup balsamic vinegar
½ cup old vine zinfandel
1 cup beef stock
1 stick cinnamon
to taste sea salt and freshly ground black pepper
1 teaspoon violet mustard

Add honey, onions, and marjoram to reserved skillet over medium heat. Cook until lightly caramelized, stirring often. Add vinegar and wine. Reduce by half. Add stock and cinnamon. Bring to simmer. Reduce by half. Remove cinnamon stick. Transfer sauce to blender. Purée until smooth. Strain through fine sieve. Return to pan. Whisk in mustard. Season with salt and pepper.

PRESENTATION

1 tablespoon unsalted butter
2 green apples
4 sprigs marjoram
to taste sea salt and freshly ground black pepper
4 Braised Endives (recipe on page 224)

Preheat oven to 375°F. Bake chops 8 minutes or until internal temperature reaches 150°F. Rest 2 minutes. Meanwhile, core apples. Cut each apple crosswise into 4 slices, discarding end pieces. Melt butter in large skillet over medium-high heat until lightly brown and foamy. Add apples. Cook both sides to golden brown. Cut pork chop in half crosswise. Arrange on center of warm serving plate. Spoon sauce onto plate. Garnish with endive, apples, and marjoram sprig.

NEW ZEALAND

The drive from the wine country of Waipara to Christchurch was flanked by harbors to the south, plains and mountains to the north and the Pacific Ocean to the east. I arrived at Barry's Bay Estate where deer, sheep, and cattle grazed on native bush overlooking Akaroa harbor. Perched at 2,200 feet above sea level, the hilly terrain was shadowed by snow-dusted mountain peaks. This ranch is just one of the 1,500 producers of Cervena farm-raised venison. The meat is lean, flavorful, healthy, easy to prepare, and a good way to surprise your friends by bringing a new twist to dining at home. Get a great bottle of shiraz for the sauce and enjoy a glass with dinner. —BERNARD

CAPE GOOSEBERRY GLAZED VENISON LOIN
Boniato, Charred Eggplant, Licorice Shiraz Reduction

SERVES 4

BONIATO

2 pounds boniato sweet potatoes
⅓ cup crème fraîche
2 tablespoons maple syrup
2 tablespoons dark rum
pinch cayenne pepper
to taste sea salt

Preheat oven to 450°F. Wrap potatoes individually in foil. Bake until soft in center. Peel. Place pulp in mixing bowl. Mash until smooth. Fold in crème fraîche, maple syrup, and rum. Season with cayenne and salt. Keep warm.

EGGPLANT

3 tablespoons olive oil
2 small Chinese eggplants, halved lengthwise
to taste sea salt and freshly ground black pepper

Add olive oil to large skillet over medium-high heat. Slice eggplant in half lengthwise. Season with salt and pepper. Cook 2 minutes on each side or until tender. Keep warm.

VENISON

1½ pounds venison loin, trimmed
2 tablespoons grapeseed oil
1 cup shiraz wine
3 tablespoons balsamic vinegar
1 tablespoon brown sugar
1 pod star anise
1 cup beef stock
2 leaves sage
½ ounce dark chocolate, 85% cocoa
1 teaspoon unsalted butter
to taste sea salt and freshly ground black pepper

Cut venison into four 6-ounce medallions. Season with salt and pepper. Add oil to large skillet over high heat. Sear medallions 2 minutes on each side. Transfer to baking sheet. Set aside. Return skillet to stove top. Add shiraz, vinegar, sugar, and star anise. Reduce to thick syrup. Add beef stock and sage. Reduce by half. Remove from heat. Whisk in chocolate. Season with salt and pepper. Strain through fine sieve. Whisk in butter. Keep warm.

GOOSEBERRY GLAZE

2 cups cape gooseberries, halved
¼ cup sugar

Remove husk from gooseberries. Cut berries in half. Transfer to saucepan over medium heat. Stir in sugar. Crush berries with fork. Simmer 5 minutes to syrupy consistency. Strain through coarse sieve. Set aside.

PRESENTATION

⅓ cup vegetable stock
1 tablespoon unsalted butter
12 asparagus tips, peeled
to taste sea salt and freshly ground black pepper
4 cape gooseberries, husk on
4 pods star anise

Preheat broiler to high. Meanwhile, add stock, butter, asparagus, salt and pepper to saucepan over medium-high heat. Cover. Simmer 1 minute or until al dente. Spoon gooseberry glaze on top of venison. Place under broiler 1 minute or until desired doneness. Spoon boniato into 2-inch ring in center of warm serving plate. Place eggplant beside boniato. Spoon sauce onto plate. Place venison on top. Garnish with asparagus, gooseberry and star anise.

Upon entering the village of Guérande, or "White Land," I could almost taste the sea salt in the misty ocean air. White pyramids of salt line both sides of the road leading into town. For the residents of Guérande, salt is their history, their present, and their future. *Fleur de sel* or "flower of salt" is the cream of the salt crop—hand-harvested by collectors who scrape only the top layer from evaporated salt ponds—the best portion of the best salt in the world. The briny mineral flavors in fleur de sel are wonderful and a great seasoning for earthy foods like veal and mushrooms. Do be careful—the coarse, uneven grain of fleur de sel makes it easy to over-apply. —RON

FLEUR DE SEL RUBBED FREE RANGE VEAL TENDERLOIN

Savory Corn Cake, Hen of the Wood Mushrooms, Sage Tomato Sauce

SERVES 6

VEAL

- **3 pounds** veal tenderloin, trimmed
- **3 tablespoons** chopped parsley leaves
- **1 teaspoon** freshly ground black pepper
- **1 teaspoon** fleur de sel
- **3 tablespoons** unsalted butter

Preheat oven to 375°F. Rub veal tenderloin with parsley, black pepper, and fleur de sel. Melt butter in large oven-proof skillet over medium heat until golden brown and frothy. Sear veal tenderloin on all sides. Transfer skillet to oven. Cook 8 minutes for medium rare, or until desired doneness. Remove from skillet. Rest 5 minutes. Degrease skillet. Return to stoveop over medium heat to prepare sauce.

TOMATO SAUCE

- **¼ cup** red wine vinegar
- **2 tablespoons** honey
- **½ teaspoon** cracked black peppercorns
- **2 cups** chopped vine ripened tomatoes
- **¼ cup** chopped shallots
- **1 tablespoon** chopped tarragon leaves
- **1 clove** garlic, crushed
- **2 tablespoons** extra virgin olive oil
- **to taste** sea salt and freshly ground black pepper

Add vinegar, honey, and peppercorns to skillet. Reduce until syrupy. Add tomatoes, shallots, tarragon and garlic. Season with salt and pepper. Simmer 15 minutes, stirring occasionally. Transfer mixture to blender. Puree until smooth. Strain through coarse sieve. Return to stovetop over medium heat. Reduce to sauce consistency. Whisk in olive oil. Season with salt and pepper.

NECTARINE BEIGNET

- **1 quart** canola oil for frying
- **½ cup** tempura batter mix
- **1 tablespoon** chopped lemon thyme leaves
- **1 cup** sparkling cider
- **2 small** nectarines, pitted, cut into ¼-inch thick rings
- **1 cup** rice flour

Heat oil in heavy sauce pot to 350°F. Add tempura batter mix and thyme to mixing bowl. Stir in cider. Do not over mix. Set aside. Dredge nectarine in rice flour. Dip immediately into prepared tempura mix. Deep fry one at a time for 20 seconds or until golden crisp. Transfer to paper towel-lined plate to remove excess oil.

PRESENTATION

- **12** medium size white asparagus, peeled
- **½ cup** vegetable stock
- **2 tablespoons** unsalted butter
- **1 tablespoon** honey
- **¼ teaspoon** fleur de sel
- **pinch** freshly ground white pepper
- **1 cup** hen of the wood mushrooms, stemmed
- **6 sprigs** tarragon
- ****Savory Corn Cake** (recipe on page 224)

Add asparagus, vegetable stock, butter, honey, fleur de sel and pepper to large skillet over medium heat. Bring to simmer. Cover. Cook 4 minutes or until tender. Add mushrooms to pan. Cover. Cook 30 seconds. Turn off heat. Cut veal tenderloin into 12 slices. Invert corn cake onto center of hot serving plate. Spoon sauce at base of cake. Arrange 3 slices veal atop sauce. Garnish with asparagus, mushrooms, nectarine beignet, and tarragon.

In the medieval town of Montepulciano, we stayed with my friend Alex, owner of La Falconara Bed and Breakfast, a seventeenth-century farmhouse surrounded by olive groves and vineyards overlooking the Chiana Valley. Strolling the cobbled streets, guided by the light of the moon, we visited a secret restaurant, known only to the villagers, for a Tuscan feast. Like a scene from *Babette's Feast*, quail, rabbit, lamb, porcini, pasta, and gnocchi were prepared for dinner. The ingredients were mastered with the delicate touch of a magician by an all-woman brigade. Fluffy pillows of sweet potato gnocchi were blanketed with white truffles, shaved tableside. When making gnocchi, it is important not to overmix the dough or add too much extra flour—the dumplings should melt in your mouth! —BERNARD

ROASTED VEAL RIBEYE CHOP
Parmesan Puff, Sweet Potato Gnocchi, Lemoncello Sauce

SERVES 4

PARMESAN PUFF

2 ounces unsalted butter, softened
2 ounces diced white bread, no crust
2 ounces parmesan cheese

Add butter, bread, and parmesan cheese to food processor. Pulse until it forms a sticky dough. Divide into four portions. Shape each into 2-inch disk. Refrigerate at least 2 hours.

VEAL

4 12-ounce veal chops, frenched
2 tablespoons grapeseed oil
½ cup chopped shallots
½ cup Marsala wine
¼ cup lemoncello liqueur
1½ cups beef stock
1 teaspoon chopped tarragon leaves

1 teaspoon whole grain mustard
1 teaspoon butter
to taste kosher salt and coarse black pepper
4 sprigs thyme

Season chops with salt and pepper. Add oil to large skillet over high heat. Sear chops 2 minutes on each side. Transfer to baking sheet. Return skillet to medium heat. Add shallots. Cook 30 seconds, stirring constantly. Add Marsala and lemoncello. Reduce by half. Add beef stock. Reduce by two thirds. Strain through fine sieve. Whisk in tarragon, mustard, and butter. Adjust seasoning. Transfer sauce to sauce dish. Keep warm. Preheat oven to 375°F. Top each veal chop with parmesan disk. Bake 8 minutes for medium rare or until desired doneness. Arrange gnocchi and vegetables in center of large serving plate. Lean veal chop against. Garnish with thyme sprigs.

GNOCCHI

1 pound Idaho russet potatoes
1 pound yams, whole
2 teaspoons salt
⅛ teaspoon freshly ground white pepper
⅛ teaspoon freshly ground nutmeg
1 egg, beaten
1 tablespoon brown sugar
1¼ cups all purpose flour

½ pound broccolini
4 large green asparagus, stalks peeled
2 tablespoons unsalted butter
½ cup currant tomatoes
2 teaspoons chopped fresh thyme leaves
to taste sea salt and freshly ground black pepper

Add potatoes to large pot of lightly salted cold water. Place over high heat. Bring to simmer. Cook until fork tender, 30–50 minutes depending on size. Remove from water. Peel potatoes. Immediately pass through ricer or food mill into large mixing bowl. In separate bowl, whisk egg, salt, pepper, nutmeg, and sugar. Fold into potatoes. Fold in ¼ cup flour at a time. Turn dough onto floured surface. Knead briefly, adding just enough flour to prevent sticking. Divide dough into 4 equal parts. Let sit uncovered 15 minutes. On floured surface, roll each into ½-inch diameter logs. Cut logs crosswise into pillow shapes. Freeze half the gnocchi in single layer on cookie sheet for future use. Bring large pot of lightly salted water to boil. Working in 2 batches, add gnocchi to water, cooking two minutes or until they float to the surface. Remove with slotted spoon to oiled cookie sheet. Cook broccolini and asparagus in same water 1 minute or until al dente. Transfer to plate. Melt butter in nonstick skillet over medium heat until golden brown and foaming. Add gnocchi. Cook until lightly browned on all sides. Add broccolini, asparagus, tomatoes, and thyme. Cook until heated through. Season with salt and pepper.

UNITED STATES

Fourth of July is the one day of the year that no matter what city, village, or town you may be in, you are sure to find festivities. I love taking my family to new places to see what we will discover. One such day, we arrived in Nauvoo, Illinois mid-morning. Within an hour we were touring the streets of Old Town in a covered wagon, chatting with locals and other visitors about the day's activities. The best tip I received during the ride was from a local shop owner who told me about Nauvoo's artisan blue cheese. No surprise to my family, my sentiment changed from "where do we see the fireworks?" to "where do we taste this blue cheese?" Here is a picnic style dish inspired by that discovery, and what a discovery it was—delicious! —RON

MAPLE CHILI SMOKED ANGUS NEW YORK STEAK
Three Potato Salad, Yellow Wax Beans, Blueberry Blue Cheese Butter

SERVES 6

THREE POTATO SALAD

2 large sweet potatoes
1 pound Yukon gold potatoes
1 pound Peruvian purple potatoes
1 cup thinly sliced red onion
½ cup finely diced celery stalk
1 apple, peeled, cored, diced
½ cup mayonnaise
½ cup sour cream
1 lemon, zested, juiced
1 clove garlic, minced
1 teaspoon fennel seeds
¼ cup chopped parsley leaves
to taste sea salt and freshly ground
    black pepper

Preheat oven to 400°F. Wash sweet and Yukon gold potatoes. Pierce with fork. Wrap individually in foil. Transfer to baking sheet. Bake 30–50 minutes or until tender. Add purple potatoes to pot of lightly salted cold water. Bring to simmer. Cook until tender. Drain. Chill all potatoes overnight. Peel purple and sweet potatoes. Cut all potatoes into ½-inch pieces. Transfer to large mixing bowl. Fold in remaining ingredients. Season with salt and pepper.

BUTTER

⅓ cup unsalted butter, softened
⅓ cup Nauvoo or Maytag blue cheese
¼ cup dried blueberries
2 tablespoons dark rum
to taste freshly ground black pepper

Add all ingredients to large mixing bowl. Beat with wooden spoon until smooth. Transfer mixture to piping bag without tip. Pipe onto large sheet of wax paper, forming 6-inch-long log. Roll wax paper to wrap butter. Freeze until firm. Slice into 6 medallions. Discard paper.

WAX BEANS

2 tablespoons hazelnut oil
12 chives, 6-inches long
½ pound yellow wax beans, trimmed
to taste sea salt and freshly ground
    black pepper

Bring 1 quart lightly salted water to boil in large pot. Add chives. Cook 10 seconds. Transfer to ice bath. Add beans to boiling water. Cook 3 minutes or until tender. Transfer to ice bath. Drain in colander. Divide beans into 6 equally sized bundles. Tie each bundle tightly with chive. Transfer to small skillet over medium heat. Drizzle hazelnut oil atop. Season with salt and pepper. Cover. Heat 2 minutes, or until bundle is hot in center.

STEAKS

6 twelve-ounce prime grade New York
    steaks
⅓ cup dark rum
¼ cup sherry wine vinegar
⅓ cup pure maple syrup
2 tablespoons Worcestershire
¾ cup chopped scallions
1 tablespoon red chile flakes
2 cloves garlic, minced
1 tablespoon chopped rosemary leaves
½ teaspoon hickory smoke liquid
** high-heat canola oil spray

Place steaks in nonreactive shallow dish. Whisk remaining ingredients in mixing bowl. Pour mixture over steaks. Turn to coat. Refrigerate 6 hours. Preheat grill to medium high. Lightly coat with canola oil spray. Remove steaks from marinade. Transfer marinade to small saucepan set on grill to heat. Grill steaks 2–3 minutes on each side for medium rare, or until desired doneness, basting often with marinade. Transfer steaks to large warm serving plates. Place potato salad beside. Stand wax bean bundle against steak. Top steak with butter.

MEXICO

In the Central Mexican town of Pátzcuaro, with its famous lake and colorful highlands, I entered a local grind shop. Every Sunday, the town's women arrive carrying their buckets of mole ingredients. Each creates her own blend, using toasted chiles, roasted nuts, sesame seeds, browned garlic, bitter chocolate, and other secret ingredients. I loved watching the grind master pour the contents of each bucket into the feeder and catch the spicy aromatic paste in the hopper below. I inhaled the enticing earthy aromas stirred up by the hot friction of the grinder's blades and tried to imagine how each meal would taste if I were dining at their house that night. —RON

FILET MIGNON TIERRA Y MAR
Ancho Cacao Sauce, Crab Stuffed Squash Blossom

SERVES 4

SQUASH BLOSSOM

8 whole chives, 6-inches long
2 tablespoons goat cheese
¼ cup grated Monterey jack cheese
1 teaspoon lemon zest
¼ cup stemmed, diced dried figs
6 mint leaves, minced
1 tablespoon tequila
4 squash blossoms
½ cup crab meat, shelled
2 tablespoons extra virgin olive oil
to taste sea salt and freshly ground black pepper

Preheat oven to 350°F. Blanch chives in boiling water 10 seconds. Transfer to ice bath. Combine goat cheese, jack cheese, lemon zest, figs, mint, and tequila in large mixing bowl using wooden spoon. Fold in crab meat. Season with salt and pepper. Carefully open blossoms. Fill with crab mixture. Tie with blanched chives. Brush baking dish with 1 tablespoon olive oil. Lay blossoms in dish. Drizzle with remaining olive oil. Season with salt and pepper. Bake 15 minutes or until hot in center.

FILET MIGNON

4 eight-ounce choice-grade filet mignon, center cut
to taste sea salt and freshly ground black pepper
1 tablespoon grapeseed oil
¼ cup cilantro leaves
1 tablespoon toasted pepita seeds
**Arroz Verde (recipe on page 226)

Season filet mignon with salt and pepper. Add oil to skillet over medium-high heat. Sear 4 minutes on each side for medium rare, or to desired doneness. Pack rice into a 2-inch round cookie cutter in center of warm serving plate. Place filet besides. Top each filet with a squash blossom. Spoon sauce at base of filet. Garnish with cilantro sprigs and pepita seeds.

ANCHO CACAO SAUCE

2 dried guajillo chiles
2 tablespoons sesame seeds
2 tablespoons corn oil
⅓ cup raw peanuts
½ cup chopped white onion
3 cloves garlic
½ teaspoon cloves
⅓ cup raisins
½ cup peeled, seeded, diced tomatoes
1½ cups beef stock
1 ounce chopped dark chocolate, 85% cocoa
to taste sea salt and freshly ground black pepper

Cut chiles in half lengthwise. Discard stems. Transfer chile seeds to large skillet over medium heat. Add sesame seeds. Toast until golden brown, stirring constantly. Transfer to coffee grinder. Grind to fine powder. Return skillet to medium-high heat. Add oil. Roast chiles 5 seconds on each side. Transfer to plate. Add peanuts to skillet, stirring constantly until golden brown. Transfer to plate. Add onion, garlic, cloves and raisins to skillet. Cook 3 minutes or until caramelized, stirring often. Add tomatoes, chiles, peanuts, and 1 cup of stock. Bring to simmer. Reduce liquid by half. Transfer to blender. Add remaining beef stock. Purée until smooth. Strain through fine sieve into small saucepan. Bring to simmer. Turn off heat. Whisk in sesame mixture and chocolate. Season with salt and pepper. Keep warm.

KOREA

The city of Jeonju in South Korea has a few attributes I can relate to—a passion for soccer, a film festival, and lots of rural farms. It is also sister city to my home town, San Diego. Traveling between Seoul and Jeonju, I discovered the fertile Honam plain, adorned by paddies of rice growing in thin pools of water. Cattle and pigs grazed peacefully on rural farms, checking out the train as we rolled by. Koreans use rice flour to make their traditional *pajeon*, or spring onion pancakes. Cooking them in a cast iron skillet ensures a golden, crispy texture that brings the essence of Korea to your kitchen. —BERNARD

KALBI GLAZED TRI TIP
Spring Onion Pancake, Stir Fried Vegetables

SERVES 6 FAMILY STYLE

TRI TIP

3 pounds beef tri tip, trimmed
½ cup soy sauce
¼ cup brown sugar
⅓ cup apricot nectar
2 tablespoons sesame oil
½ teaspoon sambal chili sauce
1 teaspoon grated peeled ginger
2 tablespoons seasoned rice vinegar
3 cloves garlic, chopped
2 tablespoons chopped cilantro leaves
1 tablespoon chopped mint leaves
1 stalk lemongrass, sliced thinly crosswise
** high heat canola oil spray

Place tri tip in large resealable bag. Transfer remaining ingredients to blender. Purée until smooth. Pour into bag. Seal. Marinade overnight. Preheat grill to medium-high. Lightly coat grates with canola oil spray. Remove tri tip from bag. Transfer marinade to small saucepan set on grill to heat. Grill tri tip on all sides, turning and basting often with marinade to caramelize evenly. Cook to 130°F internal temperature for medium rare, or until desired doneness. Remove from heat. Rest 5 minutes. Strain marinade into serving dish. Cut tri tip crosswise into thin slices. Transfer to serving platter.

PANCAKES

½ cup rice flour
½ cup whole wheat flour
½ teaspoon fine sea salt
⅛ teaspoon ground white pepper
¼ teaspoon ground turmeric
¼ cup soju wine
¾ cup soda water
1 cup bean sprouts
1 tablespoon black sesame seeds
½ cup thinly sliced spring onions
2 tablespoons canola oil

Sift flours, salt, pepper, and turmeric into large mixing bowl. Make a well in the center of the flour mix. Add soju and water to the well. Using wire whisk, stir small circles in the center of the well, moving progressively outwards until you have a smooth batter. Fold in bean sprouts, sesame seeds, and onions. Add 1 teaspoon oil to 8-inch nonstick skillet over medium heat. Ladle ⅓ cup batter into skillet. Cook 2 minutes or until golden brown. Flip. Cook 1 more minute or until golden. Transfer pancake to serving platter. Repeat process with remaining batter.

VEGETABLES

2 tablespoons peanut oil
½ cup sliced water chestnuts
½ cup broccoli florets
½ cup sliced peeled carrots
½ cup sugar snap peas, cut in half on bias
½ cup julienned red bell pepper
6 shiitake mushrooms, stemmed, halved
⅓ cup grapefruit juice
1 tablespoon hoisin sauce
2 tablespoons dried seaweed flakes
¼ cup cilantro leaves
to taste sea salt and freshly ground black pepper
to taste hot chile oil

Add oil to wok over high heat. Stir fry vegetables 3 minutes or until tender. Add grapefruit juice and hoisin sauce. Toss to coat. Season with seaweed flakes, cilantro, salt, pepper, and chile oil. Transfer to serving dish.

I agree with Coventry Patmore who described the East Sussex town of Rye as "a little bit of the Old World living on in pleasant ignorance of the new." At the end of January, a freezing rain and howling winds welcomed me to this medieval town. Looking for warmth and a bite to eat, I ducked into The Mermaid Inn. I took refuge by the crackling fire, and warmed up to a conversation with local gents, sharing lofty stories over a pint of stout. An earthy meal of braised beef, spuds. and the king of cheeses, Stilton, made the evening unforgettable. Adding stout beer to the braising liquid contributes a rich heartiness to this dish. —BERNARD

STOUT BEER BRAISED BEEF SHORT RIBS
Stilton Whipped Butternut, Molasses Cider Barbecue Sauce

SERVES 6

BARBECUE SAUCE

- 2 tablespoons unsalted butter
- ½ cup chopped red onions
- 2 cloves garlic, crushed
- 1 teaspoon chile powder
- 3 cups diced red plums
- 2 tablespoons grated peeled ginger
- 4 cups diced tomatoes
- 1 tablespoon mustard seeds
- 12 ounces hard apple cider
- ½ cup molasses
- ½ cup cider vinegar
- to taste sea salt and freshly ground black pepper

Melt butter in large saucepan over medium heat. Add onion, garlic, chile powder and plums. Cook without browning 5 minutes, stirring often. Fold in remaining ingredients. Season with salt and pepper. Simmer 30 minutes or until jam consistency, stirring often to avoid scorching. Transfer mixture to blender. Puree until smooth. Adjust seasoning. Set aside.

BUTTERNUT SQUASH

- 1 tablespoon unsalted butter
- ¼ cup white wine
- ¼ cup apple juice
- 1 teaspoon brown sugar
- 2 pounds peeled, seeded, chopped butternut squash
- ¼ cup crème fraîche
- 3 ounces Stilton blue cheese
- ¼ cup chopped walnuts
- 2 tablespoons chopped chives
- to taste sea salt and freshly ground black pepper

Add butter, wine, apple juice. and sugar to skillet over medium heat. Simmer until syrupy. Add squash. Season with salt and pepper. Cover. Cook 20 minutes or until soft. Uncover. Continue cooking until liquid evaporates. Turn off heat. Mash until smooth. Fold in crème fraîche, Stilton, walnuts and chives. Adjust seasoning. Keep warm.

SHORT RIBS

- ⅓ cup dark brown sugar
- 1 orange, zested, juiced
- 1 tablespoon Madras curry powder
- 1 tablespoon chili flakes
- 1 tablespoon smoke liquid
- 1 tablespoon thyme leaves
- ½ teaspoon sea salt
- ½ teaspoon freshly ground black pepper
- 4 pounds boneless beef short ribs, trimmed
- 3 tablespoons grapeseed oil
- 2 cups diced red onion
- 2 cups diced peeled carrots
- 2 cups diced peeled celery root
- 2 pints stout beer
- 2 bay leaves
- 3 cups beef stock

Preheat oven to 300°F. Combine first eight ingredients in large mixing bowl. Add short ribs. Toss to coat. Refrigerate overnight. Add oil to large Dutch oven over high heat. Sear ribs on all sides. Set aside. Add onions, carrots. and celery. Cook 5 minutes or until lightly browned, stirring often. Return ribs to vegetables. Add stout beer, bay leaves. and beef broth. Bring to simmer. Cover pot. Place in oven. Cook 2½ hours or until ribs are fork tender. Transfer ribs to baking sheet. Return pot to medium-high heat. Reduce liquid by two thirds. Skim and discard fat. Strain liquid through fine sieve into saucepan, pressing on vegetables to extract maximum flavor. Adjust seasoning. Keep warm.

PRESENTATION

**Baby Fennel (recipe on page 224)

Preheat oven to 450°F. Coat ribs generously with barbecue sauce. Bake 10 minutes or until hot. Mold butternut squash in 2-inch ring in center of large warm serving plate. Overlap ribs besides. Garnish with baby fennel. Spoon sauce onto plate.

S GALLERY

BRAISED BABY FENNEL 224

AVOCADO FRITTERS 224

EGGPLANT TAGINE 224

SAVORY CORN CAKE 224

SAFFRON BRAISED ENDIVE 224

FIVE MUSHROOM BREAD PUDDING 225

BENGALI SPICED LEEK CASSEROLE 225

GLOBETROTTER RATATOUILLE 225

PLUM SPICED BLACK THAI RICE 226

KUMQUAT COCONUT MOCHI GOME 226

ARROZ VERDE 226

WILD RICE AND LENTIL RAGOUT 226

KAFFIR LIME ASIAN CRAB STICKY RICE 227

SUNCHOKE WATERCRESS RISOTTO 227

BIRYANI INDIAN SPICED RICE 227

ALMOND SWEET POTATO CROQUETTE 228

LINGUIÇA PURPLE POTATO HASH 228

TRUFFLE FINGERLING STEAK FRIES 228

FIG GOAT CHEESE POTATO GRATIN 229

WASABI CHIVE WHIPPED POTATOES 229

BLUE CHEESE TWICE BAKED POTATO 229

FIG CHUTNEY 230

PAPAYA SWEET PEPPER CHUTNEY 230

HONEY LIQUOR SHALLOT MARMALADE 230

CARDAMOM RUM PEAR CHUTNEY 230

BEETROOT JAM 230

5-SPICE PICKLED CRABAPPLES 231

SUN DRIED FRUIT MUSTARD SEED PRESERVES 231

RHUBARB RASPBERRY JAM 231

CRANBERRY RELISH 231

VEGETABLES

BABY FENNEL

SERVES 6

12 baby fennel, trimmed
1 pod star anise
2 tablespoons butter
1 cup white grapefruit juice
½ cup white wine
¼ teaspoon sea salt
⅛ teaspoon freshly ground white pepper

Preheat oven to 350°F. Lay fennel in small casserole dish. Add remaining ingredients. Cover with plastic wrap, then foil. Bake 30 minutes or until tender.

SAVORY CORN CAKE

SERVES 6

2 cups sweet corn kernels
1 cup heavy cream
⅛ teaspoon cayenne pepper
2 large eggs
2 large egg yolks
2 tablespoons truffle oil
to taste sea salt and freshly ground black pepper
1 tablespoon unsalted butter, softened

Preheat oven to 300°F. Add corn, cream, and cayenne to saucepan over medium heat. Bring to simmer, stirring often. Transfer to blender. Purée until smooth. Add eggs, egg yolks, and truffle oil. Season with salt and pepper. Purée until smooth. Butter six 4-ounce ramekins. Divide mixture between ramekins. Transfer to paper towel-lined roasting pan. Add hot water halfway up sides of ramekins. Bake 40 minutes or until set. Remove from oven. Rest 20 minutes. Run blade of paring knife between cake and ramekin to loosen.

AVOCADO FRITTER

SERVES 6

2 quarts canola oil for frying
1 cup tempura batter mix
2 tablespoons finely chopped Thai basil leaves
pinch cayenne pepper
2 cups cold soda water
3 avocados, seeds removed, peeled, cut into eight wedges each
to taste sea salt

Heat oil in heavy sauce pot to 365°F. Whisk tempura batter mix, basil, cayenne pepper, and soda water in mixing bowl. If mix is too thick add small amount of water. Dip avocados in tempura. Fry four wedges at a time 20 seconds or until golden brown. Transfer to paper towel-lined plate. Sprinkle with sea salt.

BRAISED ENDIVE

SERVES 6

6 Belgian endive
1 tablespoon olive oil
1 cup apple juice
3 tablespoons cider vinegar
1 lemon, zested, juiced
¼ cup honey
pinch saffron threads
2 bay leaves
⅛ teaspoon sea salt
⅛ teaspoon freshly ground white pepper

Preheat oven to 375°F. Add olive oil, apple juice, vinegar, lemon zest, lemon juice, honey, saffron, bay leaves, salt and pepper to medium saucepan. Bring to boil. Cut endives in half. Place in single layer in baking dish. Pour broth over endive. Cover tightly with plastic wrap and foil. Bake 20 minutes or until tender.

EGGPLANT TAGINE

SERVES 6

3 tablespoons olive oil
1 cup diced red onion
6 cups ½-inch diced peeled eggplant
½ teaspoon sea salt
¼ teaspoon freshly ground black pepper
4 cloves garlic, minced
2 teaspoons paprika
1 tablespoon grated ginger
1 teaspoon cumin seeds
2 cups tomato juice
2 lemons, zested, juiced
2 pinches saffron threads
1 cup garbanzo beans
¼ cup dark raisins
⅓ cup green olives, pitted, quartered
1 tablespoon extra virgin olive oil
¼ cup toasted almonds, whole
6 sprigs cilantro
to taste sea salt and freshly ground black pepper

Add olive oil to large deep skillet over medium heat. Add onions, eggplant, salt, pepper, garlic, paprika, ginger, and cumin. Cover. Cook 5 minutes, stirring often. Add tomato juice, lemon juice, lemon zest, and saffron. Fold in garbanzo beans. Simmer 20 minutes or until liquid coats eggplant, stirring often. Fold in raisins and olives. Transfer to tagine dish. Drizzle extra virgin olive oil atop. Cover with tagine lid to keep warm. Before serving, garnish with almonds and cilantro sprigs.

FIVE MUSHROOM BREAD PUDDING

SERVES 6

¾ **pound** shiitake mushrooms
¾ **pound** oyster mushrooms
¾ **pound** portobello mushrooms
¾ **pound** chanterelle mushrooms
1 **tablespoon** unsalted butter
1 **one-pound** loaf brioche
¼ **cup** grapeseed oil
to taste sea salt and freshly ground
    black pepper

2 **tablespoons** chopped parsley leaves
1 **teaspoon** chopped thyme leaves
½ **cup** white port
¼ **cup** finely chopped shallots
½ **cup** dried porcini mushrooms
3 **cups** heavy cream
5 **extra large** eggs

Preheat oven to 350°F. Cut stems from shiitake and oyster mushrooms. Remove stems and scrape gills from portobello mushrooms. Trim stems of chanterelle mushrooms. Thinly slice shiitakes, oysters, and chanterelles. Dice portobellos. Butter 9x13-inch baking dish. Lightly trim and discard crust from brioche. Cut brioche into 1-inch cubes. Add oil to large skillet over medium-high heat. Add all mushrooms. Season with salt and pepper. Cook 8 minutes or until liquid evaporates, stirring often. Transfer to large mixing bowl. Add brioche, parsley, and thyme. Toss. Set aside. Add white port, shallots, dried porcinis and cream to sauce pot over medium heat. Bring to simmer. Remove from heat. Cover. Steep 10 minutes. Transfer to blender. Purée until smooth. Whisk eggs in large mixing bowl until smooth. Whisk in hot cream mixture in slow stream. Season with salt and pepper. Add to mushroom brioche mixture. Toss to ensure that all of the bread is saturated with custard. Transfer to buttered baking dish. Cover tightly with plastic wrap then with aluminum foil. Bake 25 minutes. Remove foil and plastic wrap. Bake additional 15 minutes or until set and skewer inserted in center comes out clean.

GLOBETROTTER RATATOUILLE

SERVES 6

3 **tablespoons** olive oil
¾ **cup** diced red onion
6 **cloves** garlic, slivered
1 **pod** star anise
1 **cup** diced seeded yellow bell pepper
1 **cup** diced Japanese eggplant
¼ **cup** mirin
¼ **cup** white balsamic vinegar

½ **cup** diced zucchini
4 vine ripened tomatoes, diced
1 **teaspoon** sambal
1 **cup** diced peeled chayote squash
¼ **cup** chopped Thai basil leaves
to taste sea salt and freshly ground
    black pepper
1 **tablespoon** pumpkin seed oil

Add olive oil to large deep skillet over medium heat. Add onions, garlic, star anise, yellow bell pepper, and eggplant. Cook 5 minutes without browning, stirring often. Add mirin and white balsamic. Bring to simmer. Add zucchini, tomato, sambal and chayote. Cook 10 minutes or until chayote are tender. Adjust seasoning. Fold in Thai basil. Transfer to lidded serving dish. Drizzle with pumpkin seed oil. Cover to keep warm.

BENGALI SPICED LEEK CASSEROLE

SERVES 6

1½ **teaspoons** cumin seeds
½ **teaspoon** fennel seeds
½ **teaspoon** mustard seeds
¼ **teaspoon** black peppercorns
¼ **teaspoon** ground turmeric
2 **tablespoons** unsalted butter
2 **cups** thinly sliced leeks, white part only
½ **cup** finely sliced shallots
¼ **cup** white wine
½ **cup** vegetable stock
1 green apple, cored, ¼-inch diced
½ **cup** finely diced carrots
¼ **cup** crème fraîche
to taste sea salt
½ **cup** bread crumbs
2 **tablespoons** chopped parsley leaves
¼ **cup** feta cheese

Preheat oven to 375°F. Add cumin, fennel seeds, mustard seeds and peppercorns to skillet over medium-low heat. Toast 2 minutes or until mustard seeds start to pop, stirring constantly. Transfer to spice grinder. Add turmeric. Process until coarsely ground. Melt butter in saucepan over medium heat. Add leeks and shallots. Cook 5 minutes without browning, stirring often. Add white wine and spice mixture. Simmer until liquid evaporates. Add vegetable stock, apples, and carrots. Cook until liquid is absorbed. Fold in crème fraîche. Season with sea salt. Transfer to casserole dish. In small bowl, combine bread crumbs and parsley. Sprinkle evenly over leeks. Crumble feta cheese over top. Bake 15 minutes. Serve piping hot.

RICE

PLUM SPICED BLACK THAI RICE

SERVE 6

1 cup black Thai rice
1½ cups vegetable stock
¼ teaspoon togarashi
1 tablespoons honey
2 tablespoons seasoned rice vinegar
1 tablespoon mirin
½ cup diced sun dried plums
1 tablespoon light sesame oil
3 tablespoons nigiri sake wine
to taste sea salt and freshly ground black pepper

Thoroughly rinse black rice in colander under cold running water. Drain. Combine rice and stock in large saucepan. Cover with tight fitting lid. Place over medium heat. Bring to boil. Reduce to simmer. Cook 12 minutes or until water is absorbed. Transfer rice to large mixing bowl. Fold in remaining ingredients. Season with salt and pepper. Transfer to lidded serving dish. Cover to keep warm.

KUMQUAT COCONUT MOCHI GOME

SERVES 6

8 kumquats
2 tablespoons unsalted butter
½ cup minced Maui onions
1 cup mochi gome sticky brown rice
1 cup vegetable stock
1 cup coconut milk
¼ cup chopped cilantro leaves
½ cup toasted, chopped macadamias
1 cup ¼-inch diced seeded zucchini
to taste sea salt
⅛ teaspoon cayenne pepper

Cut kumquats in half. Remove and discard flesh. Finely chop peel. Melt butter in saucepan over medium heat. Add onion. Cook 2 minutes without browning, stirring often. Add rice and kumquat. Stir to coat. Add stock and coconut milk. Bring to simmer. Cover. Cook 25 minutes or until liquid is absorbed. Fold in cilantro, macadamias and zucchini. Season with sea salt and cayenne pepper. Cover pan 2 minutes. Transfer to lidded serving dish. Cover to keep warm.

ARROZ VERDE

SERVES 6

2 cups long grain white rice
1 cup cilantro leaves
4 cloves garlic
½ cup diced onion
½ cup diced celery
½ cup pepita pumpkin seeds, toasted
3½ cups chicken stock, cold
¼ cup safflower oil
½ teaspoon sea salt
½ teaspoon freshly ground black pepper

Add rice to large bowl. Cover with hot water. Soak 15 minutes. Drain. Spread onto cookie sheet in thin layer for 15 minutes or until dry. Add cilantro, garlic, onion, celery, pepitas, chicken stock, salt and pepper to blender. Purée until smooth. Add oil to sauce pot over medium heat. Add rice. Cook 5 minutes or until lightly browned, stirring often. Transfer to colander to drain oil. Return pot to medium-high heat. Add vegetable mixture. Bring to simmer. Stir in rice. Cover. Simmer 15 minutes. Remove from heat. Let stand, covered, 5 minutes. Fluff with fork. Season with salt and pepper.

WILD RICE AND LENTIL RAGOUT

SERVES 6

¾ cup wild rice
½ cup diced pancetta
¼ cup finely chopped shallots
½ cup finely diced peeled carrots
½ cup julienned leeks, white part only

3 cloves garlic, minced
2 bay leaves
1 cup diced button mushrooms
½ cup white wine
3¾ cups vegetable stock

¾ cup black beluga lentils
½ cup blanched green peas
¼ cup extra virgin olive oil
** sea salt and freshly ground black pepper

Rinse wild rice under cold running water. Transfer to colander to drain. Add pancetta to stock pot over medium-high heat. Cook until golden brown. Add shallots, carrots, leeks, garlic, bay leaves, and mushrooms. Cook 2 minutes, stirring often. Stir in rice. Pour in white wine and vegetable stock. Bring to simmer. Cover. Cook 20 minutes. Stir in lentils. Cover. Cook additional 25 minutes or until lentils are tender and rice is split open. Fold in peas and extra virgin olive oil. Season with salt and pepper. Transfer to lidded serving dish. Cover to keep warm.

KAFFIR LIME ASIAN CRAB STICKY RICE

SERVES 6

3½ cups vegetable stock
2 tablespoons light sesame oil
1 tablespoon unsalted butter
4 cloves garlic, minced
⅓ cup minced shallots
1 cup Arborio rice
¾ cup plum wine
¼ teaspoon sambal chile sauce
½ teaspoon green curry paste
1 stalk lemongrass, crushed
3 kaffir lime leaves
¼ cup mascarpone
3 tablespoons lime juice
¼ cup freshly grated parmesan cheese
½ pound fresh jumbo lump crab meat, shelled
2 tablespoons finely chopped flat leaf parsley
2 tablespoons finely chopped cilantro leaves
to taste sea salt and freshly ground black pepper

Bring vegetable stock to a simmer in sauce pot. Keep hot while preparing rice. Add sesame oil and butter to large pot over medium heat. Add garlic and shallots. Cook 1 minute without browning, stirring constantly. Stir in rice until coated with oil. Add plum wine, sambal, green curry paste, lemongrass and kaffir lime leaves. Bring to simmer. Cook 1 minute, stirring often. Add one third of the hot stock. Using a wooden spoon, stir rice occasionally until liquid is absorbed and leaves a clear wake behind the spoon. Repeat process twice with remaining broth, cooking until rice is al dente. Total cooking time should be 15 to 20 minutes. Remove from heat. Discard kaffir lime leaves and lemongrass. Fold in mascarpone, lime juice, parmesan, crab meat, parsley, and cilantro. Season with salt and pepper. Transfer to lidded serving dish. Cover to keep warm.

SUNCHOKE WATERCRESS RISOTTO

SERVES 6

3½ cups vegetable stock
2 tablespoons unsalted butter
½ cup minced white onion
1 cup arborio rice
2 cups ¼-inch diced peeled sunchokes
½ cup white port wine
¼ cup crème fraîche
½ cup watercress juice
¼ cup grated 5-year aged Gouda cheese
1 teaspoon chopped sage leaves
to taste sea salt and freshly ground black pepper

Bring vegetable stock to a simmer in sauce pot. Keep hot while preparing rice. Melt butter in large pot over medium heat. Add onions. Cook 1 minute, stirring constantly. Add rice and sunchokes. Cook 2 minutes, stirring often. Add port wine. Bring to simmer. Add one third of the hot stock. Using a wooden spoon, stir rice occasionally until liquid is absorbed and leaves a clear wake behind the spoon. Repeat process twice with remaining broth, cooking until rice is al dente. Total cooking time should be 15 to 20 minutes. Remove from heat. Stir in crème fraîche and watercress juice. Fold in cheese and sage. Season with salt and pepper. Transfer to lidded serving dish. Cover to keep warm.

BIRYANI INDIAN SPICED RICE

SERVES 6

1 cup basmati rice
2 tablespoons unsalted butter
¼ cup diced white onion
¼ cup diced carrots
1 teaspoon red chile powder
1 Anaheim pepper, seeded, thinly sliced
1 tablespoon peeled, grated ginger
3 cloves garlic, slivered
1 teaspoon garam masala
pinch saffron threads
¼ teaspoon sea salt
1½ cups vegetable stock
½ cup organic plain yogurt
1 teaspoon rose water
¼ cup chopped mint leaves
¼ cup chopped cilantro leaves
¼ cup toasted, chopped cashews
¼ cup raisins

Rinse rice in colander under cold running water for 30 seconds. Drain thoroughly. Melt butter in large sauce pot over medium heat. Add onions, carrots, chile powder, anaheim pepper, ginger, and garlic. Cook 5 minutes, stirring often. Add garam masala, saffron, sea salt and rice. Cook 2 minutes, stirring often. Add vegetable stock. Bring to low simmer. Cover. Cook 20 minutes or until stock is fully absorbed. Remove from heat. Fold in remaining ingredients. Season with salt and pepper. Transfer to lidded serving dish. Cover to keep warm.

POTATOES

ALMOND CRUSTED SWEET POTATO CROQUETTE

SERVES 6

4 medium sweet potatoes
2 tablespoons cornstarch
5 large eggs
½ cup extra sharp cheddar cheese
¼ cup maple syrup
1 teaspoon chopped parsley leaves
1 teaspoon chopped sage leaves
¼ teaspoon hot paprika
⅛ teaspoon grated nutmeg
to taste sea salt and freshly ground black pepper

2 quarts canola oil
⅓ cup milk
1 cup panko bread crumbs
1 cup sliced almonds, chopped
1 tablespoon poppy seeds
2 cups all purpose flour
to taste flaky sea salt

Preheat oven to 375°F. Wrap potatoes individually in foil. Bake 45 minutes or until fork tender. Transfer to cutting board. When cool enough to handle, peel, mash, and chill. Measure 4 cups sweet potato pulp. Add to food processor with cornstarch. Pulse to blend. Add 2 eggs, cheese, maple syrup, parsley, sage, paprika, and nutmeg. Process until smooth. Season with salt and pepper. Transfer to pastry bag fitted with ¾-inch straight tip. Pipe mixture into long straight lines onto wax paper-lined baking sheet. Cover with plastic wrap. Freeze 1 hour. Heat oil in heavy bottom pot to 350°F. Whisk 3 eggs and milk in mixing bowl until smooth. Combine bread crumbs, almonds and poppy seeds in shallow bowl. Place flour in large plate. Cut sweet potato lines into 3-inch pieces. Roll in flour to coat. Shake off excess flour. Dip in egg mixture. Roll in breadcrumb mixture. Fry six at a time 2 minutes or until golden brown. Transfer to paper towel-lined dish to remove excess oil. Sprinkle with salt. Serve immediately.

TRUFFLE FINGERLING STEAK FRIES

SERVES 6

2 quarts grapeseed oil for frying
2 pounds fingerling potatoes, washed
2 tablespoons truffle oil
2 tablespoons chopped flat leaf parsley

¼ cup freshly grated Parmesan
8 sun dried plums, thinly sliced
1 teaspoon sea salt flakes
¼ teaspoon freshly ground black pepper

Heat oil in deep-fryer to 375°F degrees. Quarter potatoes lengthwise. Rinse under cold running water. Drain in colander. Pat dry thoroughly with towels. Divide into 4 batches. Fry potatoes until golden brown and crispy, stirring often. Drain, shaking basket to remove excess oil. Transfer to mixing bowl. Toss with remaining ingredients.

LINGUIÇA PURPLE POTATO HASH

SERVES 6

2 tablespoons safflower oil
3 cups diced peeled purple potatoes
1 cup peeled pearl onions
½ cup Madeira wine
1 cup ¼-inch diced peeled celery root
2 cloves garlic, crushed
1 cup peeled, diced linguiça sausage
1 teaspoon paprika
1 teaspoon dried orange peel
1 tablespoon chopped oregano leaves
½ cup chicken stock
to taste sea salt and freshly ground black pepper

Preheat oven to 375°F. Add oil to Dutch oven over medium-high heat. Add potatoes and onions. Cook 5 minutes or until lightly caramelized, stirring often. Add Madeira. Bring to simmer. Fold in celery root, garlic, linguiça, paprika, orange peel, oregano and chicken stock. Season with salt and pepper. Transfer to oven. Bake 20 minutes or until lightly browned on top, bubbly around edges, and vegetables are tender.

PRESERVED FIG GOAT CHEESE POTATO GRATIN

SERVES 6

¼ cup hazelnut meal
½ cup muesli cereal
2 tablespoons chopped parsley leaves
1 teaspoon chile powder
2 tablespoons hazelnut oil
2 pounds Yukon gold potatoes
1 tablespoon olive oil
2 cups diced leeks, white part only, washed
1 teaspoon anise seeds
½ cup Marsala wine
1 cup sun dried mission figs, stemmed, quartered
1½ cups heavy cream
6 ounces goat cheese
to taste sea salt and freshly ground black pepper

Preheat oven to 350°F. Add hazelnut meal, muesli cereal, parsley, chile powder, and hazelnut oil to food processor. Pulse to coarse meal. Set aside. Add potatoes to large stock pot. Cover with lightly salted cold water. Place over medium high heat. Bring to simmer. Cook until tender. Drain. Transfer to ice bath to chill. Peel. Dice into ½-inch cubes. Add oil to large skillet over medium heat. Add leeks and anise seed. Cook 3 minutes without browning, stirring often. Add Marsala and figs. Cook until liquid is reduced by two thirds. Add cream. Bring to simmer. Stir in goat cheese. Transfer to large mixing bowl. Fold in potatoes. Season with salt and pepper. Transfer to 8x8-inch baking dish. Sprinkle evenly with mueslix mixture. Bake 30 minutes or until crust is golden and bubbling in center.

WASABI CHIVE WHIPPED POTATOES

SERVES 6

2½ pounds russet potatoes
¼ pound spinach leaves
1 cup watercress leaves
½ cup heavy cream
3 tablespoons wasabi paste
¼ cup chopped chives
¼ pound melted unsalted butter
to taste sea salt and freshly ground white pepper
1 tablespoon toasted sesame seeds

Peel and wash potatoes. Cut into quarters. Transfer to large stock pot. Cover with cold, lightly salted water. Place over medium-high heat. Bring to simmer. Cook until fork tender. While potatoes are cooking, wash spinach and watercress leaves thoroughly. Spin dry. Chop leaves. Transfer to blender. Add cream to large stock pot over medium-high heat. Bring to simmer. Pour over leaves in blender. Add wasabi and chives. Puree until smooth. Set aside. Drain potatoes. Immediately pass through ricer or food mill set over large mixing bowl. Fold in cream mixture and butter. Season with salt and pepper. Transfer to serving dish. Sprinkle with sesame seeds.

AUVERGNE BLUE CHEESE TWICE BAKED POTATO

SERVES 6

3 large baking potatoes, about ¾ lb. each, washed
2 tablespoons safflower oil
½ tablespoon coarse sea salt
6 sprigs thyme
3 large egg yolks
2 tablespoons crème fraîche
2 tablespoons unsalted butter
1 tablespoon chopped parsley leaves
4 ounces Auvergne blue cheese, crumbled
½ cup sun dried cherries
¼ cup chopped pecans
3 large egg whites
dash cream of tartar
to taste sea salt and freshly ground black pepper

Preheat oven to 375°F. Prick potatoes with fork. Rub with oil and sea salt. Tightly wrap each potato in foil with thyme sprigs. Bake 1 hour or until tender. Transfer to cutting board. Discard foil and thyme. When cool enough to handle, cut in half lengthwise. Using spoon, gently scoop out pulp to form a boat shape. Transfer pulp to large mixing bowl. Mash until smooth. Fold in egg yolks, crème fraîche, butter, and parsley. Fold in cheese, cherries, and pecans. Season with salt and pepper. Whip egg whites with cream of tartar in large bowl until stiff peaks form. Gently fold egg whites into potato mixture. Divide mixture between potato boats. Transfer to wax paper-lined baking sheet. Bake 20 minutes or until piping hot and golden brown. Transfer to warm serving platter.

PRESERVES

FIG CHUTNEY

MAKES 1 CUP

½ cup sun dried figs, stemmed, quartered
¼ cup brandy
¼ cup sherry wine
2 tablespoons malt vinegar
3 tablespoons brown sugar
½ cup thinly sliced red onion
2 teaspoons yellow mustard seeds

Combine all ingredients in saucepan over medium heat. Simmer until liquid is absorbed, stirring occasionally. Set aside. Cool completely. Transfer to resealable glass jar. Refrigerate.

CARDAMOM RUM PEAR CHUTNEY

MAKES 2 CUPS

1 pound sun dried pears, diced
1¼ cups vanilla rum
5 pods green cardamom
¼ cup verjus
¼ cup honey
¼ cup sherry vinegar
½ cup diced red onions
¼ teaspoon sea salt
¼ teaspoon freshly ground white pepper

Combine all ingredients in large sauce pot over medium heat. Bring to simmer. Cook 15 minutes or until liquid is reduced by two thirds, stirring occasionally. Remove from heat. Cool completely. Transfer to resealable glass jar. Refrigerate.

PAPAYA SWEET PEPPER CHUTNEY

MAKES 1 CUP

1 tablespoon olive oil
1 teaspoon ground cumin
1 teaspoon ground coriander
1 tablespoon finely minced fresh ginger
1 cup diced red onion
½ cup lime juice
¼ cup honey
2 large red sweet bell peppers, roasted, peeled, diced
2 large papayas, peeled, seeded, diced
to taste sea salt and freshly ground black pepper
to taste cayenne or hot pepper sauce

In large nonstick skillet, heat olive oil. Add cumin and coriander. Cook 1 minute. Add ginger and onion. Cook until just brown, about 8 minutes. Add lime juice, honey and red peppers. Cook until tender, about 5 minutes. Add papaya. Cook until softened and hot, about 2 minutes. Balance seasonings with salt, pepper and cayenne or hot pepper sauce to taste. Remove from heat. Cool completely. Transfer to resealable glass jar. Refrigerate.

HONEY LIQUOR SHALLOT MARMALADE

MAKES 1 CUP

1 cup finely diced shallots
½ cup honey liquor
½ cup Gewürztraminer wine
2 tablespoons light brown sugar
¼ cup apricot jelly
½ teaspoon sea salt
⅛ teaspoon cayenne pepper
¼ teaspoon freshly ground black pepper

Combine all ingredients in saucepan over medium heat. Bring to simmer. Cook 20 minutes or until to jam consistency. Remove from heat. Cool completely. Transfer to resealable glass jar. Refrigerate.

BEETROOT JAM

MAKES 1 CUP

2 tablespoons grapeseed oil
1 cup thinly sliced red onions
1½ cups peeled, grated red beets
1 dried red chiles
½ teaspoon thyme leaves
¼ cup apricot jam
2 tablespoons sherry vinegar
1 tablespoon granulated sugar
to taste sea salt and freshly ground black pepper

Add grapeseed oil to saucepan over medium heat. Add onion, beet, chiles and thyme. Cook 30 minutes or until liquid evaporates, stirring occasionally. Add apricot jam, vinegar, and sugar. Cook 10 minutes or until jam consistency. Season with salt and pepper. Discard chiles. Remove from heat. Cool completely. Transfer to resealable glass jar. Refrigerate.

5-SPICE PICKLED CRABAPPLES

MAKES 2 QUARTS

2 pounds crabapples
2 cups champagne vinegar
1⅓ cups water
½ cup honey
2 teaspoons pickling spices
2 teaspoons ginger powder
2 teaspoons ground cardamom
2 teaspoons ground turmeric
1 teaspoon ground cinnamon
1 teaspoon anise powder

Wash apples. Transfer to large stock pot. Add remaining ingredients to saucepan over medium high heat. Bring to boil. Immediately pour liquid over apples. Place large plate into pot atop of apples, making sure they are fully submerged. Cool to room temperature. Transfer apples to resealable glass jar. Pour in liquid. Seal. Refrigerate 2 weeks.

SUN DRIED FRUIT MUSTARD SEED PRESERVE

MAKES 2 QUARTS

1 cup finely diced sun dried apricots
1 cup finely diced sun dried red plums
1 cup finely diced sun dried figs
1 cup finely diced sun dried apples
1 cup sun dried blueberries
1 cup sun dried cherries
¼ cup brown mustard seeds
1 tablespoon cracked black pepper
¼ cup granulated white sugar
3 pods whole star anise
2 cups Riesling wine
1 cup honey liquor

Combine all ingredients in large mixing bowl. Transfer to resealable glass jar. Seal. Refrigerate 6 months. Serve as accompaniment to cheese, charcuterie, and grilled meats.

RHUBARB RASPBERRY JAM

MAKES 2 CUPS

4 cups diced fresh rhubarb
2 cups sugar
1 tablespoon fresh lemon juice
½ cup Chambord liqueur
½ teaspoon ground cardamom
2 pints raspberries
¼ cup diced crystallized ginger

Combine rhubarb, sugar and lemon juice in large sauce pot. Stir. Cover. Refrigerate overnight. Place over medium heat. Add Chambord and cardamom. Cook until sugar dissolves, stirring occasionally. Bring to simmer. Cook 20 minutes or until mixture thickens slightly. Add raspberries. Return to simmer. Cook 10 minutes or until jam consistency, stirring occasionally. Remove jam from heat. Fold in ginger. Cool completely. Transfer to resealable glass jar. Refrigerate.

CRANBERRY RELISH

MAKES 2 CUPS

1 pound fresh cranberries
1 cup sun dried cranberries
1 teaspoon grated ginger
½ cup orange juice
½ cup honey
2 tablespoons red wine vinegar
1 stick cinnamon
¼ teaspoon freshly ground black pepper
½ teaspoon sea salt

Place all ingredients in saucepan over medium heat. Cook 20 minutes or until relish consistency, stirring occasionally. Remove from heat. Cool completely. Transfer to resealable glass jar. Refrigerate.

INDIAN MANGO PICKLES

MAKES 2 CUPS

4 mangoes, under ripe
2 tablespoons mustard oil
½ cup thinly sliced shallots
2 teaspoons garam masala
2 ½ cups rice vinegar

2 cups water
2 teaspoons sea salt
¼ cup sugar
24 leaves mint

Peel mangoes. Cut flesh lengthwise into ¼-inch wide strips, discarding pit. Place in resealable glass jar with mint. Add mustard oil to saucepan over medium heat. Add shallots and garam masala. Cook 3 minutes, stirring often. Add vinegar, water, sea salt and sugar. Bring to boil. Immediately pour into jar. Cool to room temperature. Seal. Refrigerate 2 weeks. Serve as accompaniment to poultry, seafood and pork.

DESSERTS

ECUADOR

Lauralee and I departed from Quito in her old army jeep to deliver a wedding cake for her friend Pablo, who is a cook at one of the city's best restaurants. Little did we know that the delivery of the cake would take place in the quaint village of Pujili, much farther inland than we expected. The small market town in the high plateau of the Andes Mountains awaited us.

On that sunny morning, we stopped in Tumbaco. Sipping a delicious cup of organic Zaruma coffee from the province of El Oro, I watched the hummingbirds in the hyacinth trees fight for sweet nectar. As copilot and cake handler, it was quite an adventure balancing the boxes on my knees as we traveled through the glorious mountain region near Cotopaxi, Ecuador's second-highest mountain. We made it!

We met the parents of the bride at the busy central square in Pujili. Sunday morning is market day and the locals were nicely dressed in colorfully woven attire, an Andean tradition. Guided by their handlers, a traffic jam of llamas and burros packed with vegetables, sacks of potatoes, dried meats, and alpaca wool were marched toward their stalls. For a wedding gift, we chose a one-of-a-kind, handcrafted pottery overflowing with a bouquet of morning glories, estrellas de mar, calla lilies, and daisies.

At the wedding, beautiful centerpieces of woven baskets were filled with freshly picked Andean herbs, adding a fragrant aroma to the atmosphere. Multicolored rose petals were scattered around the courtyard to celebrate the union. We feasted on tropical fruits from the region including taxo, maracuya, pitahaya, noni, naranjilla, araz, tree tomatoes, and my favorite—babacos.

The aroma of quinoa, barley, plantains, and yucca simmering in huge cauldrons of soup filled the air, a staple in the diet of highlanders. The father of the bride brought shrimp, squid, and concha from his coastal village of Puerto Cayo to make ceviche. Naturally, I jumped into the kitchen to help the family cook. We made small morocho empanadas filled with beef and root vegetables, toasted corn flour cakes served with fresh farmers cheese, and *encocado de pescado*—a braised white fish in coconut milk sauce.

My favorite entrees were *seco de chivo*—a stew made with goat meat, beer, and naranjilla juice, and *pernil*—a roasted leg of pork marinated in annatto, garlic, cumin and olive oil. Proving that Ecuador's culinary landscape is truly endless, the celebration was completed with the main offering, a sacred indigenous tradition of *cuy*—guinea pig roasted on sticks, served with beans and hominy.

Lauralee's wedding cake formed the centerpiece of the dessert table. Each of the five tiers was a different flavor inspired by the five geographical zones of Ecuador. Her spun sugar bride and groom were surrounded with miniature delicacies made by the two grandmothers. The "fiesta of dulces" included alfajores, peanut caramel manizanos, condensed milk mignones, white chocolate dipped guayabas, and pineapple tomatillos. As a storm hovered over the mountains in the distance, we headed into the house. We toasted, sung and danced through the night, embracing this far away culture at the top of the world.

—BERNARD

BAHAMAS

I discovered the pleasure of mixing different flavors of ice cream as a kid on a family vacation in the Bahamas. Right on the harbor was a big ice cream shop complete with balloons, music, and caramel apples. The abundance of choices made me dizzy with excitement. When I couldn't decide between banana and praline ice cream, the kind man behind the counter put a scoop of each in my bowl. Take a look at what he started! —RON

DIZZY MONKEY'S PLANTATION ICE CREAM PIE
Chocolate Spiced Rum Sauce

SERVES 8

CRUST

3 cups chocolate cookie crumbs
½ cup unsalted butter, melted

Combine cookie crumbs and melted butter in mixing bowl. Press into bottom and sides of 9-inch spring form pan. Place in freezer.

PIE

1 cup chopped white chocolate
1 cup chopped roasted hazelnuts
1 cup crumbled Butterfinger™ bars
1½ quarts praline ice cream, softened
1½ quarts banana ice cream, softened

Combine white chocolate, hazelnuts and Butterfingers in mixing bowl. Pack praline ice cream into prepared spring form pan. Sprinkle with half of white chocolate mixture. Mound banana ice cream atop. Sprinkle evenly with remaining white chocolate mixture. Cover with plastic wrap. Freeze overnight.

PINEAPPLE CONFIT

3 cups diced, cored, peeled pineapple
½ cup granulated sugar
1 vanilla bean, split, scraped
1 stick cinnamon

Add all ingredients to sauce pot over low heat. Cook 30 minutes until thick and syrupy. Remove from heat. Cool. Refrigerate.

PLANTAIN CHIPS

3 tablespoons granulated sugar
1 tablespoon ground cinnamon
2 quarts canola oil for frying
2 green plantains

Combine sugar and cinnamon in small bowl. Set aside. Heat oil in heavy sauce pot to 350°F. Using mandoline slicer, carefully cut plantains lengthwise ⅛-inch thick. Fry plantain slices in batches of three until crispy. Transfer to paper towel lined plate. Sprinkle immediately with sugar mixture.

SAUCE

1¼ cups chopped dark chocolate, 72% cocoa
¼ cup unsalted butter
1 cup heavy cream
1 vanilla bean, split, scraped
½ cup granulated sugar
¼ cup spiced rum

Add chocolate and butter to large mixing bowl set over pot of barely simmering water, ensuring bottom of bowl does not touch water. Stir until melted. Remove from heat. Bring heavy cream, vanilla, and sugar to boil in saucepan over medium heat. Remove vanilla bean. Pour cream over chocolate. Whisk until smooth. Stir in rum. Return vanilla bean to sauce. Keep warm.

PRESENTATION

8 sprigs mint
8 chocolate sticks

Remove pie from spring form pan. Cut into 8 wedges, running knife under hot water between slices. Place 1 wedge in center of serving plate. Spoon chocolate sauce at base. Garnish with pineapple confit, mint, chocolate stick, and plantain chip.

ITALY

Harvest time in the picturesque region of Valpolicella is truly spectacular. Multicolored crates of amarone grapes are stacked as high as the rooftops. After resting for over three months, the grapes will bring a lush flavor of dark, dried fruit to the wine. In this recipe, reducing the wine intensifies the deep cherry flavors inherent in amarone. Experiment using different containers, such as tea cups, when making this pot de crème. It brings excitement to the table. Use an old vine zinfandel if you cannot locate amarone. —RON

SUN DRIED CHERRY AMARONE POT DE CRÈME
Three Citrus Biscotti

SERVES 6

THREE CITRUS BISCOTTI

1¼ cups all purpose flour
1½ teaspoons baking powder
⅓ cup almond meal
¾ cup coarsely chopped almonds
⅛ teaspoon freshly ground black pepper
1 teaspoon sea salt
¼ cup unsalted butter, softened
¼ cup granulated sugar
¼ teaspoon vanilla extract
1 orange, zested
1 lemon, zested
1 tangerine, zested
2 tablespoons lemoncello liqueur
1 large egg

Preheat oven to 325°F. Line cookie sheet with silicone baking pad. Combine flour, baking powder, almond meal, chopped almonds, black pepper, and salt in large mixing bowl. In separate bowl, cream butter and sugar. Beat in vanilla, orange zest, lemon zest, tangerine zest, lemoncello, and egg. Add flour mixture. Beat with wooden spoon until well blended. Transfer dough to prepared cookie sheet. Form into 3 by 12-inch loaf. Bake 30 minutes. Remove from oven. Cool 10 minutes. Lower heat to 275°F. Cut loaf crosswise into ½-inch thick slices. Lay slices on cookie sheet. Bake 15 minutes. Flip over biscotti. Bake additional 15 minutes. Transfer to wire rack to cool.

POT DE CRÈME

½ cup sun dried cherries
2 cups amarone wine
⅓ cup brown sugar
6 large egg yolks
1 tablespoon granulated sugar
2 cups heavy cream
1 teaspoon vanilla extract

Preheat oven to 275°F. Soak cherries in ¼ cup amarone for 2 hours. In saucepan over medium high heat, add remaining amarone and brown sugar. Reduce to ½ cup. Cool. Whisk egg yolks and granulated sugar in mixing bowl until thick and ribbony. Stir in amarone reduction. Add cream and vanilla to saucepan over medium heat. Bring to simmer. Add to yolk mixture in slow stream, whisking continuously. Strain through fine sieve. Skim foam. Place six 5-ounce ramekins in paper towel-lined roasting pan. Divide cherries among ramekins. Pour cream mixture into ramekins. Pour enough hot water into the pan to come halfway up sides of ramekins. Bake 40 minutes or until pot de crème is set but jiggly in center. Transfer ramekins to wire rack to cool. Refrigerate overnight.

PRESENTATION

12 cherries with stems

Place pot de crème in center of serving plate. Serve with biscotti and cherries.

One Saturday every June, the quaint, tranquil town of Trenton, South Carolina celebrates the harvest at their annual Peach Festival. I discovered this event during my first month in culinary school and imagined returning one day when I had a family. Ten years later, on a sunny day, we arrived. After the parade, we indulged in delicious peach ice cream, peach preserves, and peach pie. The real centerpiece was the good old-fashioned peach cobbler, bubbling in a deep-dish cast iron pan, followed by local music under the stars. The best cobblers are made from fruits in the peak of the season. —RON

CAST IRON SKILLET SOUTHERN PEACH COBBLER
Peanut Brittle, Coconut Ice Cream

SERVES 6

COCONUT ICE CREAM

1 cup heavy cream
½ cup whole milk
1 cup coconut cream
½ cup packed coconut flakes
½ vanilla bean, chopped
2 large egg yolks
¼ cup granulated sugar
¼ cup coconut liqueur

Combine all ingredients in blender except coconut liqueur. Purée until smooth. Transfer to saucepan over medium heat. Bring to simmer, stirring constantly. Remove from heat. Strain through fine sieve into stainless steel bowl set over ice bath to stop cooking process. Cool completely. Add coconut liqueur. Place in ice cream machine and process according to manufacturer's instructions. Transfer to chilled container. Cover tightly. Store in freezer.

PEANUT BRITTLE

** canola oil spray
1 cup granulated sugar
½ cup water
½ cup light Karo syrup
1¼ cups shelled raw peanuts
⅛ teaspoon sea salt
1¼ teaspoons baking soda
1 teaspoon unsalted butter

Coat cookie sheet with canola oil spray. Set aside. Combine sugar, water, and Karo syrup in heavy bottom pot over medium-high heat. Cook to 240°F on candy thermometer. Add peanuts and salt. Cook until 290°F, stirring often with wooden spoon. Remove from heat. Stir in baking soda and butter. Be careful as mixture will foam. Beat 15 seconds with wooden spoon. Immediately transfer to prepared cookie sheet. Spread to ¼-inch-thick using spatula. Cool. Break into pieces.

PEACH COBBLER

8 peaches, pitted, sliced into eighths
1 tablespoon orange blossom water
1 teaspoon almond extract
½ teaspoon vanilla extract
¼ cup peach schnapps
½ cup almond meal
½ cup all purpose flour
¼ cup rolled oats
½ cup unsalted butter, cut into small cubes
¾ cup brown sugar
1 teaspoon cinnamon
½ teaspoon all spice

Preheat oven to 350°F. Combine peaches, orange blossom water, almond extract, vanilla extract, and peach schnapps in large mixing bowl. Sprinkle almond meal evenly on top. Toss until fruit is evenly coated with almond meal. Divide peaches between 6 individual baking dishes. Add flour and oats to mixing bowl. Using fingertips or a pastry cutter, incorporate butter to a coarse meal, being careful not to melt butter. Mix in sugar and spices. Cover peaches evenly with topping. Bake 30 minutes or until top is golden and juices are bubbling. Remove from oven. Place scoop of ice cream on top of each cobbler. Garnish with peanut brittle.

Entering the city of Fez through the gate of Bab Boujeloud, I stopped to take in the fascinating display of culture. I made my way through the labyrinth of streets towards the Fez market, swept up in the overwhelming crowd of shoppers. My tour guide, Dahlil, invited me to his grandmother's house for the most important ritual of the day—mint tea and pastries. At an afternoon tea ceremony, I learned that pouring the tea from a silver pot high above a small glass is a Moroccan tradition that enhances the delicate mint flavor. —BERNARD

HIBISCUS INFUSED LEMON BAR
Almond Cumin Crust, Spearmint Tea

SERVES 8 FAMILY STYLE

ALMOND CUMIN CRUST

½ cup unsalted butter
⅓ cup granulated sugar
1 teaspoon vanilla extract
¾ cup almond meal
¼ teaspoon cumin seeds
1 cup all purpose flour
2 large eggs
1 large egg, beaten

Preheat oven to 325°F. Lightly butter 13x5x1-inch tart pan with removable bottom. Beat remaining butter, sugar and vanilla in large mixing bowl until creamy. Mix in almond meal, cumin seeds, and flour using wooden spoon. Beat in 2 eggs to form dough. Transfer to floured work surface. Knead briefly. Wrap in plastic. Refrigerate 2 hours. Return to floured work surface. Knead just to make pliable. Roll to 13x5-inch rectangle, ⅛-inch thick. Ease gently into tart pan. Prick dough with fork. Refrigerate 30 minutes. Line dough with parchment paper. Fill with pie weights or beans. Bake 10 minutes. Remove weight and parchment. Brush shell with beaten egg. Bake additional 5 minutes or until golden. Remove from oven. Cool on wire rack.

HIBISCUS LEMON CURD

3 large eggs
3 large egg yolks
1 cup granulated sugar
2 tablespoons all purpose flour
½ cup dried hibiscus flowers
¼ teaspoon baking powder
1 cup lemon juice
1 lemon, zested
½ cup unsalted butter
2 tablespoons almond liqueur

Whisk eggs, egg yolks and sugar in large mixing bowl until pale yellow and ribbony. Fold in flour, hibiscus flowers, and baking powder. Slowly whisk in lemon juice and zest. Place bowl over pot of simmering water, ensuring bowl does not touch water. Whisk constantly until mixture thickens and reaches 160°F on instant read thermometer. Strain through fine sieve. Whisk in butter and almond liqueur. Pour into tart shell. Cool. Cover with plastic wrap. Refrigerate overnight. Run tip of paring knife along edges of tart pan to loosen. Unmold. Cut crosswise into 1-inch bars.

MINT TEA

1 cup packed spearmint leaves
4 bags organic green tea
1 tablespoon honey
1 teaspoon rose water
4 cups water
8 sprigs spearmint

Place mint, tea, honey, and rose water in carafe of French press coffee maker. Bring water to boil. Pour into carafe. Steep 3 minutes. Press. Pour into hot cups. Garnish with mint sprig.

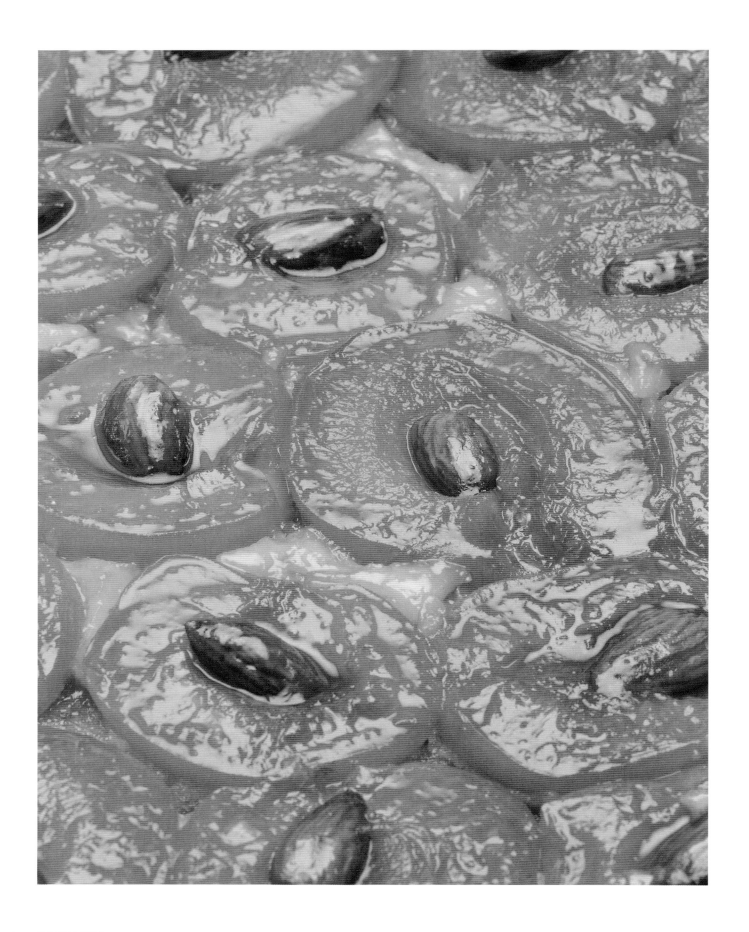

AUSTRALIA

In a fertile valley of the Australian outback sits the town of Mildura whose centerpiece, the winding Murray River, is surrounded by farms, orchards, and vineyards. My friend, Chef Stefano di Pieri is celebrated for his "slow food" principles and his mastery of ingredients from local growers, fishermen, and hunters. Peaches and apricots ripen soon after Christmas, which is summertime in Australia. They are the highlight of many dishes from sweet to savory. For this recipe, find locally grown, organic apricots and try the cake with a glass of late harvest wine, called "stickles" in Australia. —BERNARD

MILDURA CARAMELIZED APRICOT CAKE
Clover Honey Fromage Blanc

SERVES 8 FAMILY STYLE

CARAMEL

⅔ cup granulated sugar
⅓ cup unsalted butter
1 tablespoon water

Add all ingredients to 10-inch oven-proof skillet over medium-high heat. Cook until golden brown. Remove from heat. Cool 5 minutes or until caramel is hardened.

APRICOTS

12 apricots, halved, pitted
1 orange, zested
¼ teaspoon ground allspice
24 whole almonds
¼ cup apricot brandy

Combine all ingredients in large mixing bowl. Place 1 almond in center of each apricot half. Arrange apricots onto caramel in skillet, almond side down. Reserve remaining brandy mixture for batter.

BATTER

4 large eggs, separated
5 tablespoons granulated sugar
1 teaspoon vanilla extract
½ teaspoon almond extract
⅓ cup cake flour, sifted

Preheat oven to 375°F. In large mixing bowl, whisk egg yolks, 2 tablespoons sugar, and reserved brandy mixture until thick and ribbony. Whisk in flour. In separate bowl, beat egg whites to soft peaks. Add vanilla extract, almond extract, and remaining sugar. Beat until stiff peaks. Fold into yolks using rubber spatula. Pour batter evenly over apricots. Bake 30 minutes or until skewer inserted in center of cake comes out clean. Remove from oven. Let stand 15 minutes. Place skillet on stovetop over high heat 15 seconds or until caramel loosens and cake moves freely in the pan. Place large serving platter on top of skillet. Carefully and quickly invert cake onto serving platter. Cut into wedges.

FROMAGE BLANC

¾ cup fromage blanc or ricotta cheese
⅛ teaspoon freshly ground white pepper
⅛ teaspoon flaky sea salt
2 tablespoons clover honey

Whisk fromage blanc, pepper and sea salt until well combined. Transfer to serving bowl. Drizzle honey on top.

Kahlúa, with its deep coffee notes, makes a fitting companion to chocolate. The Aztecs regarded chocolate for its mystical powers and healing properties, and called it the "food of the gods." Nowadays, it's food for everyone! This tart is a wonderful way to experience the synergy of these flavors. Using dark chocolate with at least 72 % cocoa content is a must for this not-too-sweet treat. Remember—putting "eat chocolate" on your to-do list every day will ensure you get something done! —RON

CHOCOLATE KAHLÚA TART
Crystallized Ginger Crema Fresca

SERVES 8

WALNUT CRUST

1 tablespoon unsalted butter, softened
⅓ cup chopped walnuts
3 tablespoons sesame seeds
1 cup all purpose flour, sifted
2 tablespoons granulated sugar
½ teaspoon sea salt
¼ cup walnut oil
1 lemon, zested, juiced
1 large egg, beaten

Preheat oven to 375°F. Butter 9-inch fluted tart pan with removable bottom. Combine walnuts and sesame seeds on cookie sheet. Bake 5 minutes until toasted. Cool. Transfer to food processor. Combine with flour, sugar, and salt. Process until walnuts are finely ground. Transfer to large mixing bowl. Make well in center of mixture. Pour in oil, lemon juice, and zest. Stir with wooden spoon until dough forms a ball. Transfer to floured work surface. Roll to 11-inch circle, ⅛-inch thick. Gently ease dough into tart pan. Press dough into the edges and sides of pan. Prick dough with a fork. Refrigerate 30 minutes. Line dough with parchment paper. Fill with pie weights or beans. Bake 10 minutes. Remove weights and parchment. Brush shell with egg. Bake additional 5 minutes or until golden. Cool on wire rack.

CHOCOLATE ESPRESSO FILLING

5 ounces chopped dark chocolate, 72% cocoa
½ cup unsalted butter, diced
4 large eggs
3 large egg yolks
¾ cup granulated sugar
½ cup Kahlúa liqueur
1 cup espresso coffee, cold
2 tablespoons brown sugar
1 envelope powdered gelatin

Lower oven to 350°F. Add chocolate and butter to large mixing bowl set over pot of barely simmering water, ensuring bottom of bowl does not touch water. Stir until melted. Whisk eggs, egg yolks, and sugar in mixing bowl until pale yellow and ribbony. Stir in Kahlúa and ⅓ cup espresso. Whisk into chocolate. Remove from heat. Strain through fine sieve into prepared tart shell. Bake 18 minutes or until set. Transfer to wire rack to cool. Combine brown sugar and remaining espresso in small saucepan. Sprinkle gelatin over surface of liquid to bloom. Place over medium heat. Stir constantly until gelatin dissolves. Do not boil. Remove from heat. Cool to room temperature. Evenly ladle over tart. Refrigerate overnight. Unmold.

CRYSTALLIZED GINGER CREMA

¼ cup heavy cream
½ cup crème fraîche
1 teaspoon lime juice
pinch sea salt
2 tablespoons honey
¼ cup diced crystallized ginger

Whisk heavy cream, crème fraîche, lime juice, salt, and honey in mixing bowl, until consistency of whipped cream. Fold in ginger. Cover. Refrigerate 3 hours.

PRESENTATION

2 slices crystallized ginger
8 sprigs mint

Cut tart into 8 slices. Place 1 slice in center of large serving plate. Place a dollop of ginger crema on top. Slice ginger into fine strips. Place atop cream. Garnish with mint sprig.

The beautiful Loire river snakes through Brittany and Anjou, near my childhood home. Majestic pear, apple, and cherry orchards tower over the banks of the river, heaven for bees and fishermen alike. After a day of fly fishing with my father, I would gather apples then rush home and bake our family's tarte tatin—a rich, buttery, caramelized apple cake topped with homemade ice cream. Choose Granny Smith, Fuji, Gala, or Jonagold apples. Using a cast iron pan allows the caramel and apples to cook evenly. —BERNARD

MY GRANDMOTHER'S APPLE TARTE TATIN
Pistachio Ice Cream

SERVES 8 FAMILY STYLE

PASTRY

1 cup whole wheat flour
1 lemon, zested, juiced
1 tablespoon poppy seeds
½ teaspoon thyme leaves
⅓ cup unsalted butter, chilled, cubed
1 large egg, beaten
2 tablespoons Grand Marnier liqueur

Combine flour, lemon zest, poppy seeds, and thyme in large mixing bowl. Using fingertips or a pastry cutter, incorporate butter to a coarse meal, being careful not to melt butter. Make well in center. Add egg, lemon juice, and Grand Marnier. Using wooden spoon, stir in small circles in center of bowl, working progressively outwards to make dough. Form into a ball. Turn out onto floured work surface. Roll to 1-inch thick disk. Cover with plastic wrap. Refrigerate 1 hour.

TARTE TATIN

4 pounds medium apples
¼ cup lemon juice
¾ cup granulated sugar
¼ teaspoon ground cinnamon
½ cup unsalted butter, diced
½ teaspoon vanilla extract
½ teaspoon anise extract

Preheat oven to 375°F. Peel and core apples. Cut in halves. Toss with lemon juice. Mix sugar with cinnamon, vanilla extract, and anise extract in small bowl. Spread half of mixture in 9-inch cast-iron skillet. Dot half the butter over sugar. Drizzle with vanilla and anise extract. Tightly arrange apples in skillet, standing up, with all of the apples on the perimeter facing the same direction and remaining apples packed tightly into the center. Sprinkle remaining sugar mixture over apples. Dot with remaining butter. Place skillet on baking sheet. Bake 40 minutes. Roll pastry to 11-inch circle. Place over apples. Tuck overlapping dough into pan. Bake 30 minutes or until pastry is golden brown and juices are bubbly. Remove from oven. Let rest 10 minutes. Place skillet over medium-high heat. Cook 2 minutes or until caramel on the edges becomes mahogany brown. Remove from heat. Place oversized serving platter on top of skillet. Quickly invert tarte tatin onto serving platter, being careful as caramel is very hot. Serve hot.

PISTACHIO ICE CREAM

2 cups shelled raw pistachios
1 cup granulated sugar
¼ cup pistachio oil
12 large egg yolks
5 cups heavy cream
½ cup chopped dark chocolate, 85% cocoa
¼ cup shelled toasted pistachios

Combine raw pistachios, ¾ cup sugar, and oil in food processor. Process 3 minutes or until mixture forms a paste. Whisk egg yolks and remaining sugar in large mixing bowl until pale yellow and ribbony. Add cream to large saucepan over medium heat. Bring to boil. Add to yolk mixture in slow stream, whisking continuously. Return to saucepan over low heat. Cook, stirring constantly, until custard thickens enough to coat back of a spoon or until 165°F on candy thermometer. Strain through fine sieve into large bowl. Whisk in pistachio paste. Cool. Cover tightly with plastic wrap. Refrigerate 3 hours or until chilled. Transfer to ice cream machine. Add chocolate. Freeze according to manufacturer's instructions. Cover. Freeze overnight. Scoop into chilled serving bowl. Garnish with toasted pistachios.

SOUTH AFRICA

On a photo safari in the eastern cape of South Africa, with the serene Lebombo Mountains in the background, I sat perched on a hilltop watching hippos and buffalos bathe in the mud of a waterhole. Further east, where the elephants roam, the plump, yellow berries of the unique marula tree are ripened by the heat of the glaring sun. This unusual fruit is prized for its rich flavor, and is used to make the cream liqueur Amarula. The nutty, caramel taste of the drink creates the ultimate crème brûlée. If you need a substitute for Amarula, Baileys® is spot on! — BERNARD

AMARULA CRÈME BRÛLÉE
Rooibos Tea Spiced Cookies

SERVES 8

COOKIES

** canola oil spray
½ cup water
2 tablespoons rooibos tea leaves
1½ cups all purpose flour
¼ teaspoon baking soda
¼ teaspoon cream of tartar
¼ teaspoon turmeric powder
½ teaspoon ginger powder
½ cup packed brown sugar
¼ cup unsalted butter, cut in small pieces
1 large egg
2 tablespoons milk
⅔ cup sultana raisins
½ cup toasted chopped pecans
1 large egg white, lightly beaten
1 tablespoon turbinado sugar

Preheat oven to 350°F. Grease cookie sheet with canola oil spray. Add water and rooibos tea leaves to small saucepan over low heat. Bring to simmer. Reduce until 1 tablespoon liquid remains. Remove from heat. Cool. Transfer saucepan to refrigerator until fully chilled. Sift flour, baking soda, cream of tartar, turmeric, and ginger into large mixing bowl. Mix in sugar. Cut butter into flour mixture using fingertips or pastry cutter. Whisk egg and milk into tea reduction. Strain through fine sieve into flour mixture. Add raisins and pecans. Mix with wooden spoon to form a dough. Turn onto heavily floured work surface. Flour dough and rolling pin. Roll dough ¼-inch thick. Cut into 2½-inch rounds using a cookie cutter. Transfer to prepared cookie sheet. Gather scraps into ball and repeat process. Brush surface of cookies with egg white. Sprinkle with turbinado sugar. Bake 12 minutes. Cool.

CRÈME BRÛLÉE

12 large egg yolks
¾ cup granulated sugar
3 cups heavy cream
⅛ teaspoon ground nutmeg
1 vanilla bean, split, scraped
½ cup Amarula cream liqueur

Preheat oven to 300°F. Whisk egg yolks and sugar in large mixing bowl until pale yellow and ribbony. Combine cream, nutmeg, and vanilla bean in large saucepan over medium heat. Bring to simmer. Add to yolk mixture in slow stream, whisking continuously. Stir in Amarula. Strain through fine sieve. Skim foam. Place eight 6-ounce ramekins in paper towel-lined roasting pan. Pour cream mixture into ramekins. Pour enough hot water into the pan to come halfway up sides of ramekins. Bake 40 minutes or until crème brûlée is set but jiggly in center. Transfer ramekins to wire rack to cool. Refrigerate overnight.

PRESENTATION

8 tablespoons turbinado sugar
8 sprigs mint
24 raspberries

Spread 1 tablespoon sugar evenly over top of each custard. Caramelize to mahogany brown using crème brûlée torch or blow torch. Garnish with mint sprig, raspberries, and cookies.

VENEZUELA

After two days of trekking along Venezuela's rugged northern coast with my *compadre* Atanacio, we arrived at the remote village of Chuao. Surrounded by mountains and dense forests, the townspeople quietly produce some of the best cocoa beans in the world, using techniques passed down through generations. Just the sight of the beans drying in the sun of the church courtyard was worth the trip. Remember, when preparing this timbale, take your time when melting the chocolate—don't go too fast or get it too hot. Chop the chocolate into small pieces, place them in a bowl set over barely simmering water, and melt it slowly. It should remain nice and shiny. —BERNARD

MOLTEN CHUAO CHOCOLATE TIMBALE
Mango, Lemon Ginger Confit

SERVES 4

LEMON GINGER CONFIT

2 large Meyer lemons
2 tablespoons julienned, peeled ginger
1 cup granulated sugar
¼ cup lemoncello
¼ teaspoon cracked black peppercorns

Peel lemons. Dice peel into ¼-inch cubes. Squeeze juice from pulp. Set aside. Bring 1 quart water to boil in large pot. Add lemon peel. Poach 30 seconds. Transfer to ice bath. Cool 1 minute. Return to boiling water. Repeat process three times. Transfer to saucepan over low heat. Add lemon juice and remaining ingredients. Bring to simmer. Cook 30 minutes or until syrupy.

CHOCOLATE TIMBALE

1 tablespoon unsalted butter, softened
2 tablespoons granulated sugar
4 ounces dark chocolate, 72% cocoa
½ cup unsalted butter
2 large eggs
3 large egg yolks
¼ cup granulated sugar
¼ cup cake flour, sifted
4 teaspoons cocoa nibs
1 teaspoon chopped basil leaves

Preheat oven to 375°F. Grease four 4-ounce ceramic ramekins with softened butter. Coat each with ½ tablespoon sugar. Add chocolate and butter to large mixing bowl set over pot of barely simmering water, ensuring bottom of bowl does not touch water. Whisk until well combined. Beat eggs, egg yolks and ¼ cup sugar until pale yellow and ribbony. Whisk chocolate mixture into egg mixture until well combined. Fold in flour, cocoa nibs, and basil using rubber spatula. Divide batter into ramekins. Bake 9 minutes.

PRESENTATION

1 mango
1 tablespoon powdered sugar
4 sprigs flowering basil

Peel mango. Thinly slice using mandoline or vegetable slicer. Place slices in overlapping pattern among four serving plates. Invert cakes onto center of plate. Remove ramekins. Dust lightly with powdered sugar. Spoon lemon and ginger confit around. Garnish with flowering basil sprigs.

On the island of Sardinia, off the coast of Italy, I visited the ancient city of Cagliari—a fusion of Spanish, African, and Arabic cultures. Sardinians craft a liqueur from berries harvested from myrtle trees in the north of the island. As a digestif, Mirto Rosso is made from the berries and Mirto Bianco from the leaves. I enjoyed its licorice and blackberry notes al fresco on the Piazza Constituzione, paired with local almond pastries. Experimenting back at home, I discovered that Mirto makes a wonderfully aromatic syrup to flavor cakes and tortes. —BERNARD

SARDINIAN ALMOND BISCOTTI TORTE
Mirto Myrtle Syrup

SERVES 8 FAMILY STYLE

TORTE

½ pound almond biscotti
3 tablespoons unsalted butter, melted
6 large eggs
1 cup granulated sugar
1 teaspoon vanilla extract
1 teaspoon cream of tartar
1 cup almond meal
1 tablespoon all purpose flour

Preheat oven to 325°F. Add biscotti to food processor. Process to coarse meal. Transfer to large mixing bowl. Combine with melted butter. Press into the bottom of 9-inch nonstick spring-form pan. Bake 6 minutes. Cool. Separate eggs, placing yolks in medium mixing bowl, whites in a large mixing bowl. Beat yolks with ¼ cup sugar and vanilla until pale yellow and ribbony. Beat egg whites until frothy. Add cream of tartar. Continue beating, slowly adding remaining sugar until stiff peaks form. Fold egg whites into yolks, followed by almond meal and flour. Pour mixture into prepared springform pan set on cookie sheet. Bake 45 minutes or until wooden skewer inserted in center comes out clean. Remove from oven. Cool to room temperature. Unmold torte. Transfer to serving platter.

SYRUP

1 cup lemon juice
¾ cup Mirto Myrtle liqueur(or Campari)
½ cup water
¾ cup granulated sugar
1 tablespoon lemon zest
10 pods whole star anise

Combine all ingredients in sauce pot over medium-high heat. Bring to simmer. Cook 15 minutes or until syrupy. Remove from heat. Cool.

PRESENTATION

3 lemons
½ cup toasted sliced almonds

Remove star anise pods from syrup. Set aside. Brush syrup onto top and sides of torte. Cut lemons crosswise into thin slices. Shingle around edge of the torte. Sprinkle torte with toasted almonds. Garnish with star anise pods.

TURKEY

After leaving the beautiful fishing village of Yumurtalik, Turkey, for an inland reprieve in the rich valley of Adana, I discovered an abundance of stone fruit trees in full harvest. Seeing the orchard's intense and juicy fruits hanging from overstocked branches made me think of the old Turkish proverb "eat sweetly, speak sweetly." Turkey has a long history of delectable desserts, inspired by their rich agriculture and love for sweets. Here is one example. —RON

ADANA NECTARINE CAKE
Arak Fig Confit, Lemon Verbena Yogurt

SERVES 8 FAMILY STYLE

THE CAKE

- **1 tablespoon** unsalted butter, softened
- **3 tablespoons** turbinado sugar
- **2 cups** powdered sugar
- **⅔ cup** self rising flour
- **2 cups** almond meal
- **8 large** egg whites, lightly beaten
- **½ cup** unsalted butter, melted
- **2 tablespoons** almond oil
- **2 tablespoons** whole milk
- **1** orange, zested
- **3** nectarines, pitted, diced
- **½ cup** jumbo dark raisins
- **1 sprig** thyme

Preheat oven to 375°F. Grease an 8 by 8-inch baking dish with softened butter. Coat with turbinado sugar. Set aside. Sift powdered sugar and flour into large mixing bowl. Combine with almond meal. Add egg whites, melted butter, almond oil, milk, and orange zest. Beat with wooden spoon until well incorporated. Fold in nectarines and raisins. Pour mixture into prepared dish. Bake 1 hour or until skewer inserted in center of cake comes out clean. Remove from oven. Garnish with thyme sprig. Serve warm.

LEMON VERBENA YOGURT

- **2 tablespoons** granulated sugar
- **1 tablespoon** minced fresh lemon verbena leaves
- **2 teaspoons** thyme leaves
- **½ teaspoon** vanilla extract
- **1 cup** organic plain yogurt

Place sieve over large bowl. Line with four layers dampened cheesecloth. Whisk sugar, lemon verbena, 1 teaspoon thyme leaves, vanilla, and yogurt in mixing bowl. Pour into sieve. Cover. Refrigerate overnight. Discard water. Transfer yogurt to serving bowl. Sprinkle with remaining thyme leaves.

FIG CONFIT

- **1 cup** dried mission figs
- **¾ cup** prune juice
- **¼ cup** Arak liquor
- **1 teaspoon** mustard seeds
- **¼ teaspoon** ground cinnamon

Dice mission figs, discarding stems. Transfer to saucepan over medium heat. Add remaining ingredients. Bring to simmer. Cook until liquid becomes thick and syrupy. Transfer to serving dish.

Whakatane is home to the spectacular Eastern Bay of Plenty in New Zealand. At Julian Berry Farm, I picked a basket of ripe, plump, juicy berries straight from the vine and had the ultimate loganberry ice cream at the outdoor café, overlooking the trestle rows of vines. That afternoon, I went back to the cottage to recreate this recipe, taught to me as an apprentice by my mentor, Chef George Paineau. Berries are most flavorful when in season. This is the perfect time to process them into jams. To freeze freshly picked berries, spread them in a single layer on a tray, cover with plastic wrap, then freeze until solid. Pack berries into resealable bags, remove the air, and freeze for up to 3 months. —BERNARD

WHAKATANE WILD BERRY GRATIN
Ti-Toki Sabayon, Almond Macaroon

SERVES 6

ALMOND MACAROON

** canola oil spray
1¼ cups blanched whole almonds
¾ cup granulated sugar
1 large egg white
¼ teaspoon almond extract
⅛ teaspoon sea salt
12 whole almonds, shelled

Preheat oven to 350°F. Lightly grease baking sheet with canola spray or line with silicone pad. Add blanched almonds and sugar to food processor. Process to fine meal. Add egg white, almond extract, and salt. Pulse until combined. Roll into 12 balls, 1 inch in diameter. Transfer to baking sheet, leaving 2-inch space between each cookie. Press 1 almond into center of each cookie, flattening slightly with fingertips. Bake 8 to 10 minutes or until golden brown. Cool on wire rack. Transfer to serving bowl.

TI-TOKI SABAYON

½ cup heavy cream
2 teaspoons honey
¼ teaspoon vanilla extract
6 large egg yolks
¼ cup granulated sugar
⅓ cup Ti-Toki liqueur (or Myers's dark rum)
1 tablespoon lemon juice

Whip cream, honey, and vanilla to stiff peaks in large mixing bowl. Cover. Refrigerate. Add yolks, sugar, Ti-Toki, and lemon juice to large mixing bowl set over pot of simmering water, ensuring that bottom of bowl does not touch water. Beat with handheld electric mixer or wire whip until fluffy, ribbony, and thick. Transfer bowl to ice bath. Continue beating until cooled. Fold whipped cream into yolk mixture using rubber spatula.

PRESENTATION

1 cup blackberries
1 cup raspberries
1 cup quartered stemmed strawberries
1 cup blueberries
1 tablespoon powdered sugar
6 sprigs mint

Preheat broiler to medium-high. Divide berries equally among 6 shallow, heat-proof serving bowls. Spoon sabayon evenly on top. Place under broiler for 20 seconds or until surface of sabayon turns golden brown. Monitor constantly to avoid burning. Dust sabayon with sugar. Garnish with mint sprig. Serve with macaroons.

In the Punjab, the bright colors of turbans and kameezes are mirrored in all aspects of life, including food. Saffron and other spices mingle with sliced nuts and toasted seeds, bringing vibrant hues to local dishes. In a posh suburb of Mumbai, I experienced freshly puffed *naan*, fragrant curry, *paratas*, and *pulaos* for a true taste of the Punjabi Northern State. A flavorful rice pudding brought the experience to a dramatic finale, as colorful as the culture itself. For me, this dish contributes to why they call Punjabi the "smiling soul of India." —BERNARD

PUNJABI EXOTIC RICE PUDDING
Vanilla Sesame Cookies

SERVES 8 FAMILY STYLE

RICE PUDDING

2 cups coconut milk
3 tablespoons brown sugar
1 vanilla bean, split, scraped
¼ teaspoon ground ginger
¼ teaspoon ground cardamom
⅛ teaspoon cloves
2 pinches saffron threads
2½ cups water
¼ teaspoon sea salt
1 cup basmati rice
¼ cup golden raisins
½ cup diced pitted dates
¼ cup toasted coconut flakes

Preheat oven to 375°F. Combine coconut milk, brown sugar, vanilla, ginger, cardamom, cloves, and saffron in saucepan over medium-high heat. Bring to boil. Remove from heat. Steep 10 minutes. Discard vanilla bean. Add water and salt to large saucepan over medium-high heat. Bring to boil. Add rice. Bring back to boil. Reduce heat to low. Cover. Simmer 20 minutes or until water is absorbed. Transfer rice to large mixing bowl. Stir coconut milk mixture into rice. Fold in raisins, dates, and coconut flakes. Transfer to baking dish. Cover. Bake 15 minutes. Uncover. Bake additional 5 minutes or until center reaches 165°F on instant read thermometer.

COOKIES

** canola oil spray
½ cup unsalted butter, softened
¾ cup powdered sugar
2 teaspoons vanilla extract
1¼ cups all purpose flour, sifted
2 tablespoons white sesame seeds, toasted
2 tablespoons half and half
2 tablespoons black sesame seeds

Preheat oven to 350°F. Grease cookie sheet with canola oil spray. Cream butter, sugar, and vanilla in small mixing bowl until light and fluffy. Fold in flour and 1 tablespoon white sesame seeds. Add 1 tablespoon half and half. Turn out dough onto lightly floured work surface. Roll ¼-inch thick. Cut into rectangles and crescent shapes using cookie cutter. Transfer to prepared cookie sheet. Brush cookies lightly with remaining half and half. Sprinkle with remaining white and black sesame seeds. Bake 15 minutes or until lightly golden. Cool. Transfer to serving platter.

Most of the kitchen disaster stories I have heard involve soufflés, the chic French word for "puffed up." Don't be scared. This recipe is easy to make. To prep ahead of time, fill soufflé cups with batter then refrigerate up to 4 hours. Increase cooking time by 2 minutes. The key for success is in using the highest quality chocolate, such as the one favored by Belgium's master chocolatiers—Callebaut. At home, the girls always ask for soufflé with vanilla bean ice cream in the center. They love the "chaud-froid" effect—icy on the tongue, warm in the heart. —RON

CALLEBAUT CHOCOLATE SOUFFLÉ
Mandarine Napoleon Crème Anglaise

SERVES 8

SOUFFLÉ

2 tablespoons unsalted butter, softened
8 teaspoons granulated sugar
10 ounces chopped dark chocolate, 72% cocoa
3 tablespoons unsalted butter
6 large egg yolks
6 large egg whites
⅛ teaspoon cream of tartar
pinch sea salt
¼ cup granulated sugar
4 ounces dark chocolate, 72% cocoa, cut into 8 pieces

Preheat oven to 375°F. Butter eight 6-ounce soufflé dishes. Coat each dish thoroughly with 1 teaspoon sugar. Place on baking sheet. Set aside. Add chocolate and 3 tablespoons butter to large mixing bowl set over pot of barely simmering water, ensuring bottom of bowl does not touch water. Stir until melted. Remove from heat. Whisk in egg yolks, one at a time. In separate mixing bowl, beat egg whites, cream of tartar, and pinch of salt to soft peaks. Add sugar. Beat to stiff peaks. Whisk quarter of egg whites into chocolate. Gently fold in remaining egg whites, using rubber spatula. Neatly spoon mixture into prepared soufflé dishes. Insert one piece chocolate into center of mixture. Bake in center of oven 12 minutes or until nicely puffed.

CRÈME ANGLAISE

¾ cup granulated sugar
6 extra large egg yolks
2 cups whole milk
2 cups heavy cream
1 vanilla bean, split
¼ cup Mandarine Napoleon® liqueur

Whisk sugar and egg yolks in mixing bowl until pale yellow and ribbony. Add milk, cream, and vanilla bean to saucepan over medium-high heat. Bring to simmer. Add milk mixture to egg yolks in slow stream, whisking constantly. Return mixture to saucepan over medium heat. Bring mixture to 180°F, stirring constantly with high heat-proof rubber spatula. Do not boil. Strain through fine sieve into stainless steel bowl set over ice bath, to stop cooking process. Whisk to cool quickly. Return vanilla bean to crème Anglaise. Stir in Mandarine Napoleon®. Refrigerate. Transfer to sauce dish.

PRESENTATION

2 tablespoons powdered sugar

Dust top of soufflé with powdered sugar before serving. At the table, tell your guests to puncture center of soufflé with dessert spoon and pour in crème Anglaise.

The big island of Hawaii is the heart of Kona coffee country. During the holidays, lights twinkle and musicians stroll the streets playing festive tunes on ukuleles. The rich aroma of the famous brew mixes with the smell of fried pastries, filling the jungle air with anticipation. These spring rolls capture the island flavors of banana, macadamia, and coconut. Making them is a fun project for the whole family! —RON

BANANA CHOCOLATE SPRING ROLLS
Kona Caramel Ice Cream

SERVES 8 FAMILY STYLE

KONA CARAMEL ICE CREAM

¼ cup water
¾ cup granulated sugar
1 vanilla bean, split in half, scraped
2 cups heavy cream
¾ cup whole milk
3 tablespoons finely ground Kona coffee beans
½ teaspoon togarashi pepper
10 large egg yolks
2 tablespoons brown sugar

Add water, sugar, and vanilla bean to large, deep saucepan over medium heat. Cook until sugar dissolves. Increase heat to high. Cook without stirring until syrup turns to a deep amber-colored caramel. Remove from heat. Slowly add cream, being careful as mixture will bubble heavily. Return the pan to low heat. Whisk until smooth. Set aside ½ cup caramel. Stir milk, coffee beans, and togarashi into remaining caramel in saucepan. Whisk egg yolks and brown sugar in large mixing bowl until pale yellow and ribbony. Slowly add one cup caramel mixture into egg yolks, whisking constantly. Whisk tempered egg yolk mixture into remaining caramel mixture in saucepan over medium heat. Bring mixture to 180°F, stirring constantly with high heatproof rubber spatula. Do not boil. Strain through fine sieve into stainless steel bowl set over ice bath to stop cooking process. Whisk to cool quickly. Refrigerate until well chilled. Transfer to ice cream maker and process according to manufacturer's instructions. Fold reserved caramel into ice cream to create swirl. Cover. Freeze overnight. Scoop into chilled serving bowl.

SPRING ROLLS

2 large bananas, peeled
16 7½-inch square spring roll wrappers
2 large egg whites, lightly beaten
1 cup chopped Callebaut chocolate, 72% cocoa
1 cup chopped toasted macadamia nuts
⅓ cup shredded sweetened coconut
2 quarts canola oil for frying

Cut each banana in half crosswise. Cut each half into quarters lengthwise. Work with 1 spring roll wrapper at a time. Cover remaining wrappers with damp paper towel. Lay spring roll wrapper on dry work surface. Place one piece banana 2 inches from bottom of wrapper. Top with 1 tablespoon chocolate, 1 tablespoon macadamia, and 1 teaspoon coconut. Lightly brush edges with egg white. Fold bottom edge over filling. Roll upwards 1 complete turn. Fold in sides. Continue rolling to form tight cylinder. Repeat with remaining ingredients. Heat oil in heavy sauce pot to 300°F. Fry 2 spring rolls at a time until golden brown. Drain on paper towels.

PRESENTATION

2 tablespoons powdered sugar
2 tablespoons cocoa powder

Arrange spring rolls on large serving platter. Dust spring rolls with sugar and cocoa. Serve with ice cream.

What better way to contemplate the glorious history of Florence than with a scoop of gelato or sorbetto in hand? The imagination of Florence's gelaterias reflects the city's artistic spirit. The festival of flavors in the display cases—lemon basil, pistachio, bitter chocolate, rose petal, and many more, are matched only by the vibrant hues of yellow, white, brown, green, and almost every shade of red. The possibilities are endless, so get yourself an ice cream maker and have your own culinary Renaissance! —RON

ORCHARD HARVEST SORBETS

Tellicherry Pepper Blood Orange, 4 Lemon Essence, Persimmon Cardamom Pistachio

YIELDS 1 QUART EACH

TELLICHERRY PEPPER BLOOD ORANGE

½ teaspoon Tellicherry black peppercorns
½ teaspoon juniper berries
1 cup granulated sugar
2½ cups blood orange juice
1 teaspoon angostura bitters

Add peppercorns and juniper berries to spice grinder. Pulse to coarsely ground. Transfer to large mixing bowl. Combine with remaining ingredients. Whisk to dissolve sugar. Refrigerate overnight. Strain through fine sieve into ice cream machine and process according to manufacturer's instructions. Transfer to chilled container. Cover tightly. Store in freezer.

4 LEMON ESSENCE

1 cup water
1⅓ cup granulated sugar
2 stalks lemongrass, cut into 3-inch lengths, crushed
4 sprigs lemon thyme
1 cup Meyer lemon juice
3 tablespoons Hangar One® citron "Buddha's Hand" vodka

Add water, sugar, and lemongrass to saucepan over medium heat. Simmer 5 minutes. Add thyme. Cover. Remove from heat. Cool to room temperature. Strain through fine sieve. Combine with lemon juice and vodka. Place in ice cream machine and process according to manufacturer's instructions. Transfer to chilled container. Cover tightly. Store in freezer.

PERSIMMON CARDAMOM PISTACHIO

3 pounds fuyu persimmons, ripe
1 lemon, juiced, zested
1 cup water
1 cup granulated sugar
5 pods cardamom
¾ cup chopped toasted pistachios
¼ teaspoon fleur de sel

Peel and dice persimmons, discarding seeds. Transfer to blender with lemon juice and zest. Add water, sugar, and cardamom to saucepan over medium heat. Bring to boil. Add to blender. Purée until smooth. Strain through fine sieve. Refrigerate until thoroughly chilled. Place in ice cream machine and process according to manufacturer's instructions. Fold in pistachios and fleur de sel. Transfer to chilled container. Cover tightly. Store in freezer.

The architecture of Morelia, the jewel of Mexico's colonial cities, shimmers in pink stone. Throughout the town, green and violet jacarandas are entwined with bugambilia, hugging the trunks of the ancient oak trees. *Paletas*, a local popsicle made of pureed fruit, water, and a touch of sugar, are available at shops all along the main boulevard. These three sorbet recipes are our takes on the frozen, fresh fruit creations that Morelia is famous for. —RON

MORELIA SWEET ICE
Zen Green Tea Apple Verjus, Blackberry Ruby Port, Island Passion Fruit

YIELDS 1 QUART EACH

ZEN GREEN TEA APPLE VERJUS

1½ cups green verjus
¾ cup granulated sugar
3 ounces green tea powder
5 large green apples
1 lime, juiced
¼ teaspoon togarashi

Add verjus, sugar and green tea powder to saucepan over medium-high heat. Bring to simmer. Remove from heat. Refrigerate until thoroughly chilled. Peel, core, and chop apples. Toss with lime juice. Transfer to blender. Add syrup and togarashi. Purée until smooth. Place in ice cream machine and process according to manufacturer's instructions. Transfer to chilled container. Cover tightly. Store in freezer.

BLACKBERRY RUBY PORT

1 cup water
¾ cup granulated sugar
4 pods star anise
3 cups blackberries
½ cup ruby port wine

Add water, sugar, and star anise to saucepan over medium heat. Bring to simmer. Add blackberries. Simmer 10 minutes. Remove star anise. Transfer to blender. Add port wine. Purée. Strain to remove seeds. Refrigerate until thoroughly chilled. Place in ice cream machine and process according to manufacturer's instructions. Transfer to chilled container. Cover tightly. Store in freezer.

ISLAND PASSION FRUIT

¾ cup water
1 cup light brown sugar
2 tablespoons spiced rum
¾ cup passion fruit purée or pulp
½ cup diced pineapple
¼ cup tangerine juice
1 teaspoon grated fresh ginger

Add water and sugar to saucepan over medium heat. Bring to boil. Cool. Add to blender with remaining ingredients. Purée. Strain through fine sieve. Refrigerate until thoroughly chilled. Place in ice cream machine and process according to manufacturer's instructions. Transfer to chilled container. Cover tightly. Store in freezer.

Absinthe was first distilled in Switzerland in 1797. The bright green liquor, affectionately nicknamed "The Green Fairy," was born. Many famous artists and writers, including Van Gogh, Baudelaire, and Verlaine, believed it stimulated their creativity. Truffles are a grand finale to any dining experience. What more symbolic way to conclude our adventure than with this recipe—a clever union of Switzerland's most sensual ingredients—absinthe and chocolate. To give you something extra to remember us by, we added a little spice for good measure. Farewell, until we meet again! —BERNARD AND RON

GREEN FAIRY CHOCOLATE TRUFFLES
Cocoa Powder Dust

MAKES 32 TRUFFLES

TRUFFLES

¾ cup heavy cream
3 tablespoons unsalted butter
12 ounces finely chopped dark chocolate, 72 % cocoa
¼ cup absinthe liquor

Add cream and butter to saucepan over medium heat. Bring to simmer. Turn off heat. Add chocolate. Whisk until smooth. Stir in absinthe. Transfer to 9x9-inch baking dish. Refrigerate 1 hour or until set. Scoop mixture onto wax paper-lined baking sheet using a half-ounce ice cream scoop. Refrigerate 30 minutes. Roll each portion in palms of hands to form a ball. Return to wax paper. Cover. Refrigerate 2 hours.

COATING

1½ pounds finely chopped dark chocolate, 72 % cocoa
2 cups cocoa powder
⅛ teaspoon cayenne pepper

Add chocolate to mixing bowl set over pot of simmering water, ensuring that bottom of bowl does not touch water. Melt, stirring often. Sift cocoa powder and cayenne pepper into deep baking dish. Set aside. Quickly dip chocolate balls in melted chocolate one at a time for 3 seconds. Retrieve with fork, tapping stem of fork on side of bowl to remove excess chocolate. Transfer to cocoa powder. Roll to coat. Let set 2 minutes. Transfer to serving bowl. Store extras in airtight container.

RESOURCES

HEAT OF THE MOMENT

One of the most basic functions in the kitchen is transferring energy from a heat source to food—simply known as "cooking." Throughout the ages many methods have evolved to achieve this, each designed for a specific result. Here are some tips to ensure success when "cooking with fire."

GRILLING

The high heat of a grill effectively caramelizes the surface of foods while locking in moisture. The best temperature is 550°F. Positioning grates 4 inches above the heat source ensures even cooking. In case of flare-ups, keep a spray bottle filled with water handy to extinguish. Trimming excess fat from meat before grilling will reduce flare-ups. An instant-read thermometer is the best way to determine when food is properly cooked. Use tongs to turn food, as a fork pierces meat allowing flavorful juices to escape. Cooking fish on a cedar plank is a fun way to bring a wonderful, smokey flavor to your grilling.

BAKING

Baking is a general term which refers to cooking foods, savory or sweet, in an oven. Reduce the heat by 25°F when using an ovenproof glass dish instead of a metal baking pan. When placing pans in an oven, they should be staggered to ensure even heat circulation. Precise measurment of ingredients is the key to successful baked goods. Baking a sheet of cookies without rotating is a good method for determining hot spots in the oven. Always bake cakes on the center rack to ensure even cooking. As a safety net, always set your timer 5 minutes earlier than the recipe calls for.

ROASTING

Roasted foods are cooked using an oven or other heat source, such as a tandoori or rotisserie, to attain a golden brown surface. Individual portions or small pieces are roasted quickly at high heat. Large cuts of meat may be roasted slowly at moderate heat to achieve a caramelized surface while retaining succulent juices. Using a properly calibrated oven and rotating the food occasionally will help ensure a perfect roast. Potatoes and root vegetables added to a meat roast will absorb pan juices, creating a one-dish meal. Basting often during the roasting process adds flavor and prevents drying.

SEARING

Searing is a quick and convenient way to cook food over very high heat to trap in juices and flavor. For thin or small pieces, searing may be all that is needed. Searing and baking in combination is a common way of cooking thicker cuts of seafood, meats, and poultry. It is beneficial to dry the surface of foods before searing as moisture interrupts the browning process. A cast iron skillet is best for searing because of its ability to retain heat. The 1-inch rule: Leave 1 inch of space between each protein when searing to avoid heat loss in the pan, which would result in less development of flavor.

POACHING

Poaching is a delicate cooking method where heat is transferred slowly to a food's interior without browning the surface. The food is submerged in a lightly simmering liquid. For fish, it is better to start the product in a cold poaching liquid and bring to a simmer. The result will be evenly cooked and tender. When poaching, never bring liquid to a full boil. Boiling is an aggressive cooking method not suitable for proteins, as they become tough. Fortify poaching liquid with aromatics such as lemongrass, herbs, and spices to elevate the flavor. Leftover poaching liquid can be used as a stock or soup.

BLANCHING

Blanching is a method that improves the texture of certain foods, most often green vegetables. The other objective is to intensify color and minimize nutrient loss. The first step is to briefly submerge ingredients in lightly salted, boiling water. The second step, called "shocking," is to transfer the ingredients to an ice bath. This stops the cooking process to retain color, nutrients and crispiness of the vegetables. Using 1 gallon of lightly salted boiling water per 1 pound of vegetables is the ratio for perfect blanching. This technique is a great way to prep corn for the grill and green beans for a salad on a warm summer night.

FRYING

When frying, oil is the medium used to transfer heat to food. Pan-fried foods, such as fish and potato cakes, are cooked in ¼ inch of oil and flipped during the cooking process. Deep fried foods are fully submerged in the oil. Most foods should be deep fried between 350° and 375°F. The best oils for frying have a neutral flavor and a high smoking point, such as grapeseed oil and canola oil. When deep frying, your ingredients should swim freely in the oil for a crispy golden brown crust and tender inside. After frying, cool, strain, and store oil in a tight container for later use. Oil used to fry seafood should be reused only for seafood.

SAUTÉEING

A specific style of frying—sauté—comes from the French word *sauter*, "to jump." It describes cooking foods in small amount of fat at high heat in a large pan with frequent movement to the product. It is beneficial to add a little oil when sautéeing with butter. This will prevent the butter from burning. Sautéeing promotes an even caramelization of ingredients that have a high sugar content, such as onions, fruits, carrots and scallops. Salt spongy foods, like mushrooms and eggplant, in the beginning of sautéeing to expedite the cooking process by drawing out moisture.

WOKKING

"Wok Hay" is a Chinese expression that means "hot breath," "energy" or "spirit." Cooking in a wok is a way of life in the Asian kitchen, using a deep, bowl-shaped metal pan over high heat. Oil is heated with aromatics such as ginger, garlic, and chiles until sizzling. Small cuts of meat and vegetables are tossed around quickly until cooked. Cooking in a wok happens very fast, so be sure to have all ingredients prepared before you start. Always use sesame oil as a seasoning, adding at the last minute to protect the aroma. A wok is an all-purpose kitchen utensil. To create a steamer: Add 2 cups of water to your wok and set a bamboo steamer basket inside and cover with lid. It can also be used for deep frying, braising, and blanching.

BRAISING

Braising is the complex and colorful cousin of poaching. Foods are cooked slowly in an enriched liquid in a covered vessel for the purpose of tenderizing. This can be done on the stove top or in the oven. Always brown meats prior to braising. Adding an acidic ingredient to the cooking liquid, such as wine or tomatoes, helps in the tenderizing process and adds flavor. Vegetables, such as endive, salsify, whole carrots, and celery hearts can be braised in a broth flavored with saffron, white wine, spices, and aromatic herbs. Short ribs, pot roast, brisket, shanks, oxtail, and cheeks take well to braising. Our favorite pan for braising is a Dutch oven or other sturdy pot with tight fitting lid to trap steam and heat inside.

THE KITCHEN DRAWER

Fancy equipment is not essential to successful cooking. Having spent the majority of our lives cooking, both professionally around the world and leisurely at home with friends and family, we have grown attached to certain tools and gadgets. Here is our top 20 list of wise investments for you to collect:

CAST IRON

We love cast iron for its durability, versatility, heat retention, and even heat distribution. It can be used on the stove top or in the oven. Apply a thin layer of vegetable oil to cast iron cookware after each use to prevent rusting. Dutch ovens are perfect for slow braising meats in the winter and baking cornbread year round. If you do not have a grill, a cast iron griddle pan is the perfect substitute. With a lot of use, cast iron skillets become nonstick.

SILICONE BAKING MAT

You will be amazed the first time you use this mat. Nothing sticks to it! Caramel, batters, taffy, and peanut brittle—it all slides right off. No more peeling wax paper from the bottom of your cookies. For the best care, never scrape, cut, or fold silicone mats as they will become damaged. When Ron and the kids make fortune cookies, they are always in luck, thanks to the silicone mat Bernard stuffed in their stocking one Christmas.

BOUILLON STRAINER

This is the best tool for straining sauces, broths, stocks, and all other types of liquids. Called *chinois* in French, a bouillon strainer has a cone-shape and a very fine mesh. It is most popular in professional kitchens for refined sauces. Most of the sauce recipes in this book require straining through a fine sieve. We highly recommend you make this a part of your kitchen collection. For easy cleaning, rinse your chinois immediately after each use. If possible, hang chinois when storing to avoid damage to the mesh.

KITCHEN SHEARS

Kitchen shears are specially designed scissors for the kitchen. We use them in our home kitchens as the perfect tool to open shrimp and cut through lobster shells and whole chicken. Bernard grows fresh herbs, tomatoes, and lemongrass in his garden and uses kitchen shears to clip his harvest. Ron trims artichoke leaves and snips sprigs of spearmint for mojitos. Get a pair.

SQUEEZE BOTTLES

Squeeze bottles are great fun in the kitchen. They are an easy way to dispense sauces, oils, balsamic syrup, and other condiments. At home, a squeeze bottle can make the difference between home-style and elegant presentations. To make fine lines, dots and drops, use a small nozzle. We used this tool to create the presentation on top of Chilled Carrot Tangerine Velouté, pg. 59.

WOK

Two types of woks are available on the market. One has handles on both sides while the other has a single long handle on one side. We prefer the single handle because it is easier when tossing ingredients when stir frying. The best woks are made from carbon steel and can be seasoned in the same way as cast iron. It has pores that absorb oil and become sealed when heated. The more you use your wok, the more seasoned and nonstick it becomes. Using a wok ring over the stove top distributes heat up the sides of the wok, simulating the pit cooking of China.

MICROPLANE GRATER

Zesting is one of the most rewarding activities in the kitchen. It allows you to reap the essential oils from citrus peel, leaving the pith behind. The Microplane Zester is our favorite one for making fluffy shreds very fast. The tool looks like a woodworking rasp, with a large handle and a very long stainless steel zesting blade. It can also be used for shaving Parmesan cheese, truffles, chocolate, ginger, and even ice. If we had to choose one tool that we cannot do without, this is it.

THERMOMETERS

Thermometers are often overlooked, but should be at the top of your list for food safety and accurate cooking. We recommend that you have the following types:
1. Instant-Read Thermometer—roasts and poultry.
2. Deep Frying Thermometer—accurate and safe cooking.
3. Oven-Safe Thermometer—accurate baking, a must have.
4. Refrigerator Thermometer—Don't trust the built-ins, they do not stay calibrated.

FISH SPATULA

Commonly called a "fish slice," this spatula is slotted, allowing liquid or fat to stay behind when the food is being lifted. It is thin and flexible, making it a very versatile tool in the kitchen. It was originally invented for removing fish from a frying pan, but it is our favorite multitasker. You can even get a left-handed one. Our favorite is from Wusthof Cutlery.

LARGE CUTTING BOARD

There's nothing worse than a cutting board that is too small for the job. In Bernard's home, his oak butcher block is the soul of the kitchen. Ron is attached to his bamboo board—the wood is sustainable, softer on the knives, and does not stain. Whichever style you choose, remember, the bigger the better.

WHISK

A good whisk is essential to good cooking. It is a handheld tool used for blending, whipping, incorporating air, and eliminating lumps in food. Use a stainless steel balloon whisk for foams and emulsions such as meringue, whipped cream, and hollandaise sauce. French whisks are a must for everything from sauces to dressings. The teardrop shape allows it to get into the corners of bowls, pots, and skillets.

COFFEE GRINDER FOR SPICES

We like to have one coffee grinder dedicated to spices. It is most effective for grinding woody or hard spices like star anise and peppercorns. Grind spices just before using to ensure fresh flavor and potency. Processing dried mushrooms to a fine powder is a great way to enhance mushroom dishes. A tablespoon of uncooked rice whirled in your grinder is a great way to clean it.

DIGITAL SCALE

Essential for quick and precise measurement of ingredients for baked goods and spice blends. Look for a scale that measures in both grams and ounces, and has a tare feature for convenient use. Taring a scale means zeroing out the reading so that you can measure the next ingredient without removing the existing one. Get one with a four minute auto shutoff feature to maximize the battery life.

KNIVES

A knife should feel like an extension of your hand. You should try holding a variety of knives before deciding on one. The shape, weight and comfort level will determine your personal favorite. A sharp knife is a safe knife. Our favorites are Japanese knives, such as Shun brand, forged from one single piece of steel. Bernard's rule: designate a small serrated knife for tomato and citrus use. High acid ingredients dull the blade. Ron's rule: to prevent damage, never place wooden handled knives in the dishwasher.

MANDOLINE VEGETABLE SLICER

The fastest and most effective way to thinly slice or shave ingredients, especially vegetables, is with a mandoline slicer. Instead of moving the blade over the food, as you do with a knife, you move the food over the blade. This creates perfect onion rings, potato chips, coleslaw, and rainbow colored vegetable threads. Mandolines are very sharp—to prevent an accident use the safety guard and keep your eyes on the blade, not your fingers.

WOODEN SPOONS

Bernard has a kitchen fetish—wooden spoons. His collection of different shapes and sizes from around the world are used on a daily basis. Ron, the practical one, likes them for being non-conductive and easy on pots and pans—perfect for risotto. We both agree they make great serving utensils, bringing a note of earthiness to the table.

SWIVEL PEELER

This is the best and most effective peeler for fruits and vegetables, such as the white asparagus in the Spanish Tuna Crudo, pg. 101. They have a slingshot Y-shape and a blade that adjusts to the contour of the ingredient. Swivel peelers are fantastic for shaving aged cheeses like Parmesan or Gouda on your favorite salad or creating chocolate shavings for desserts. They can be used left- or right-handed—a plus in the kitchen.

PASTRY BRUSH

Have one in your drawer for applying liquid ingredients such as oil or eggwash to the surface of baked items, or for basting your favorite roast. Between uses, wash pastry brushes in hot soapy water or the dishwasher to remove oil residue. Dry thoroughly before storing. Choose a pastry brush with soft bristles that are at least 1-inch long and tightly bound to the handle. For food-safe use, always purchase from a kitchen store. Silicone brushes are great as well.

MEASURING CUPS AND SPOONS

We prefer stainless steel measuring cups and spoons for their durability and nonporous surfaces that do not absorb odors and are easy to clean and sanitize. For easy reading of liquid measurements, the OXO angled measuring cups are best. It's also good to have metric cups and spoons, especially nowadays with so many metric recipes available from around the world.

MORTAR AND PESTLE

Working with a mortar and pestle brings a certain spirituality to cooking. With all the technology of modern devices, the mortar and pestle remains superior for processing ingredients. The process of crushing to release essential oils is more effective than the chopping action of a blade. There are many types of mortar and pestles made from different materials. Durable and nonporous, granite is best for all-purpose use because it is easy to clean and won't develop off aromas or harbor bacteria.

OUT OF A BIND

Missing an ingredient in a recipe? Don't fret! Our recipes are flexible, and we are sure you will be able to create a delicious and exciting meal with what you have on hand. Here are some guidelines to help you in that critical moment when you are in the middle of preparing a recipe and discover something is missing.

A general rule of thumb is to analyze if the missing ingredient is sweet, sour, bitter, salty, or spicy. Look for a replacement that has similar traits and flavor, keeping in mind the ethnicity of the recipe. Write your notes on this book so you never lose them. Feel free to experiment and trust your senses— that's what cooking is all about.

OILS

We cook with a large variety of oils and use many of them as a seasoning instead of a cooking medium. A drizzle of high quality oil greatly enhances a dish. Finishing oils are usually interchangeable. Here is a guide of characteristics to help you choose a substitute:

Light Nut Oils—hazelnut, almond, walnut, macadamia, cashew, pecan, pine nut
Green Nut Oils—pistachio, pumpkin
Fragrant Fruit Oils—extra virgin olive, avocado
High Heat for searing or wokking—grapeseed, canola, safflower, peanut
Multipurpose—corn, canola, sunflower, pure olive oil
There is no substitute for truffle oil!

All oils, especially unrefined oils, should be refrigerated after opening to prevent oxidation and rancidity.

VINEGARS

We use a variety of vinegars in our cooking. Here is a list of vinegars that are compatible:

Fruit Flavored Vinegars—raspberry, cider, fig, coconut
Wood-Aged Vinegars—balsamic, sherry, banyuls, icewine, vincotto
Blond Vinegars—Champagne, apple cider, white wine, rice, malt, cane
Red Vinegars—raspberry, red wine, ume plum, cranberry
Asian Vinegars—seasoned rice, brown rice, black rice, ume plum, palm
Verjus—verjus is a sour juice made from unripened red or white grapes
No vinegar in the house? Use lemon juice.

SPICES

Always keep spices in small quantities stored in a sealed container away from direct light. If you have a lot of individual spices on hand, have fun creating your own blends.

Woodsy—cinnamon, cassia, allspice, clove, nutmeg, star anise, juniper berry
Fragrant—cardamom, anise seeds, ginger, fennel seeds, caraway
Accents—celery seeds, mustard seeds, caraway, poppy seeds, sumac
Chiles—paprika, chile powder, cayenne, togarashi, chile flakes, ancho, espelette
Earthy—turmeric, coriander, annatto, curry powder, cumin, wattleseed
There is no substitution for saffron or vanilla.
Fennel Pollen Spices can be found at chefbernard.com.

FRUITS AND VEGETABLES

Some of our favorites we like to play with:

Alliums—Shallot, leek, cipollini, pearl onions, scallions
Beans—green beans, Chinese long beans, haricots verts, yellow wax beans
Citrus Oil—lemongrass, lemon zest, lemon myrtle, orange peel
Berries—All berries in season are exchangeable
Crispy—Jicama, water chestnut, asian pear, green apple, cucumber
Exotic—persimmon, dragon fruit, kiwi, mango, papaya, gooseberry, cherimoya
Fragrant—artichoke heart, asparagus, sunchokes, cardoon
Mushrooms, Exotic—chantrelles, morels, oysters, hon-shimeji, Maitake, porcini
Mushrooms, Staple—cremini, button, portobello, shiitake
Roots—fennel, celeriac, parsnips, rutabaga, salsify, carrots, sunchokes
Stone Fruits—peach, nectarine, apricot, plum, cherry
Summer Squash—chayote, zucchini, Rond de Nice, crook neck, pattypan
Tart—pomegranate, sour cherries, cranberry, lime, yuzu
Tuber—boniato, yam, sweet potato, Okinawa purple potato
Winter Greens—bok choy, swiss chard, baby savoy cabbage, spinach, arugula

HERBS

If possible, grow your own herbs and pick just before using for optimum flavor.

Easiest Herbs to Grow—rosemary, mint, parsley, thyme, sage, lemongrass

Delicate Herbs—parsley, chervil, tarragon, mint, basil

Fragrant—rosemary, sage, thyme, oregano, lemon balm, bay leaf, cilantro, lavender

Dried Herbs—1 teaspoon dried herbs equals 1 tablespoon chopped fresh herbs.

Herbs should be chopped using a very sharp knife so that they don't bruise or lose potency and essential oils.

WINE AND SPIRITS

Always use high quality wines when cooking, so you can enjoy it as well.

Dry White Wines—chardonnay, sauvignon blanc, chenin blanc, Champagne

Light Body Red Wines—pinot noir, sangiovese, Beaujolais, plum

Bold Red Wines—zinfandel, malbec, shiraz, cabernet, amarone

Fortified—Marsala, Madeira, sherry, tawny and ruby port, Muscat, sweet vermouth

Sweet Wines—mirin, sweet vermouth, late harvest wines, viognier

When substituting a non-alcohol liquid for an alcohol, keep the volume of liquid the same as called for in the recipe. Use white grape juice for brandy, tangerine juice for grand marnier, and pomegranate juice for red wine. When substituting one alcohol for another use a similar proof and style.

SEAFOOD

The key to great results when cooking fish is freshness. If you find a fresher fish than the one in our recipe, substitute it.

Flaky White Fish—seabass, striped bass, snapper, halibut, grouper, perch

Thin and Delicate—sole, flounder, John Dory, orange roughy

High Oil Content—salmon, trout, arctic char, steelhead, cod, pompano

Raw Preparation—tuna, Kampachi, salmon, yellowtail, scallops, prawns, mackerel

Barbecue friendly—swordfish, wahoo, mahi mahi, tuna, salmon, yellow tail, prawn, lobster

Steamers—clams, cockles, mussels, crab, lobster

Braising Favorites—monkfish, squid, halibut, salmon, sardines

MEATS

A good butcher will help you choose the right cut for your cooking plans. Here are some of our favorites:

Braising—lamb shanks, short ribs, chicken thigh, osso bucco, duck legs

Stew Cuts—lamb shoulder, pork butt, chuck roast, beef cheeks, oxtail, chicken legs

Oven Roasts—leg of lamb, whole chicken, rib roast, turkey, veal chop, Cornish hen

Barbecue Friendly—New York strip, bone-in ribeye, lamb chops, tri tip, pork tenderloin, flat iron, skirt steak

Pan Seared—filet mignon, venison loin, veal tenderloin, pork tenderloin, ostrich, duck breast, quail

Meatloaf—ground turkey, chicken, veal, buffalo, top sirloin

Kebabs—chicken thigh, lamb shoulder, beef top round, pork shoulder, venison leg, ostrich fan fillet

BAKING

Baking is scientific. The results depend on chemical reactions that require precise measurement of ingredients and following the recipe exactly. If you are missing a specific ingredient, we recommend the website www.baking911.com for a comprehensive substitution chart. These are our basics:

1 teaspoon baking powder	¼ teaspoon baking soda plus ⅝ teaspoon cream of tartar
baking soda	no recommended substitution
cream of tartar	no recommended substitution
1 cup brown sugar	1 cup granulated sugar plus 2 tablespoons molasses
1 cup milk	1 cup soy milk or rice milk
1 oz. unsweetened chocolate	knead 3 tablespoons cocoa powder with 1 tablespoon butter
5 oz. semisweet chocolate	3 oz. unsweetened chocolate plus 3 tablespoons sugar
1 cup self-rising flour	1 cup all-purpose flour plus 1¼ tsp baking powder plus ¼ tsp salt
crème fraîche	sour cream strained through cheese cloth overnight
fromage blanc	fresh Greek yogurt strained through cheese cloth overnight

CONVERSION TABLES

U.S. MEASUREMENTS	CONVERSION TO GRAMS				
	GRANULATED SUGAR	BROWN SUGAR	CONFECTIONERS SUGAR	ALL PURPOSE FLOUR	BUTTER
1 teaspoon	4	4.2	2.7	2.1	4.8
1 tablespoon	12	12.5	8	6.2	14.3
¼ cup	48	51	32.5	25	57
⅓ cup	64	67	43	33	76
½ cup	96	101	65	50	115
⅔ cup	128	134	87	66	153
¾ cup	144	151	98	75	172
1 cup	192	202	130	100	229

U.S. VOLUME	METRIC VOLUME	METRIC WEIGHT
1 teaspoon	5 ml	3 grams
1 tablespoon	15 ml	9 grams
¼ cup	60 ml	36 grams
⅓ cup	80 ml	48 grams
½ cup	120 ml	72 grams
⅔ cup	160 ml	96 grams
¾ cup	180 ml	108 grams
1 cup	240 ml	144 grams
1 pint	480 ml	288 grams
1 quart	960 ml	576 grams
1 gallon	3840 ml	2304 grams

GAS MARK	FAHRENHEIT	CELSIUS	DESCRIPTION
¼	225°	110°	very cool
½	250°	130°	—
1	275°	140°	cool
2	300°	150°	—
3	325°	170°	moderate
4	350°	180°	moderate
5	375°	190°	—
6	400°	200°	moderately hot
7	425°	220°	hot
8	450°	230°	—
9	475°	240°	very hot
10	500°	260°	—

U.S. WEIGHT	METRIC WEIGHT
1 ounce	30 grams
1 pound	454 grams

INDEX OF RECIPES BY COUNTRY